Peace Movements
International Protest and World Politics since 1945

April Carter

Longman
London and New York

LONGMAN GROUP UK LIMITED
Longman House, Burnt Mill, Harlow,
Essex CM20 2JE, England
and Associated Companies throughout the world.

*Published in the United States of America
by Longman Inc., New York*

First published 1992

British Library Cataloguing-in-Publication Data
Carter, April
  Peace movements. – (The postwar world)
  I. Title   II. Series
  303.6

ISBN 0–582–02774–8
ISBN 0–582–02773–X pbk

Library of Congress Cataloging-in-Publication Data
Carter, April.
  Peace movements / April Carter.
    p.   cm. — (The Postwar world)
  Includes bibliographical references.
  ISBN 0–582–02774–8 (csd).   — ISBN 0–582–02773–X (ppr)
  1. Peace movements—History. I. Title. II. Series.
JX1952.C363 1992
327. 1'72'09—dc20   91–3953
                                                              CIP
                                                              AC

Set in Linotron 202 10/12 Bembo
Produced by Longman Singapore Publishers (Pte) Ltd.
Printed in Singapore

PEACE MOVEMENTS

The Postwar World
General Editors: A.J. Nicholls and Martin S. Alexander

As distance puts events into perspective, and as evidence accumulates, it begins to be possible to form an objective historical view of our recent past. *The Postwar World* is an ambitious new series providing a scholarly but readable account of the way our world has been shaped in the crowded years since the Second World War. Some volumes will deal with regions, or even single nations, others with important themes; all will be written by expert historians drawing on the latest scholarship as well as their own research and judgements. The series should be particularly welcome to students, but it is designed also for the general reader with an interest in contemporary history.

Contents

Abbreviations

ABM	See glossary of strategic terms
CFDT	Conféderation française démocratique de travail (Democratic Confederation of Labour)
CIA	Central Intelligence Agency (in USA)
CND	Campaign for Nuclear Disarmament
CO	Conscientious Objector
CODENE	Comité pour le Désarmament Nucleaire (Committee for Nuclear Disarmament)
CSCE	Conference on Security and Cooperation in Europe
EEC	European Economic Community
END	European Nuclear Disarmament
FBI	Federal Bureau of Investigation (in USA)
FDP	Frei Demokratische Partei (Free Democratic Party)
FOR(I)	Fellowship of Reconciliation (International)
GDR	German Democratic Republic (East Germany)
INF	See glossary of strategic terms
IKV	Interkerkelijk Vredesberaad (Inter-Church Peace Council)
IRA	Irish Republican Army
KOS	Komitet Oporu Spolecznego (Polish Committee for Social Resistance)
MRP	Mouvement Républicain Populaire
NATO	North Atlantic Treaty Organization
PCI	Partito Comunisto Italiano
PLO	Palestine Liberation Organization
PSOE	Partido Socialista Obrero Espanol (Spanish Socialist Workers' Party)
PSU	Parti socialiste unifié (United Socialist Party)

SALT	See glossary of strategic terms
SANE	Committee for a Sane Nuclear Policy
SDI	See glossary of strategic terms
SDP	Social Democratic Party (in Britain in 1980s)
SPD	Sozialdemokratische Partei Deutschlands (West German Social Democratic Party)
UN	United Nations
WILPF	Women's International League for Peace and Freedom
WRI	War Resisters' International

Glossary of Strategic Terms

ABM Anti-Ballistic Missile   ABM defences developed in the USA and USSR in the 1960s were composed of missiles designed to destroy incoming ballistic missiles. A Treaty to limit ABM deployments was agreed in 1972.

cruise missile   Cruise missile is a generic term to distinguish cruise missiles from ballistic missiles.   Cruise missiles can be launched from the ground, sea or air. The 1979 NATO 'dual-track' decision envisaged deployment of ground-launched cruise missiles in Western Europe, commonly denoted by peace campaigners opposing them as 'cruise'.

INF Intermediate-range nuclear forces   INF denoted the intermediate range SS 20 mobile ballistic missiles being deployed by the Soviet Union inside the USSR in the 1970s and early 1980s, NATO decided to deploy the Tomahawk ground-launched cruise missiles in 1979, and NATO also decided to deploy the Pershing II ballistic missiles in West Germany. The 1987 INF Treaty eliminated all three classes of missile in Europe and the SS 20s in the USSR.

Neutron bomb   An enhanced radiation warhead designed for use on the battlefield.

SALT Strategic Arms Limitation Talks   The SALT bilateral negotiations between the USA and USSR ran from 1969 to 1979 and were focused primarily on limiting intercontinental ballistic missiles (ground- and sea-launched) on both sides. The role of bombers and air-launched and sea-launched cruise missiles were contentious issues in the talks. The USA and USSR signed an Interim Agreement in 1972 (SALT I) and a more far-reaching treaty in 1979 (SALT II).

SDI Strategic Defence Initiative (popularly known as 'Star Wars'). SDI was a programme launched by President Reagan in 1983 and was a much more ambitious attempt to develop defences against ballistic missiles than the earlier ABM plans, drawing on a much wider range of technologies. Supporters of arms control opposed SDI partly on the grounds that it would breach the ABM Treaty of 1972 (denied by the administration).

START Strategic Arms Reduction Talks These talks, which began in 1982, were the successor to SALT.

tactical nuclear weapons Short range nuclear weapons which could be launched by artillery, missiles or aircraft during battle. Both NATO and the USSR deployed thousands ready for use in a European war.

Editorial Foreword

The aim of this series is to describe and analyse the history of the World since 1945. History, like time, does not stand still. What seemed to many of us only recently to be 'current affairs', or the stuff of political speculation, has now become material for historians. The editors feel that it is time for a series of books which will offer the public judicious and scholarly, but at the same time readable, accounts of the way in which our present-day world was shaped by the years after the end of the Second World War. The period since 1945 has seen political events and socio-economic developments of enormous significance for the human race, as important as anything which happened before Hitler's death or the bombing of Hiroshima. Ideologies have waxed and waned, the industrialised economies have boomed and bust, empires have collapsed, new nations have emerged and sometimes themselves have fallen into decline. While we can be thankful that no major armed conflict has occurred between the so-called superpowers, there have been many other wars, and terrorism has become an international plague. Although the position of ethnic minorities has dramatically improved in some countries, it has worsened in others. Nearly everywhere the status of women has become an issue which politicians have been unable to avoid. These are only some of the developments we hope will be illuminated by this series as it unfolds.

The books in the series will not follow any set pattern; they will vary in length according to the needs of the subject. Some will deal with regions, or even single nations, and others with themes. Not all of them will begin in 1945, and the terminal date may similarly vary; once again, the time-span chosen will be appropriate to the question under discussion. All the books, however, will be written by expert historians drawing on the latest fruits of scholarship, as well as their own expertise and judgement. The series should be particularly welcome to students, but it is designed also for the general reader with an interest in contemporary history. We hope that the books will stimulate scholarly discussion and encourage specialists to look beyond their own particular interests to engage in wider controversies. History, and particularly the history of the recent past, is neither 'bunk' nor an intellectual form of stamp-collecting, but an indispensable part of an educated person's approach to life. If it is not written by historians it will be written by others of a less discriminating and more polemical disposition. The editors are confident that this series will help to ensure the victory of the historical approach, with consequential benefits for its readers.

A. J. Nicholls
Martin S. Alexander

Preface and Acknowledgements

This book covers the period 1945–90, a period in which world politics were largely defined in terms of the Cold War and confrontation between the USA and USSR. During this period there were numerous local wars, but the main peace campaigns in the West were directed against the threat of nuclear war between the superpowers. The major exception was the movement against the war in Vietnam. Much of this book, therefore, concentrates on the first and second phases of the nuclear disarmament movement and there is a chapter on the opposition to the American involvement in Vietnam. There have, however, been many campaigns of resistance to particular wars, attempts to promote reconciliation during conflict, and protests against the role of the military in society. These are the subject of the final chapter.

The aim of this book is to indicate the world-wide scope of peace activity and to show how autonomous peace groups have arisen in a great variety of political and cultural contexts. More space is, however, given to campaigns in Europe and North America than to other parts of the world. This focus does reflect the fact that, with the exception of Japan, peace movements have generally been stronger in the parliamentary democracies of Western Europe, the USA and Canada; though during the 1980s this became less true. But my own perspectives and sources of information have influenced my geographical emphasis. Similarly, I have given especial weight to nuclear disarmament and pacifist activities in the UK. This is again partly justified by the prominence of British peace organizations within the transnational movements, but influenced by my own greater knowledge and by the fact that this book is initially directed at a British readership.

Because this book describes a great many peace campaigns, it necessarily provides a brief overview and cannot enter into the detail required for a full understanding. My aim has been to indicate the scope of these campaigns, how they were organized, their aims, tactics and policies. Major ideological, tactical or organizational controversies do figure, but there is not space to consider more minor difficulties and disputes. In order not to confuse the reader, I have mentioned only a few key personalities in various peace movements. There are hundreds of individuals who have played an important, and sometimes controversial, role in peace activity whose names are missing here. Where people well known outside peace movements have lent their support, I have sometimes named them to give an indication of the standing enjoyed by the campaign.

It is clearly important to know how many people have supported particular campaigns, and what sort of people they are, but it is often hard to answer these questions. Peace groups normally have a mailing list, but seldom formal membership. Large campaigns have local groups of varying and fluctuating size, and affiliations with a range of other organizations. Supporters with no organizational links may sometimes join in demonstrations or wear a badge. The size of demonstrations is used both by peace movements and by observers as one important measure of the breadth of popular support, but estimates of numbers attending marches and rallies tend to vary widely, with the organizers claiming high figures and the police offering much lower estimates. Public opinion polls offer some indication of support for the policies or the tactics of demonstrators, but polls, too, are controversial sources of evidence. Poll questions tend to elicit superficial and over-simplified responses and the results can usually be significantly influenced by the wording of the question. Despite all these caveats, I have tried to indicate the size and type of active support and the extent of passive sympathy in the wider population for major campaigns.

An earlier version of the Introduction was published in Czech by Charter 77 in 1984 as the first of a series of essays on peace and disarmament issues. The rest of the book is new, though it draws indirectly on some of my earlier writings.

I am very grateful to the War-Resisters' International, the Women's International League for Peace and Freedom and the International Peace Bureau for making materials available to me. I also benefited from the opportunity to consult a wide range of peace periodicals and newsletters at the Commonweal Collection in the J. B. Priestley Library, University of Bradford. Many thanks are due to Penelope

Hall for her very competent help with typing. I am greatly indebted to Peter van den Dungen for bibliographical advice, Howard Clark for offering me his inside knowledge on Chapters 7 and 8, and to my editors for much helpful advice and criticism of the book as a whole. I remain responsible for any errors of fact which may have been overlooked, and for the inevitably contentious interpretations and judgements of specific peace campaigns.

Introduction

The peace protests which captured public attention in the years since 1945 took place in response to immediate dangers, but they were, nevertheless, linked to a much longer history of peace campaigning. Some of the organizations now active in opposing war and war preparations date from earlier in this century. Some go back very much further: the Quakers, for example, arose in the seventeenth century. Moreover, recent campaigners not only respond to contemporary concerns and arguments but draw also on a much longer tradition of thinking about the problems of war and peace. There are many continuities between past and present peace action, and to gain a full understanding of the present we need to begin by looking very briefly at the history of thought and action relating to peace before the Second World War.

ORIGINS OF PEACE ACTIVITY

The belief that war is immoral is rooted in early Christianity, which at first prompted a pacifist refusal to take part in war. In due course Christian belief was adapted to political realities and the requirements of rulers, as St Augustine and later Catholic philosophers elaborated the doctrine of Just War. In addition to a specifically Christian rejection of war there is a humanist strand of thought, which stresses the brutalizing and corrupting nature of warfare, that can be traced back to classical Greece. Humanism surfaced in the Renaissance and led thinkers like Erasmus to denounce the barbarities of war. Later, secular rationalism prompted theorists in early eighteenth-century Europe to propose forms of international organization to secure permanent peace. One of the best-known treatises was by St Pierre, who published his essay on *Perpetual Peace* in 1712. Towards the end of the century both Rousseau and Kant produced their own critical reflections on this topic, raising questions about the relevance of the internal organization of states if the aim of international peace was to be realized.

The first organized peace groups, however, were founded immediately after the Napoleonic Wars, in the USA and in Britain. The growth of peace activity might be seen as part of the new spirit of democracy which prompted popular agitation not only for extension of the franchise but for a range of social and humanitarian reforms, and created aspirations for the transformation of society. It is, nonetheless, significant that the new peace societies were founded after a Europe-wide conflict that had effectively lasted twenty-five years. The Napoleonic Wars are often seen as marking a critical change in the nature of modern war, popularizing the idea of 'the nation in arms' and promoting a new form of total war. Certainly the wars prompted a romantic nationalism and a glorification of war and the figure of the soldier. But there was also awareness of the destructiveness and waste of war, of the thousands of fighting men killed, the ravages of famine and the burned and sacked towns and villages.[1] Goya's etchings of 'The Disasters of War' depicted the mutual atrocities resulting from the Spanish people's guerrilla resistance to the Napoleonic army of occupation.

The first peace societies also drew upon a much earlier commitment to oppose war, since Quakers played a key role in founding them, aided by Unitarians and other free-thinking Protestants. The Quaker commitment to peace stemmed from their belief in recapturing the spirit of early Christianity and conviction that waging war was incompatible with respecting 'that of God in every man'. While a number of religious sects which arose at the time of the Reformation believed bearing arms was forbidden by the Christian gospels, most of these were primarily concerned about personal morality and salvation, and so avoided compromise with the world of politics. The Quakers, however, were formed during the religious and political ferment of the English Civil War in the 1640s, and under one of their leaders, William Penn, were able to found a Quaker government in America. So they always had a concern with the politics of this world. Indeed, Penn anticipated St Pierre in drawing up his own plan for a league of states to preserve international peace. Quakers therefore quite naturally sponsored peace groups, which also drew on the ideas of early nineteenth-century liberalism.

The first peace societies stressed that differences between states could be settled without recourse to war, and relied heavily on the role of enlightened public opinion and on rational discussion of conflicting interests. The American Peace Society, created in 1828 through the merger of thirty-six societies from different areas, called in its constitution for 'amicable discussion and arbitration' between states, and for 'settling all controversies by an appeal to reason'. The institutional basis for devising such settlements was to be a 'Congress of Nations whose decrees shall be enforced by public opinion that rules the world'.[2] In order to promote and mobilize public opinion, the new peace societies engaged in extensive pamphleteering, sent speakers on long lecture tours and founded their own periodicals. The British Society, which laid particular emphasis on the power of the press, began to publish the *Herald of Peace* in 1819, and the first American peace paper was the *Friend of Peace*, founded in 1821. The franchise was still restricted, but the peace societies did not limit themselves to mobilizing those who had the vote. Women were involved early on in peace activity, while campaigners like the American Elihu Burritt set out to recruit workers in both the USA and Britain.

FROM THE 1840s TO THE CRIMEAN WAR

Thinking about peace acquired a more radical tinge when William Lloyd Garrison, best known for his efforts to abolish slavery, spelled out the implications of Christian 'non-resistance' and called for non-cooperation with all government preparations for war. Garrison drew up a Declaration of Principles for the New England Non-Resistance Society, which he helped to found in 1838. One of his colleagues, Adin Ballou, explained in more detail what was meant in a book entitled *Christian Non-Resistance*, published in 1846. Both Garrison and Ballou stressed that they were advocating not passivity, but an active moral resistance to evil, a resistance which did not involve inflicting physical violence.[3] Garrison came to condone the use of violence to end slavery, but the idea of non-resistance was later to influence Tolstoy, who had read Ballou. Tolstoy himself had an impact on the young Gandhi, who translated non-violent resistance into an effective form of political action, first in South Africa and then in India. Through Gandhi peace activists were in turn inspired by the potential of non-violent resistance to oppose injustice, occupation and war.

The original Quaker-influenced peace groups acquired a new ally in the 1840s in the Free Trade Movement, led in Britain by Richard Cobden and in the USA by Charles Sumner and William Ellery Channing. Theorists of free trade believed that trade would create such a strong economic interest in peace that even governments adhering to obsolete attitudes would be prevented from launching wasteful and destructive wars. The Free Traders gained support from businessmen for their economic defence of free trade, and were able to ally with the peace societies on a limited programme and help finance a number of international peace congresses, starting in London in 1843.

Peace societies flourished in countries where Protestantism in religion, liberalism in politics and a free enterprise economy provided a favourable setting. Hence the predominance of peace activity in Britain and the USA. The relative isolation of both these countries from the rivalries and conflicts of Europe encouraged opposition to war, although Britain could not entirely escape its great power 'obligation' to maintain a European balance of power, and the USA was to face similar dilemmas in the twentieth century. Peace organizations did spread to various parts of continental Europe, but were in the early nineteenth century often initiated by British or American activists; and the international congresses were organized and dominated by the Anglo-American groups. Continental Europeans had a different view of the ideal international order. After the Napoleonic Wars much of Europe was subjected to the enforced stability laid down at the Congress of Vienna. The Concert of Europe was designed to settle territorial boundaries, but under Austrian and Russian influence it also meant that peace was purchased at the price of suppressing liberal, democratic and nationalist aspirations. So, in the short run, armed rebellion seemed the obvious means of securing freedom from autocratic and imperial rulers. In the long run, European thinkers looked to the goal of a United States of Europe.

The Anglo-American concept of internationalism did not embrace any form of supranational organization: its vision was rather of independent sovereign states meeting in periodic conference and resolving their disputes by reasoned negotiation or voluntary acceptance of arbitration. By 1848 the theme of disarmament had been added to the platform of the second Universal Peace Congress, and an appeal was made to the two major liberal powers, Britain and the USA, to give a lead in reducing their arms. It was the ideas of the British and American peace societies which prevailed in international congresses up to 1853, though they themselves were split between the more committed pacifists and the conventional liberalism of the free trade movement. The former wished to oppose all wars and promote Christian non-resistance, the latter to give primacy to free trade. Both emphases were omitted from compromise policies designed to gain support in Europe.

Despite the very moderate programmes adopted at these congresses, and the generally respectable middle-class character of the peace societies, they attracted the hostility and contempt of the political establishment and its press. *The Times* denounced the 1843 Universal Peace Congress as a particularly extreme and pernicious example of the 'disease' of the 'fanaticism of association'. It commented scathingly on 'the vagaries and delusions of those unhappy individuals who . . . profess no less than the total abolition throughout the terrestrial globe of war . . .'[4]

The settlement of Europe imposed by the Congress of Vienna was challenged by the wave of revolutions which swept across Europe in 1848–49, and asserted democratic and nationalist justifications for violent rebellion and wars of liberation. Belief that some types of war were just and necessary, and that democratic or nationalist freedoms must be secured as the basis for just and lasting peace, had (as noted above) separated many European radicals from the Anglo-American ideology of the early peace societies. But the conflict between maintaining peace and securing justice caused a crisis among American pacifists also, over the issue of slavery. Some committed abolitionists, such as William Garrison, abandoned their pacifism and the Civil War divided the peace societies.

FROM THE CRIMEAN WAR TO THE FIRST WORLD WAR

The collapse of the first international peace movement was directly caused, however, not by the problems posed by just wars but by the outbreak of another European war based on the balance of power principle of curbing Russian territorial ambitions: the Crimean War of 1854–56. There followed a period of wars in Europe for Italian and German unification, and no international peace congress was held between 1853 and 1871. Nevertheless, new peace groups were springing up in Europe, representing the democratic republicanism which had been suppressed. The developing socialist movement also had a commitment to resist war. The convergence of various strands of radical thought with the more traditional pacifist internationalism of the early peace societies was demonstrated by the appearance of the flamboyant anarchist Bakunin at the Peace Congress of 1871. The development of the independent Socialist Internationals marked a divergence between the liberal and pacifist peace societies and the more militant war resistance espoused by the Second International. But the peace societies and the socialists held certain views in common, assuming peace would ensue once arbitrary and corrupt forms of government and sinister interests had been overthrown by popular democratic pressure. The liberals, however, relied primarily on an enlightened middle class, whereas socialists looked to the working class and the overthrow of capitalism. By the turn of the century both the peace groups and socialist parties were specifically pointing to the role of imperialist rivalries, the vested interests of armament manufacturers and the momentum of the arms race as threats to peace.

Peace societies multiplied after 1870. By 1900 there were 425 in existence, concentrated mainly, but not exclusively, in north-west Europe and the USA. Parallel to this growth of peace groups, many lawyers and parliamentarians became increasingly interested in promoting international law and international arbitration of disputes, creating their own international organizations. The predominant emphasis of the peace movement represented by the Universal Peace Congresses, held annually after 1892, was on negotiations between governments and arbitration to settle conflicts. The International Peace Bureau was set up as a permanent coordinating body to promote these aims, and it still has a secretariat in Geneva a century later. Even governments themselves were receptive to this approach in the late nineteenth century, and were often willing to accept arbitration. They met for the first time specifically to discuss peace at the Hague Conferences of 1899 and 1907, which issued Declarations prohibiting use of some particularly inhumane weapons, dum-dum bullets and poison gas. The 1907 convention also sought to prohibit deliberate killing of civilians during the course of war.

Belief in the possibility of securing peace, or at least of limiting the horrors of wars if it occurred, was destroyed by the First World War. It exposed the inadequacy of the liberal peace groups' reliance on rational compromise and awareness of common economic interests in peace, and demonstrated the strength of nationalist and *realpolitik* arguments for going to war. The outbreak of war demonstrated too that public opinion was not necessarily a force for peace, and showed how powerfully nationalism and martial attitudes could grip the popular imagination, as had the Crimean War sixty years earlier.[5] The utopian nature of socialist hopes for united working-class action to prevent war was also revealed in 1914. Many socialists were convinced, once war seemed inevitable, that a victory for Germany (or in the case of German socialists, a victory for Tsarist Russia) would disastrously strengthen the forces of reaction. Most socialist parliamentarians in all the belligerent countries voted for war credits. The Second International collapsed.

THE PEACE MOVEMENTS FROM 1914 TO 1945

War is often the greatest test of the convictions of those committed to oppose resort to armed violence. Despite the change in popular mood in 1914 many individuals did speak and write against the war, and some men refused to fight. One of the strongest grounds for resisting conscription was Christian pacifism, but men also disobeyed orders to enlist on socialist or anarchist grounds. There were liberals, too, who opposed the principle of conscription. The best known was Bertrand Russell, who helped to found the No Conscription Fellow-ship in Britain, and was jailed for an article opposing the war. Conscientious objection was adopted on the largest scale in Britain and the USA. After conscription was introduced, in 1916 in Britain, 16,500 men became COs, about 6,000 were court-martialled and over 800 of the most uncompromising resisters suffered more than two years of very harsh imprisonment – while a few were threatened with execution. The USA only entered the war in 1917, but nearly three million men were conscripted and about 4,000 refused on conscientious grounds, despite often brutal army measures to force them to obey orders. Christian pacifism was espoused by the Fellowship of Reconciliation, set up in 1914 in Britain and in 1915 in the USA. A minority of socialists continued to oppose the war, and forty-two delegates from Western and Eastern Europe met at Zimmerwald, Switzerland, in September 1915, in an attempt to reconstruct socialist internationalism.

If the outbreak of war in 1914 was disastrous for groups committed to work for peace, the total experience of the First World War proved a powerful impetus to peace sentiment and peace campaigning for the subsequent twenty years. The static trench warfare on the Western Front rapidly disillusioned the soldiers who suffered the constant shelling and horrors of the trenches, and who knew that each offensive for a small strip of ground brought mass slaughter and mutilation. The change in mood is illustrated by contrasting the poems of Rupert Brooke and their romantic patriotism with the bitter verses of Wilfred Owen and Siegfried Sassoon. The increasing anger among the common soldiers was expressed in 1917 by mutiny in the French army and by revolt on the Eastern Front among the ill-clothed and ill-fed Russian troops who supported revolution inside Russia. Although civilians were insulated from knowledge of the conditions under which the soldiers fought, the mounting death toll and casualties affected millions of families who lost sons, brothers, husbands, fathers and friends. After the war, novels, plays, films and autobiographies dramatized battles such as those fought on the Somme and at Passchendaele, recreating the terror of poison gas and helping to promote popular revulsion against war.

A succession of progressive movements and modes of thought had embraced the quest for creating permanent peace: liberalism, democratic republicanism, socialism and anarchism. The rise of feminism, which became politically significant by the 1900s, also embodied the hope that womanly influence in politics would result in an end to the peculiarly masculine pursuit of war. Women had been active in the peace campaigns of the previous century and had their own peace organizations, but by 1900 the cause of votes for women had been linked to anti-war sentiment. Feminists, like other progressives, split when war broke out in 1914, with some suffrage campaigners becoming ardent patriots and others moving into the ranks of war resisters. The First World War in fact evoked the first explicit feminist initiatives to end the fighting. One such initiative took place within the socialist movement. Clara Zetkin, a prominent anti-war socialist in Germany, managed to organize an International Women's Socialist Conference in Switzerland in 1915, bringing together women from both the warring alliances and from the neutral states. An international women's conference was also held at The Hague in 1915, initiated by a leading Dutch suffrage campaigner, to reaffirm the struggle for women's right to vote and to explore peaceful means of settling international conflicts. The women returned home to lobby their own governments. The Hague Conference gave rise to the Women's International League for Peace and Freedom (WILPF), which remained active after 1918 and mounted a major campaign round the 1932 World Disarmament Conference.[6]

After the First World War widespread anti-war sentiment was expressed in No More War demonstrations in Germany, but in the political and economic turmoil of the early 1920s only a few gave priority to peace campaigning.[7] A new anti-war international body, based on resistance to conscription, was founded in 1921 when groups from Germany, Austria, The Netherlands and Britain met in Holland to form PACO (Esperanto for 'peace'). The Dutch group was primarily inspired by anarchism, the others by a mixture of pacifism and socialism. This grouping soon changed its name to the War Resisters' International (WRI) and at its first proper international conference in 1925 there were representatives from twenty countries. The WRI could claim sections in an impressive range of countries: during the 1920s groups were allowed to exist in the Soviet Union and by the Fourth International Conference of 1934 the Secretary reported that new sections had been formed in Japan, Hong Kong, Mexico and Canada. Lithuania had been added to a long list of European countries where the WRI had groups. The WRI also had some influential supporters – Einstein cooperated with it for a time. Nevertheless, the absolutes of WRI's position in not only opposing military service but all forms of alternative service meant that its support in most countries was limited to a small minority, and it was not in agreement with other peace organizations. The WRI concentrated on support for conscientious objectors (COs) often treated harshly by military courts. (In France, for example, objectors were sent to the notorious prison camp on Devil's Island, made famous by the earlier incarceration there of Alfred Dreyfus.) The spread of fascism and the German occupation of much of Europe meant that war resisters had to confront extreme political repression. One of the founder members of PACO, a German Catholic priest, was hanged by the Gestapo in April 1944; others, for example in Holland and Norway, were active in non-violent resistance to Nazi rule.[8]

The International Fellowship of Reconciliation (IFOR) was founded in 1919. It was an explicitly Christian body, and primarily based on Protestant support, although a few Catholics cooperated with it. The IFOR was a response to the failure of the churches to transcend national interests in the First World War and an attempt to promote Christian pacifism. Despite the rather purist and exclusivist approach implied by this goal, the American section of the IFOR had some importance in the wider politics of the Left. It embraced the goal of the social transformation of society and increasingly saw capitalism as the primary cause of injustice and war. Leaders of the American FOR included a number of figures known as socialists or social reformers, including Norman Thomas and Jane Addams. But the extent of FOR's social commitment led some of its members to question whether non-violent methods were adequate to secure social justice.

9

Reinhold Niebuhr, who became one of the most eminent theological critics of Christian pacifism, left the organization in the mid-1930s calling for violent resistance to overthrow capitalism.[9] A. J. Muste, another leading figure in the FOR, also left to become a Trotskyist, but after visiting Europe in 1936 reverted to his belief in non-violence. A. J. had come with his parents from Holland in the 1890s to the Mid-West, become a Minister in the Reformed Church in 1909, but embarked upon a life-long career of radical protest when he opposed the War in 1917 and found himself leading a major textile strike in Massachusetts in 1919. After he returned to his Christian pacifism in 1936 he became one of the most respected figures in both American and international peace circles until he died in 1967. At eighty-two he was one of the 'few social activists and theorists over thirty' to whom an impatient generation of radical youth was prepared to listen.[10]

A much greater political impact was achieved by groups which during and after the First World War revived the liberal internationalist and legalistic proposals for resolving conflict. For example, a League of Nations Society was formed in Britain as early as 1915, and towards the end of the war there was increasing sympathy with the idea of an international body to prevent aggression and to arbitrate or adjudicate disputes. These ideas did influence governments and led to the creation of the League of Nations and the International Court of Justice. The League was based on the concept of collective security and so embodied willingness to use force to prevent aggression. Support for the League was therefore natural to those who sought to avoid further wars, but did not imply a strict pacifism.

The pacifist commitment not to fight in or support any war did win surprisingly widespread support for a period in the 1930s in Britain, where memories of the First World War influenced the attitudes of many to the prospect of any new war. The movement was launched when Canon Dick Sheppard issued a public appeal in 1934 for signatories to a pledge to renounce war. It became an organized campaign in 1936, with eminent support, up to 800 local groups, mass meetings and its own newspaper. The Peace Pledge Union (as it became known) was, however, founded at a time when pacifist policies became increasingly difficult to uphold, as the Left committed itself to oppose the victory of fascism in the Spanish Civil War and Hitler's aggressive ambitions became more obvious. Some eminent supporters of the pacifist cause, such as Albert Einstein and Bertrand Russell, became convinced of the need to fight fascism by military means. After war began in 1939 many former peace campaigners decided that they had to fight, although a significant minority remained committed to opposing the war and became COs. The Peace Pledge Union itself and its journal, *Peace News*, continued to uphold pacifist principles and when necessary defied wartime restrictions to do so. Provisions for conscientious objection were much more liberal than in the previous war, and about 60,000 men and 1,000 women applied to tribunals to be registered as COs.[11] Some took an absolutist stand and refused to do anything which might directly or indirectly assist the war effort; others, such as members of the Friends' Ambulance Unit, gave medical and human-itarian aid to both soliders and civilians wherever their services were required.

During the late 1930s the failure to impose economic sanctions against Italy, after it invaded Abyssinia in 1935, and the inability of the League of Nations to halt the Japanese invasion of China destroyed the hopes of those who had looked to international organization to prevent war. Peace campaigners who believed in collective security could, however, without any crisis of conscience support a war against the Axis Powers. Moreover, despite the weaknesses displayed by the League, Allied governments had decided before the Second World War was over to create a new body designed to promote international order and peace – the United Nations. During and after the war groups pursued the idea of supranational organization as a means of ensuring peace: this belief motivated the founders of the European Community and in the early post-war years inspired the campaign for world government. The World Federalists tended, however, to oppose the campaigns of the later 1950s against nuclear weapons. The more broadly based United Nations Associations supported negotiations for nuclear and conventional disarmament, but also diverged from more radical anti-nuclear and pacifist organizations.

NOTES AND REFERENCES

1. See, for example, letter written by a young officer in 1813, quoted in Geoffrey Best, *War and Society in Revolutionary Europe, 1770–1870* (London, Fontana, 1982), p. 194.
2. Quoted in F.H. Hinsley, *Power and the Pursuit of Peace: Theory and Practice in the History of Relations between States* (Cambridge, Cambridge University Press, 1967), p. 94. See also, Merle Eugene Curti, *The American Peace Crusade 1815–1860* (Durham, N. Carolina, Duke University Press, 1929).

3. Extracts from Garrison and Ballou and brief comments on their position can be found in Peter Mayer (ed.), *The Pacifist Conscience* (Harmondsworth, Penguin, 1966).
4. Quoted in Hinsley, p. 98.
5. Michael Howard, *War and the Liberal Conscience* (London, Temple Smith, 1978), pp. 45–6.
6. Jill Liddington, 'The Women's Peace Crusade: the History of a Forgotten Campaign', in Dorothy Thompson (ed.), *Over Our Dead Bodies: Women Against the Bomb* (London, Virago, 1983), pp. 180–98.
7. Martin Ceadel, *Pacifism in Britain 1914–1945* (Oxford, The Clarendon Press, 1980), p. 72.
8. Peter Brock, *Twentieth Century Pacifism* (New York, Van Nostrand Reinhold Co., 1970), pp. 110–12; and *The War Resister*, **50**, 1945 and **51**, 1946.
9. Brock, pp. 142–50.
10. Nat Hentoff (ed.), *The Essays of A. J. Muste* (Indianapolis, Bobbs Merrill, 1967), p. xiv. The essays include Muste's 'Sketches for an Autobiography'. See also, Nat Hentoff, *Peace Agitator: the Story of A.J. Muste* (New York, Macmillan, 1963).
11. Brock, pp. 158–60.

CHAPTER ONE
Defining Peace Movements and their Beliefs

INTRODUCTION

Deciding which groups should count as genuine peace organizations is more difficult than it might at first seem. 'Peace' like 'democracy' is an attractive label, which may be appropriated for propaganda purposes. The goal of peace is, moreover, too general to be in itself a distinctive aim which separates peace groups from everyone else since most people desire peace for much of the time. The bitter divisions arise over the priority to assign to ending a war as opposed to winning it – especially if vital issues are at stake – and over the absolute importance of avoiding war. Furthermore, there is often acute disagreement over how best to avoid war, and no definitive way of answering this question. To confuse the picture further, peace campaigners do not necessarily always call for peace in preference to war. Some may, as we noted in the context of movements of the last century, support certain kinds of 'Just War' as a prelude to a just peace. There are many differences of opinion between peace organizations at any one time, based on variations in their underlying moral and political philosophy and specific aims. Peace groups are in addition influenced by national cultural factors.

Given this diversity of views and goals, it is important to clarify whether there are certain criteria which apply to all peace groups, and which distinguish genuine peace organizations from bodies which claim the title, but have different purposes. It is also necessary to classify the types of peace association, and to explore underlying political theories and the political strategies adopted.

13

IDENTIFYING PEACE ORGANIZATIONS

The first question we need to resolve is what the criteria are for distinguishing authentic peace groups from other bodies which claim the title 'peace'. Since 1945 the main difficulty has arisen because of the role of the pro-Soviet World Peace Council. A number of pro-NATO organs have also been formed with the aim of attacking nuclear disarmament movements.

There are in practice a number of ways in which independent peace groups identify themselves and by which they are recognized by external observers such as journalists and historians. The first is autonomy from government or political parties. Autonomy can be compromised by organizational links, by the affiliations and role of central and local officials, and by sources of funds. Peace activists are not usually apolitical, though some may have no previous political experience or party ties, but they do need to show that they are not subservient to outside interests. Although Communist Party links have been the most sensitive issue in the West, in practice European nuclear disarmament campaigns have had more serious difficulties in keeping a distance from parliamentary socialist parties. Support from trade unions and professional associations has usually been acceptable, and religious backing has been seen as a guarantee not only of political autonomy but respectability.

The key test of autonomy is the policy pursued by a peace group. One requirement since 1945 has been non-alignment, a willingness to oppose the military action of both sides and to avoid unquestioning partisanship in disputes between the Soviet Union and the West. The second requirement, which has always existed, is commitment to criticize, and if necessary to resist, one's own government. On both these counts official peace committees within the USSR and Eastern Europe, and pro-NATO organs in the West, would not normally qualify as independent peace groups, though there are borderline cases.[1]

The final test of a peace group is the methods of protest adopted. Peace campaigns have embraced illegal action, but do not resort to violence. A peace group which deliberately sponsored violence or turned to guerrilla warfare would have become a different kind of body. For example the Weatherpeople formed a guerrilla group which emerged out of the protest movement against the Vietnam War in the USA, but once they went underground their aims and their methods were those of a revolutionary struggle. In principle the use of limited violence to resist and prevent a much greater violence might be seen as justifiable, but it has been generally accepted that it would be wholly incongruous for an organization committed to promote peace to engage in violent resistance.

CLASSIFYING PEACE ACTIVITY

Once we have decided what constitutes a genuine peace group, we need to understand the range and purposes of peace activity. A simple way of classifying peace campaigns is in terms of what they are against. Thus peace groups can be divided into those who oppose all wars and by extension all preparations for war; those who oppose a specific type of weapon; those who oppose particular policies relating to arms; and those who protest against a specific war.[2] These categories are not wholly satisfactory, because they tend to overlap and the motives for opposition are varied. Moreover, this classification excludes an important area of peace activity which is concerned not with protest but with positive attempts to end conflict through education and reconciliation, or through improving economic and social conditions. Nevertheless, a preliminary survey of peace protest is helpful.

Pacifists oppose all wars, arguing that fighting is morally wrong and that war is the greatest evil of all. Strict pacifism is usually now taken to mean personal refusal to take part in war and opposition to all types of war preparation. Pacifists hold the most consistent and uncompromising position on war, and often constitute the core of peace campaigns, both because of the strength of their convictions and their long-term organizational resources. On the other hand, the absolutism of the pacifist position is hard to reconcile with immediate political realities. So pure pacifists have always been a minority, and in order to make progress many pacifists support campaigns for more limited objectives.

Peace activists have tried to ban production, deployment and use of specific weapons because they are exceptionally destructive, indiscriminate or inhumane. Nuclear weapons are not only immensely powerful but cause burns and radiation sickness among the immediate survivors, while radioactive fallout contaminates the whole globe and results in deformity and illness among future generations. Biological warfare would spread hideous diseases indiscriminately. Chemical weapons are equally hard to control when used, but vary in their nature: mustard gas damages lungs and causes acute burns, but may

15

not be fatal; nerve gases on the other hand are deadly in minute amounts and will destroy whole communities. All these potentially genocidal weapons are clearly in a category by themselves. Since 1945 there have been two major transnational movements against nuclear weapons and more limited protests against chemical and biological weapons. The modern technology of destruction has in addition greatly strengthened the argument that war itself is the worst possible evil. Belief that the use of nuclear bombs in a war between the superpowers would be inevitable has created a new category of 'nuclear pacifism'.

Campaigns against nuclear weapons have not solely concentrated on the need for nuclear disarmament and for preventing the spread of such weapons. Protest has often focused on the testing of nuclear weapons – sometimes treated as a distinct issue – on particular nuclear bases, specific missile deployments, on mining uranium which can be used for bombs, and on the process of manufacturing warheads. Campaigners have also objected to the dangers of bombers carrying nuclear weapons (a number crashed in the 1950s and 1960s) and opposed vessels armed with nuclear weapons visiting their ports. The variety of these protests and their wider policy goals are explored in subsequent chapters.

Particular military policies may provoke opposition because they seem to increase the likelihood of war, or because they waste economic resources or have socially damaging consequences. Resistance to increases in military budgets and fears about an 'arms race' draw on these concerns. One major focus of anxiety and protest throughout this century has been the arms trade. Before and after the First World War many feared that arms manufacturers with a vested interest in selling as many arms as possible promoted war and so acted as 'merchants of death'. Since 1945 the trade in arms from the technologically developed states of the West and the Soviet bloc to the Third World has prompted much critical scrutiny. Peace researchers have charted the volume of arms sales, which rose dramatically in the 1970s, and have examined the dangers of such sales strengthening military élites, distorting economic development and exacerbating local conflicts.[3] Concern about arms sales was also expressed in the Brandt Report analysing the North–South divide.[4] Groups in the USA and Britain and many other countries organized protests against arms sales during the 1970s, and protests mounted in the late 1980s.

Moves by the military to take over agricultural land to create or to extend army bases or air bases have provoked significant local resistance in a number of cases. The best-known campaign has been waged in Southern France by the farmers of Larzac, supported by Gandhian pacifists at the Community of the Arch and by industrial and professional unions. The campaign began in 1970 and was eventually won after eleven years.[5] A little-known example is the prolonged struggle by the Shibokusa women who live at the foot of Mount Fuji to recover their land taken over by the US occupation army after 1945, but then retained by the Japanese armed forces.[6]

Opposition to a particular war is, of course, one logical expression of pacifism, and pacifists can often be found promoting resistance to conscription. Protesters also tend to stress the brutality and immorality of the methods used by their government in waging the war: for example opponents of the Boer War in Britain pointed to the use of concentration camps. The mainspring of campaigns against specific wars has, however, been anti-imperialism. This has been combined with a simple human resistance to being drafted overseas to face death or injury, especially when victory looks uncertain and the cause dubious. Conscripts may simply rebel against the grimness of army life. All these elements were present in the protests against the French War in Algeria. During 1955 and 1956 there were widespread demonstrations and petitions, some conscripts refused to leave for Algeria and women lay down in front of troop trains. A committee set up in 1958 indicted French use of torture and repression against Algerians, and by 1960 intellectuals and students were protesting bitterly. Some potential conscripts went into hiding or escaped abroad, and they were openly supported in a public manifesto signed by 121 intellectuals.[7] War resistance can, however, be extended to active support for those justly fighting for independence. In France the highly controversial Jeanson network offered direct assistance to the Algerian National Liberation Front, and in the eyes of many discredited the wider opposition. So not all forms of resistance to specific wars can count as being part of a 'peace movement'.

Anti-imperialism is not the only reason for opposing wars as unjust. Just War doctrine and popular perceptions distinguish between genuinely defensive wars and acts of aggression. So it is not surprising that the 1982 Israeli incursion into the Lebanon to crush the Palestine Liberation Organization, which could not, like the wars of 1967 and 1973, be seen as a legitimate response to a military threat from Arab states, provoked major public demonstrations against the government. The issue is not always, however, simply whether or not it is right to defend existing state borders, but the extent of those borders. Peace groups in Israel have criticized Israeli occupation of territories captured during the 1967 War. When frontiers are in dispute the

17

distinction between a war of liberation and internal 'terrorism' becomes contentious, and the position can be further confused by violent conflict between ethnic or ideological communities in the disputed territory. Peace groups may then concentrate on resisting central government use of troops to quell local uprisings or guerrilla action as in the case of the Palestinian *intifada* or Northern Ireland. Sometimes, as in South Africa, governments quite unambiguously wage war on sections of their own population. Campaigns for draft resistance in both Israel and South Africa in the late 1980s did not primarily reflect pacifism, but deep disquiet about the repressive role of the military in those societies.

RECONCILIATION AND THE ISSUE OF SOCIAL JUSTICE

The dominant emphasis of peace activity has been on opposing war and military policies, but it has always encompassed positive measures to promote mutual understanding and transnational cooperation. For example a Swiss pacifist, Pierre Ceresole, set up International Voluntary Service in 1920 to bring volunteers from different countries together in work camps to do useful work. Since 1945 many peace groups have been active in building bridges across the East–West divide through exchanging delegations or organizing conferences of professionals. In addition peace activists have often tried to engage in direct reconciliation of local communities in conflict by third-party mediation and by countering misinformation, or by bringing both sides together to alter long-term prejudices. Communal reconciliation is often linked to undertaking practical work to tackle local problems such as unemployment or housing. Christian pacifists have engaged in a number of such moves towards reconciliation in Northern Ireland, for example, and an international group worked with the United Nations in Cyprus in 1973–74 on a resettlement project for Turkish villagers driven from their homes.[8]

Positive peace-making is not always uncontentious. Because of the divisive and politically complex circumstances in which it takes place, reconciliation may be seen as traitorous and peacemakers can be charged with refusing to recognize the necessity of conflict and the need to resist injustice. So the claims of justice and the claims of reconciliation may appear to run counter to each other. Gandhian non-violence attempts to combine struggle with ultimate reconciliation, but even in non-violent campaigns resistance usually sharpens divisions. Pacifists may disagree on whether the right course is to support one side in a conflict or to try to end it. Bridge-building between East and West has also raised difficult issues for Western peace groups seeking dialogue through official channels in the East, but sympathetic to the opposition in Eastern Europe.

Whether peace should be an absolute priority or whether at times political freedom, human rights or social justice should take precedence has always been a problem for peace activists, as we saw in the Introduction. Pacifists and war resisters who do refuse to take part even in Just Wars are generally committed to promote freedom and equality, both because of their political beliefs and values, and because they argue peace can only be built on just foundations. Many of those prominent in peace campaigns have indeed been engaged in social reform or in struggles for racial equality, trade union rights or women's rights. Peace activists have in addition been prominent in opposing colonialism. Peace journals have not only given prominence to strict war resistance, but have also covered non-violent campaigns for social justice, for example Martin Luther King's role in the American Civil Rights movement, Danilo Dolci's struggle on behalf of the poor in Sicily and against the Mafia, and Cesar Chavez's attempts to organize the grape pickers of California. But when faced with the question of how far they can give political support to movements fighting violently for social change, peace groups, including pacifists, tend to be divided.

PEACE PHILOSOPHIES, POLICIES AND STRATEGIES

The detailed policies proposed by peace groups naturally depend on the problems they are facing and the immediate political context. In practice, moreover, peace organizations usually embrace a variety of views. It is, however, important to indicate the range of philosophical positions which can prompt peace activity and the prescriptions and actions that flow from them.

Since moral prohibitions play a significant role in peace protest, especially in pacifism, religious belief is one obvious basis for such protest. Christianity and Buddhism have indeed inspired pacifism and moves to promote reconciliation, but in both cases only certain sects have espoused unequivocal opposition to war.[9] Christian rebels against state militarism have also drawn on mainstream Protestantism, or Catholicism, but in opposition to the church hierarchies. Nuclear weapons have posed a profound challenge to the just war theory held by Catholics and many Protestants, but belief in deterrence, and abhorrence of Communist ideology, has modified the case for renouncing possession of them. The views of churches in different countries have been influenced too by national political factors, as we will see in later chapters. Hinduism has had an indirect influence on peace theory and action through Gandhi's thought and strategy of non-violent resistance.[10]

The predominant influence on thinking about peace, which is compatible with both Christian belief and with humanism, has been liberal internationalism. Liberalism has argued the benefits of international cooperation, and of reasoned negotiation or arbitration to resolve disputes. It suggests, too, the potential value of national gestures of goodwill, such as arms reduction, to remove misunderstanding and mistrust. Liberal views of international politics, which indicate that it is possible to avoid war, and that governments can be persuaded to follow rational cooperative self-interest, if irrational fears or unnecessary obstacles are removed, permeate the ideas of many peace groups. Even bodies founded initially on a distinct set of commitments, such as feminism, may embrace liberal internationalism, as we saw in relation to the Women's International League for Peace Freedom. The Quaker belief in 'speaking truth to power' in part embodies this approach. The strategy implicit in liberal internationalism is to provide skilled high-level mediation, formulate detailed proposals for government action, lobby and petition decision-makers and to educate the general public. Peace research to provide detailed information and ideas for negotiators and policy-makers falls within this approach.

There is, however, a less élitist and more populist form of liberalism, which also has a considerable influence on peace movement theory and strategy. Populist liberalism relies much less on the rationality of governments, which are seen as bureaucracies dominated by the power of the military and influenced by vested economic interests. This version of liberalism relies much more on the power of popular opinion to force change on reluctant establishments. So the strategy emphasis is on altering public attitudes through meetings, literature sales and other methods of popular education. But this approach also favours mobilizing public opposition through mass demonstrations and non-violent methods of protest that challenge military policy. Liberal populism has its own version of internationalism which looks to transnational movements creating pressure for change. Nuclear disarmament movements have been strongly influenced by liberal populism, though they have included elements of a more élitist liberal strategy.

Socialist internationalism has had some impact on post-war peace movements. It is difficult to characterize this theoretical approach briefly, since socialists have been divided between supporters of parliamentary socialism (very close in the West to welfare liberalism), Communists and non-Communist Marxists. The primary emphasis of parliamentary socialists has been on trying to move their parties away from unequivocal support for NATO policies, and they have sometimes encouraged liberal populist campaigns in order to do so. The role of Communists since 1945 can best be understood within the concrete international and national circumstance in which they have operated (see Chapter 2). Non-Communist Marxists place much greater reliance on mobilizing trade union support and on industrial action, and see peace campaigns only as one element in an anti-capitalist strategy. Trotskyists and other revolutionary Marxists were peripheral to the nuclear disarmament campaigns, but came to the fore in some of the protests against the Vietnam War.

Anarchist ideas have found expression in a variety of peace campaigns. At one end of the spectrum there is a Tolstoyan anarchist pacifism which rejects both the state and its war machine, but requires strictly non-violent forms of resistance. At the other is anarcho-syndicalism looking to the ultimate goal of the general strike and prepared to use violence. More diffuse anarchist ideas and attitudes have, however, been much more influential in promoting a critique of the reliance of the state on war, in encouraging repudiation of state socialism in the East as well as capitalist governments in the West, and in disseminating general distrust of hierarchical and bureaucratic organization. Within peace movements anarchism has prompted opposition to centralist organization of peace groups themselves and to reliance on individual leaders. Anarchists promote resort to various forms of direct action but unlike liberal populists, who envisage such action in the context of parliamentary democracy and ultimate respect for the system of law, anarchists see direct action as a means of repudiating existing institutions, and may be less concerned to maintain non-violence.

Anarchist attitudes to the state and to hierarchy link up with the radical feminism which began to influence peace groups in the 1970s. There are, however, important differences. Radical feminists may see the fundamental cause of war either in the male biological drive towards aggression and violence, or in the social system of patriarchy

21

which shapes differing forms of government and economy to perpetuate the subordination of women. Radical feminists therefore celebrate womanly values which repudiate war and call for peace associations and actions confined to women as a source of new strength for the women taking part. The Greenham Common peace camp in the 1980s has been the central symbol of radical feminist campaigning for peace.

The theories which underlie peace activity are all opposed to what has been since 1945 the dominant orthodoxy of international relations: 'realism'. Realism can be traced back in the history of political theory to the writings of Thucydides, Machiavelli and Hobbes, and it has been implicit in the practice of governments. Realism as an academic theory of international politics posits that conflict is inevitable between nation states, that maintaining military power is essential to promote national security, and that pursuit of disarmament is likely to precipitate disaster. Rigorous realism might suggest that nuclear war is inevitable, but many realists have relied on the stablizing role of the great powers and on nuclear deterrence. Realists have therefore supported forms of arms control which reduce the risk of accidental war or of miscalculation or pre-emptive strikes in a crisis. Some realists and some peace bodies can therefore agree on some specific strategies to reduce the risk of war, and in certain circumstances both might endorse a national policy of neutralism. There is, however, a fundamental gulf between the realist perspective and all those who hold to a more 'utopian' belief in the possibility of a peaceful world.[11]

Realism in international politics is related to a conservative perspective in national politics, both tending to assume the irredeemable wickedness of human nature and the inevitability of conflicting interests, and both tending to rely on an élite of experienced statesmen to steer their societies and to control dangerous popular pressures for utopian change. The link between realism and conservatism is also suggested by the fact that supporters of peace campaigns are drawn almost entirely from the liberal centre and the Left. The picture is, however, somewhat more complicated. Far right political groups in the West, who aim for radical change in domestic politics away from the welfare state and economic planning, and who have been prepared to risk a nuclear war with the Soviet Union in order to defeat 'godless Communism', represent an ideological dogmatism and a recklessness which is totally opposed to the more sober pragmatism associated with realist attitudes and policies. On the other hand liberalism in domestic politics is often compatible with a fundamentally realist outlook in international affairs – liberal theory has after all always allowed a role for the state in securing internal and external security.

The picture is further complicated by the fact that the ideas and vocabulary of international politics are strongly influenced by liberal internationalism, which is superimposed upon realist criteria. The USA has been especially inclined to stress ideals of liberal democracy as a basis for world order, and to urge the importance of international organization like the United Nations, international law and the desirability of disarmament. West European and other states have also, however, accepted the attractiveness of ideals of disarmament and international cooperation, and the Soviet Union has capitalized on the strength of this liberal internationalism in public consciousness in its own disarmament proposals. During the worst period of the Cold War both sides were engaged in ritualistic negotiations on general and complete disarmament, and negotiations on various forms of arms control and disarmament have continued ever since, with some limited agreements so far emerging from this process.

Peace groups opposed to nuclear arms and to other military policies have therefore had to clarify their position on negotiations. Some peace campaigns have sought to exert effective pressure to achieve success in negotiations, or to promote a particular negotiating stance – for example the Freeze proposals in the USA in the early 1980s. Peace groups have also used debates on disarmament at the United Nations to mobilize public pressure for progress in cutting arms. The UN Special Sessions on Disarmament in 1978 and in 1982 were both the focus of petitions and lobbying, and in 1982 of large demonstrations. Peace campaigners have, however, looked at the record of negotiations since 1947 on arms limitation, and many have concluded that negotiations, even if agreement is reached as in SALT I and II, instead of curbing arms, more often act as a justification and screen for a further arms build up. Peace groups therefore tend to urge unilateral measures of restraint or tokens of good faith in conjunction with negotiations, and campaigns in Europe have usually called for some forms of unilateral action. Demand for an end to nuclear tests or for removal of bases, or renunciation of particular military strategies is a logical extension of popular pressure on governments for a change of policy. Demands for unilateral action can in principle be achieved by popular pressure on one government, and government actions can be monitored by the news media and public opinion. If campaigns call for negotiations, then it is much harder to scrutinize the course of talks, which in some cases are at least nominally confidential. Moreover, blame for the failure of talks can be shifted

23

onto the other side. Demand for unilateral government action also stems logically from any uncompromising moral position on war or on weapons of mass destruction. So unilateral policies are promoted by pacifist and religious groups with a radical anti-militarist position, and are also associated with liberal populism. The more élitist forms of liberal internationalism tend to rely much more heavily on negotiations, as already noted, and to exert more discreet influence on governments.

When trying to define the distinctive policies associated with peace groups, it is broadly true that they can be characterized by their commitment to unilateral measures on arms, or by unconditional opposition to all or particular wars. This emphasis has distinguished nuclear disarmament campaigns, for example, from the more orthodox liberal internationalists associated with groups supporting the United Nations and negotiated arms control. But as we have seen, significant peace campaigns, like the American Freeze movement, have not been in any sense 'unilateralist'. Conversely, most advocates of unilateral measures support bilateral negotiations between the great powers and multilateral agreements like the Non-Proliferation Treaty. Unilateral action by one or a group of governments is seen as a way of promoting agreed disarmament measures – for example by creating a nuclear-free zone in the Pacific – not as an alternative to multilateral agreement.

Peace groups have varied in their attitudes to defence. All have feared that dominant military establishments will undermine or destroy internal democracy and pursue policies which increase the risks of war. Many have also opposed military training in schools and glorification of war and weapons in popular culture, and the political or cultural projection of exaggerated enemy stereotypes. Some peace campaigners have gone on to argue that any emphasis on national defence is misguided and hinders the struggle for peace and for social justice at home. The majority of nuclear disarmament campaigners have, however, accepted in principle the legitimacy of conventional defence – or even interim forms of nuclear deterrence.

During the 1970s and 1980s academics and peace researchers in Western Europe began to elaborate on possible conventional defence strategies which would reduce tension and the danger of war by miscalculation by demonstrating that the aim of military deployments was purely to repel direct attack, not to launch a pre-emptive strike. Researchers drew on examples of neutral European states to illustrate forms of 'non-offensive defence' and some also explored how NATO and the Warsaw Pact might alter their deployments.[12] Those who rejected any form of military defence, but also believed in the need to resist military domination by aggressive regimes, investigated past examples of popular resistance to occupation and tyranny and proposed preparations for non-cooperation and non-violent resistance to an occupation.[13] Some retired and serving military officers and strategic theorists have endorsed the idea of non-violent or 'civilian' defence, either as an alternative to military deployments or as a supplementary and fallback policy for national defence.[14] Serious research into non-violent defence is one response to the nuclear age.

NOTES AND REFERENCES

1. Reform within Communist Party states tended to give more autonomy to Peace Committees, for example in Czechoslovakia in 1968.

2. A similar three-fold classification (movements to eliminate war, to stop particular aspects of war and to stop particular wars) was developed by Bob Overy, *How Effective Are Peace Movements?* Peace Studies Papers No. 2 (Bradford University School of Peace Studies and London, Housmans, 1982). This classification is also used by Peter van den Dungen (ed.), *West European Pacifism and the Strategy for Peace* (London, Macmillan, 1985), pp. 22–3.

3. The Stockholm International Peace Research Institute (SIPRI) has regularly produced statistics and analysis of the arms trade since 1971.

4. *North–South: a Programme for Survival*, The Report of the Independent Commission on International Development Issues under the Chairmanship of Willy Brandt (London, Pan Books, 1980), pp. 20–2.

5. For an account up to 1976 see Roger Rawlinson, 'The Battle of Larzac', in A. Paul Hare and Herbert H. Blumberg, *Liberation Without Violence* (London, Rex Collings, 1977), pp. 58–72. See also Chris Jones, 'Victory at Larzac', *Peace News*, 26 June 1981, p. 6.

6. Leonie Caldecott, 'At the Foot of the Mountain: the Shibokusa Women of Kita Fuji' in Lynne Jones (ed.), *Keeping the Peace* (London, The Women's Press, 1983), pp. 98–107.

7. For brief references see Jean-Pierre Rioux, *The Fourth Republic, 1944–1958* (Cambridge, Cambridge University Press, 1987), pp. 268, 291–2.

8. A. Paul Hare and Ellen Wilkinson, 'Cyprus: Conflict and its Resolution', in Hare and Blumberg, pp. 239–47.

9. For Christian views see Roland Bainton, *Christian Attitudes Towards War and Peace* (London, Hodder and Stoughton, 1961).

10. See Joan V. Bondurant, *Conquest of Violence: the Gandhian Philosophy of Conflict* (Princeton, New Jersey, Princeton University Press, 1958), especially Chapter 4, 'Hindu Tradition and Satyagraha'.

11. For a survey of views on war and peace within political theory see Kenneth N. Waltz, *Man, the State and War: a Theoretical Analysis* (New

York, Columbia University Press, 1959). On recent approaches see Martin Ceadel, *Thinking About Peace and War* (Oxford, Oxford University Press, 1987).

12. For example Adam Roberts, *Nations in Arms: the Theory and Practice of Territorial Defence* (London, Chatto and Windus, 1976); Johan Galtung, *There Are Alternatives* (Nottingham, Spokesman, 1984); *Bulletin of Peace Proposals*, 15 January 1984; and *Bulletin of the Atomic Scientists*, **44**, 7, 1988, pp. 12–54, give brief summaries of work on non-offensive defence.

13. Gene Sharp has been researching and writing on non-violent resistance and its relevance to defence for thirty years. See, for example, Gene Sharp, *Making Europe Unconquerable: the Potential of Civilian-based Deterrence and Defence* (London, Taylor and Francis, 1985). See also Adam Roberts (ed.), *The Strategy of Civilian Defence* (London, Faber and Faber, 1967).

14. For example, Sir Stephen King-Hall, *Defence in the Nuclear Age* (London, Gollancz, 1958); B. H. Liddell Hart in Roberts, *Strategy of Civilian Defence*. The governments of Sweden, Denmark, The Netherlands and Norway commissioned research into non-violent defence possibilities during the 1970s and 1980s. Although some findings stressed the limitations of non-violent methods in meeting a variety of threats, this work elaborated strategic thought on non-military defence, see Anders Boserup and Andrew Mack, *War Without Weapons* (London, Frances Pinter, 1974).

CHAPTER TWO

The Global Context of Peace Activity since 1945

INTRODUCTION

The role of peace groups since the end of the Second World War can only be fully understood in the context of the main developments in world politics since 1945. The experience of the Second World War, and the lessons derived from it, have had an important impact on thinking about war and peace. Technological developments in weaponry, in particular the H bomb and the intercontinental missile, have transformed the nature of warfare between the great powers and so promoted widespread popular movements aiming to prevent a nuclear holocaust. However, the Cold War between the USA and USSR, which structured world politics for forty years, restricted the possibilities for peace action.

The impact of decolonization in creating a large number of new states is one of the most significant developments since 1945, shifting the focus of world politics away from the West, challenging the priorities of the Cold War and opening up new North–South tensions. So the demands of Third World countries have created new opportunities but also new problems for peace bodies in the West. The revolution in communications which has created a growing awareness of 'the global village' has also encouraged the growth of transnational movements to work for a better future for the world. The peace movement is one of these new forces, and although pre-war organizations and ideas remain important, they have responded to social and political changes. In addition, many new groupings have arisen. The peace movement in the 1980s, for example, reflected both the influence of feminism and the growing importance of environmental issues. This chapter concentrates, however, on clarifying the back-

27

ground to the upsurge of peace protest in the late 1950s and in the 1960s.

THE IMPACT OF THE SECOND WORLD WAR

The evolution of peace activity since 1814, and the strength of anti-war sentiment in many countries after 1918, suggest that peace movements can be explained partly as a reaction to the experience of modern warfare. The impact of the Second World War on public attitudes does not, however, seem to confirm this hypothesis. Within the Western Allied powers the main lessons drawn from the 1930s were that it is essential to maintain preparedness for war, and that it is fatal to appease dictators. Whereas the First World War had encouraged the belief that arms races lead to war, so spurring the search for disarmament, the Second World War prompted a conventional wisdom on the perils of disarmament. Beliefs about the lessons of 1939 strongly influenced governments in the West in the build-up of the Cold War in the late 1940s.

There were a number of reasons why the experience of war between 1939 and 1945 did not generate such widespread peace sentiment as the 1914–18 War. One reason is that the actual fighting of the war, however appalling the losses, did not engender the same sense of deadly futility as the static trench warfare of the Western Front in the First World War. The new technologies of the battle tank and of the fighter and bomber aircraft, gave scope for daring generalship and individual feats of skill and bravery. Guerrilla action against the German occupying armies provided examples of ingenuity, determination and extreme courage. Even the suffering of civilian populations from bombing and privation provided material for myth-making. The Second World War revived some of the romanticism of battle, not only in wartime propaganda but in the way it has been portrayed in the forty-five years since war ended, as numerous novels and films – and quite a few memoirs of escape or adventure – confirm.

The pain and suffering caused by the Second World War was, however, even more extreme, and the deaths more numerous, than in the First War. The most important reason why those who suffered did not in general draw pacifist conclusions was that the vast majority in the West believed the war was both necessary and just. Whereas the First World War appeared to many in retrospect as a war which should never have been fought, the revelation of the Nazi death camps strengthened the conviction that Hitler's regime was an evil which had to be overthrown. Moreover, many of the atrocities of the war were perpetrated by the German, Italian and Japanese occupation forces, and during its course those in the occupied countries of Europe longed for liberation by the armed forces of the Allies. So the horrors of war were overshadowed by the horrors of ruthless dictatorship and expansionist militarism. When Stalinism appeared to threaten a new attempt to impose a totalitarian dictatorship, not only over Eastern Europe, where Soviet armies had remained since 1945, but in the West, even some of the neutrally inclined countries of Western Europe were ready to join the North Atlantic Alliance.

In the Soviet Union itself the legacy of the war was complex. It enabled Stalin to recapture the territories of the Tsarist Empire and to extend Soviet power over Eastern Europe. The experience of the German invasion in 1941 and the enormous Soviet losses, estimated at twenty million deaths, left Soviet governments determined to maintain a bulwark of East European territory against possible future aggression. The war encouraged a strong revival of Russian nationalism and a popular desire to assert Russian prestige and ensure military strength. But simultaneously it evoked a genuine longing to avoid a new war. Both popular attitudes were encouraged by the Soviet leadership, which mobilized desire for peace under the aegis of a party-controlled Peace Committee and international peace campaigns, but also organized patriotic rituals in memory of the war and displays of military strength. The German invasion of the Soviet Union forced the USSR and the Western Allies to combine, but it remained an uneasy alliance and conflict of interests over a post-war settlement laid the basis for future East–West tension.

The Second World War was, as its name suggests, quite literally a world war, involving not only the Middle East and parts of Africa, but also having cataclysmic effects on Asia. The speed and efficiency with which the Japanese overthrew European colonialism in much of Asia helped to destroy the image of white military supremacy and encouraged the nationalist and anti-colonialist aspirations which already existed. Japanese occupation itself, however, stimulated nationalist resistance, and when Japan was defeated the resistance movements turned their attention to opposing the reimposition of Western colonial rule. Western powers varied in their willingness to abandon imperial claims. The USA granted independence to the Philippines in 1946, India and Pakistan gained freedom from the British Empire in 1947 and The Netherlands recognized an independent Indonesia in 1950. France was more intransigent in Indo-China, but was forced out after the traumatic defeat by the Vietnamese Communist forces at Dien Bien Phu, leaving the USA to back the non-Communist government created in the South.

So the main effect of the war on Asia, like the break-up of the Austro-Hungarian Empire after the First World War, was to promote nationalism and newly independent states. Asia was, however, also caught up in the developing Cold War between the USSR and the West. Victory of the Chinese Communists, in the civil war in 1949, greatly strengthened American fears of Communist expansion. Korea had been an early victim of the tension between the USA and USSR, when it was divided into US and Soviet spheres of influence at the end of the Second World War. Vietnam, after French forces withdrew, was also divided into two ideologically opposed regimes sponsored by the Soviet Union and the USA respectively.

One country in Asia which did draw specifically anti-militarist conclusions from the experience of the Second World War was Japan. Under US occupation Japan was encouraged to renounce the militarist ambitions and rigid warrior code associated with the regime of the 1930s, and specific limits on its armed forces were written into the new Japanese Constitution. By the 1970s, as Japan's economic power flourished and the USA began to see economic disadvantages in its extended global military role, the US government began to urge the Japanese to spend more on arms to contain the Soviet Union. But although groups in Japan by the 1980s favoured a resurgence of its military power, and have tried to promote a favourable image of Japan's wartime policies, there has been strong popular resistance to Japan becoming a military power. This revulsion against war and military preparations was a product of the suffering in the War, and in particular the atomic bombing of Hiroshima and Nagasaki. In Japan, the only country to have experienced the horror of nuclear attack, opposition to testing and deployment of nuclear weapons has remained strong.

Relief that the war was over, and preoccupation in Europe with rebuilding shattered national economies and creating a better society, diverted most people's attention from pondering deeply on the lessons of the war. Despite the predominant belief that the war had been necessary, there were factors which could be interpreted to support an anti-war case.

Pacifists have stressed that war crodes moral sensitivity and human sympathy, and at the same time accelerates the technology of death. Europe had first been alerted to the brutal possibilities of a new era of aerial warfare during the Spanish Civil War, when German planes

30

bombed the town of Guernica. Picasso recorded this monstrous crime in his famous painting. A few years later the monstrous had become commonplace, as not only Germany, but also Britain and the USA began to bomb cities, not just to destroy military targets or economic potential, but to break civilian morale. This policy developed from the raids on Coventry and London into the indiscriminate bombing of Dresden, the fire bombing of Tokyo and the annihilation of Hiroshima. Opposition to deliberate destruction of cities was voiced during the war by Bishop Bell of Chichester and pacifists in Britain, but moral qualms were swept aside by political and military leaders committed to use any means to gain the end of victory. The war also ensured a race by Allied scientists to develop an atomic bomb – only a theoretical possibility in 1939 – because of fear that German scientists might develop it first. After the bomb was successfully tested at Alamagordo in July 1945, the US and British governments, as previously planned, used it to bring about a rapid end to the war against Japan. Whether by August 1945 it was necessary to drop two A bombs on Japanese cities to secure a surrender, and how far the American decision was influenced by desire to contain the Soviet Union in Asia, or by its overall diplomatic strategy towards Stalin, has been the subject of historical disputes.[1] These questions have also been raised in the context of nuclear disarmament campaigns.

NUCLEAR WEAPONS AND THE COLD WAR

The bombs dropped on Hiroshima and Nagasaki ended the Second World War, and inaugurated a new era in international politics. But although there was general awareness that a new and awesome weapon had been used, and some Christians, and others, queried the morality of Hiroshima[2], most people did not immediately think deeply about the long-term implications of nuclear weapons. A few academics did, however, address the issues raised for international relations, notably Bernard Brodie, the father of nuclear deterrence theory.[3] The greatest concern about the implications for the world of the discovery of how to unleash the power of the atom was felt by the nuclear scientists who had helped to create the A bomb. Neils Bohr and his colleagues had during the war begun to argue the need for international control of atomic energy once the war was over, and scientists at the University of Chicago, headed by James Franck, urged Roosevelt not to use the atomic bomb against the Japanese but

31

instead to prepare to promote an international body to control nuclear energy.[4] Scientists in the USA were active in the immediate post-war period in lobbying for civilian control of atomic energy within their country, and pressing their government to sponsor an attempt to freeze nuclear bomb technology at its existing level and to promote international control over the peaceful development of nuclear energy.

The great power interests of the USA and the humanitarian concerns of the atomic scientists were combined in the Baruch Plan presented in 1946 to the United Nations. The plan proposed a supranational authority with powers to monitor all nuclear plants and to promote a free flow of scientific information. The USA offered to renounce its advantage in nuclear technology and to abandon its weapons in return for assurance that no other power could secretly develop the A bomb. For the Soviet Union there were three over-whelming disadvantages: (1) the USA would retain a monopoly of nuclear weapon expertise; (2) a supranational body would have the right to supervise any nuclear plants located in the USSR; (3) the Baruch proposal denied the Soviet Union a right of veto in a body which would (like the United Nations) at that period be dominated by the West. While it is doubtful whether the Soviet Union would in any circumstances have allowed the USA to retain a monopoly of the knowledge of how to make nuclear weapons, the Baruch terms helped to ensure the Soviet Government would turn down the plan.[5] As the Cold War began to dominate international politics, the pattern set by the Baruch Plan became standard in all East–West negotiations on disarmament. The USA and its allies demanded a supranational body with extensive powers of inspection as a condition of nuclear or conventional arms reduction, while the USSR saw inspection as a form of espionage and demanded equal representation and a veto on any international body. The USSR also issued ambitious plans for rapid nuclear and conventional disarmament and not only promoted its ideas at the United Nations but engaged in extensive 'peace' propaganda.

When the USSR tested its first atomic bomb in July 1949, NATO had already been founded, Communist Party control directed from Moscow had been imposed over the whole of Eastern Europe (except rebel Yugoslavia) and the Cold War had already polarized attitudes in the West. Alarmed by the rapidity with which the USSR had acquired the A bomb the USA accelerated research on the infinitely more powerful H bomb, as did the Soviet Government. In this context opposition to Western military programmes seemed almost treasonous and implied support for Soviet policies. The impression that peace activity must be pro-Soviet was greatly strengthened by the association between Communist parties and campaigns against the A bomb. The Polish Government sponsored a World Congress of Intellectuals for Peace in August 1948, and French Communists arranged a World Congress for Peace in Paris in April 1949. The World Peace Committee, which later became the World Peace Council, launched the Stockholm Peace Appeal in May 1950, involving a petition against the A bomb. Mass signatures were organized by party-sponsored Peace Committees in the USSR and Eastern Europe, while Western Communists mobilized support from many non-Communists genuinely concerned about the nuclear threat. In subsequent campaigns the anti-American slant of the World Peace Council became clearer and the obvious involvement of Communist activists ensured that not only right-wing governments denounced the peace campaigns, but socialist parties and public opinion in most Western countries reacted with distrust. The small independent peace groups that existed distanced themselves as far as possible from the World Peace Council.

The fact that development of both the A and the H bomb was so closely associated with the deepening of the Cold War was of profound importance. The discovery of how to split the atom created a threat to the future of the planet, and so demanded cooperative global solutions. Nuclear weapons, however, also posed in extreme form traditional security dilemmas for both the Soviet and US Governments, because of the vital military advantage apparently conveyed by being ahead in nuclear weapon technology. The age-old question of whether to prepare for war in order to secure peace, or whether to cut back arms to avoid war, was posed with even greater acuteness. The problems of deciding the correct strategy in a new nuclear era were compounded by the ideological clash between Western liberal capitalism and the Stalinist version of socialism.

These dilemmas were reflected in the way the scientists in the USA responded to Cold War developments. While a minority linked to the *Bulletin of the Atomic Scientists* continued to maintain that the greatest threat came from nuclear bombs, and that international cooperation to control this threat was a priority, after 1947 many accepted the necessity of the US Government's policy of 'containment' against the spread of Soviet influence and power. This larger group was, however, split again when it came to the decision whether or not the US Government should engage in a crash programme to make the H bomb. Edward Teller, the strongest advocate of the H bomb, had weighty support among the military and the bureaucracy. Scientists on the General Advisory Committee to the Atomic Energy Commission, who were asked to advise on the implications of the Soviet A bomb, accepted the need for continuing H bomb research, but opposed a crash programme.[6] The committee, chaired by Robert Oppenheimer, still hoped that this new danger to the world could be averted. Oppenheimer became a victim of McCarthyism in 1954, partly because of his role in 1949.

NUCLEAR TESTING

Public opinion did, however, become roused over the long-term effects of radiation on health and on future generations. Testing of nuclear weapons therefore began to become a major issue in the mid-1950s. The USA had tested its first thermonuclear device in 1952, followed by the USSR in 1953. The first tests of a viable US H bomb took place in March 1954 at the Bikini atoll in the Pacific. These H bomb tests had repercussions which the US Administration certainly had not anticipated. The radioactive fall-out from the Bravo explosion on 1st March showered twenty-eight Americans and 236 Marshallese on four islands close to the blast, who had to be evacuated. Although the Americans suffered less seriously from radiation sickness than the Islanders, the fact that Americans were involved in the mishap meant that news began to leak back to the USA. The Administration might, however, have been able to play down the incident and restrict knowledge of its H bomb testing if Bravo had not claimed other victims: Japanese tuna fishermen, whose boat, the *Lucky Dragon*, was about eighty-five miles away from Bikini. When the boat returned home with its crew of twenty-three, seriously ill with all the signs of radiation sickness, the *Lucky Dragon* became a new symbol of Japanese suffering from the effects of US nuclear weapons. A political furore broke out in Japan and made headlines in the American press, stimulating public debate about the extent of the danger from fall-out and long-term radiation levels and about the implications of H bombs themselves.[7] The Bikini Bomb exploded on 1st March was 15 megatons, one thousand times more powerful than the Hiroshima bomb of around 15 kilotons.

Nuclear weapons, and in particular nuclear testing in the atmosphere, became the subject of increasing public concern after 1954, and pressure mounted on the USA to halt nuclear testing and to enter into negotiations on a nuclear test ban. The most significant political pressure was exerted by Third World countries, beginning to become an important factor on the international political scene as increasing numbers of newly independent states entered the United Nations, and as both the USA and the Soviet Union competed to enlist them in the Cold War alliances. Many of these new states were not, however, willing to be drawn into a conflict which was irrelevant to their own priorities, and the Bandung Conference in April 1955 launched the Non-aligned Movement, and the Conference ended with an appeal for a moratorium on nuclear testing. India was prominent in launching this movement and also active in denouncing nuclear tests, which were producing greatly increased levels of radiation in many parts of the world. Although Soviet nuclear tests contributed to these enhanced radiation levels, the USSR saw the advantages of publicly responding to Third World concern, and from 1955 called for a test ban.

The second important element in prompting the USA and its Western allies to worry about the political implications of nuclear testing was the renewed role of scientists in the nuclear weapons debate. The main issue was the damage caused to health by increased radiation from nuclear testing. What levels of radiation resulted in real risk, and how great that risk was, both became hotly contested issues. Scientific knowledge was increasing about the possible effects of radiation in the long term, but there was still considerable uncertainty, allowing for widely varying estimates. The scientific debate was also inevitably highly politicized, and the US Atomic Energy Commission was suspected of deliberately underrating the dangers to human health. Nobel Prize winner Linus Pauling, who was strongly opposed to nuclear testing, produced estimates at the other extreme, predicting widespread cancer, particularly leukaemia, and genetic damage. Many of Pauling's colleagues, including scientists deeply concerned about nuclear fallout and the dangers of nuclear weapons, were sceptical about the scientific validity of his findings. Pauling did, however, play an important role in sparking off a public debate.

Scientific debate and protest was not of course limited to the USA. One hundred scientists in Britain signed a petition in April 1950, urging their government not to follow the USA in developing the H bomb, and Japanese scientists were active in gauging the effects of fall-out. An international petition launched by Bertrand Russell and signed by Albert Einstein and nine other eminent scientists led to the creation of the Pugwash Movement, which aimed to mobilize scientists to transcend Cold War barriers and use their expertise as an international force for peace. The first conference of scientists from both East and West and non-aligned countries was held in 1957 at the Pugwash estate in Nova Scotia of millionaire Cyrus Eaton. Pugwash produced detailed proposals in the next few years designed to help overcome the technological problems of verifying nuclear explosions, and remained a forum for Soviet bloc scientists to meet their Western colleagues. Mobilization of scientific protest across the world was more dramatically illustrated, however, when Linus Pauling presented a petition signed by 9,235 scientists to the United Nations in January 1958 calling for an end to nuclear tests.[8]

The third factor which predisposed the US Government to consider negotiating specifically on the issue of nuclear testing was growing public concern inside the USA and Western Europe. After the death of Stalin in March 1953 and the discrediting of Senator McCarthy by the end of 1954, the Cold War grip on public attitudes in the West gradually weakened. Space was created for dissent, and protest was not automatically attributed (except by the extreme Right) to a Soviet-controlled Communist conspiracy. Even in 1954 quite a number of American citizens had been disturbed enough by the fall-out from the US H bomb tests to write to the White House or to the newspapers and to risk having their names added to blacklists of supposed Communist sympathizers. Tests became an issue in the 1956 US presidential elections, and by 1957 public concern in both the USA and Britain crystallized into campaigns against nuclear testing.

The first major movement against nuclear weapons saw popular protests in many parts of the world between 1957 and 1964. Campaigners were acutely aware of the threat nuclear weapons posed to the future of life on earth, and opposed nuclear strategies which impinged upon them most directly. The central focus was, however, nuclear testing. So when the USA, USSR and UK signed the Partial Test Ban Treaty in Moscow in July 1963, which ended nuclear testing in the atmosphere and under water, concern about nuclear weapons began to fade. By 1966 opposition to the American war in Vietnam had become the centre of peace protests.

DIVISIONS IN WORLD COMMUNISM

During the first wave of demonstrations against nuclear weapons the Cold War had begun to give way to more complex relations within the Communist world and between East and West, but Cold War stereotypes still had a powerful grip on thinking about war and peace.

Much of the debate was crudely focused on whether it was better to be 'red or dead', and protesters against nuclear weapons in the West were often told to 'go to Moscow'. Changes in Sino-Soviet relations were, however, affecting the position on nuclear weapons and arms control and the future of great power confrontation. In addition, East European moves to loosen Moscow's control and pursue national roads to socialism, and the Soviet response to such moves, partially altered the nature of the Soviet bloc and had an important impact on Communist Parties and the Left in the West.

The alteration in Soviet domestic and foreign policy after the death of Stalin, which made possible a limited *rapprochement* with the West, provoked the rift with Mao's China. The post-Stalin leadership inaugurated a 'thaw' which allowed a limited degree of liberalization within the USSR and culminated in Khrushchev's 'Secret Speech' to the twentieth Party Congress in February 1956, denouncing Stalin's crimes against the Party and the post-1934 terror. Khrushchev also espoused the policy of peaceful coexistence with the West, arguing that in the age of nuclear weapons war between capitalism and socialism was no longer inevitable.

Mao openly denounced the principle of coexistence in 1957, urged revolutionary war against capitalism and imperialism, and pressed ahead with producing a Chinese atomic bomb. The final break between China and the USSR came in 1963, and the Chinese denounced the Partial Nuclear Test Ban Treaty, and fostered breakaway pro-Chinese Communist Parties. The Sino-Soviet dispute had a particularly strong impact on Communist Parties in Asia, and Chinese views on nuclear weapons influenced Japanese Communists, leading to a split in the Japanese anti-nuclear weapons movement.

For peace movements in the West, however, challenges to Soviet control over Eastern Europe, in particular the 1956 uprisings in Poland and Hungary, and the response of some Western Communist Parties, were more significant. Both the Secret Speech and the crushing of the Hungarian uprising had a profound impact on Western Communists. In Italy, the party under Togliatti saw that it could promote domestic policies suited to the political realities of Italian society and at the same time distance the party from Soviet-style Communism and direct obedience to Moscow. Togliatti proclaimed the principle of 'polycentrism' and the right of Communists to pursue national roads to socialism. It was not until 1968, however, that the Italian PCI embarked on an unambiguously independent course. Some Spanish Communists had also immediately responded to the implications of the Secret Speech, but the Spanish party did not begin to diverge openly from Moscow until the mid-1960s, when the USSR gave its backing to the Franco regime. Under Carillo, the party was to become in the 1970s one of the foremost 'Eurocommunist' parties.[9] Reform Communists in the West allied themselves with anti-Stalinist moves in Eastern Europe, for example Titoism in Yugoslavia, and later the 1968 Czechoslovak Reform Movement. The Soviet invasion of Czechoslovakia in 1968 was a crisis point, and was widely condemned by Western Communist Parties.

These changes in Western Communism had varying implications for peace organizations. Reformism tended to mean softening of the former unremitting hostility to NATO and the US military presence in Europe, so Communist Parties and their associated peace committees might not always be radical enough to suit the uncompromising position of some peace groups. On the other hand, parties and peace committees which distanced themselves from Moscow, and publicly criticized aspects of Soviet foreign and defence policy, became more acceptable allies for independent peace campaigners. So whereas the international independent peace organization set up in 1963 – the International Confederation for Disarmament and Peace – included no Communist Parties and only the Yugoslav official Peace Committee, the European Nuclear Disarmament campaign launched in 1980 involved the Italian Communist Party.[10] The World Peace Council as an international body remained, however, a representative of official Soviet policy even in the 1980s.

Revelations of the Stalinist terror and the crushing of the Hungarian uprising not only stimulated new thinking within Communist circles, it also prompted disillusioned party members to resign. The reduced attraction of official Communism for those rejecting the compromises made by Western social democratic parties with capitalist economies and with Cold War politics created space for new ideas and organizations on the left. Trotskyist parties made some converts, and had some influence on student radicals in the 1960s, but Trotskyism was too sectarian in ideology and too centralist in its organization to satisfy the spirit of 1960s radicalism. The gap was filled by the New Left.

The first strand in the New Left was created by disillusioned Communist intellectuals who left the party in 1956. Students in Britain and the USA sparked their own debates and contributed a second strand to New Left thinking. The New Left in Britain played an important role in the campaign against nuclear weapons from 1958 to 1963. The American New Left was primarily active in the Civil Rights movements and in community organizing, but also attacked

Cold War foreign policy and the war-based economy. Both the American and the British New Left moved into a more radical opposition to Western domestic and foreign policies in the later 1960s, and influenced the movement against the Vietnam War.[11]

NOTES AND REFERENCES

1. See for example Gar Alperovitz, *Atomic Diplomacy: Hiroshima and Potsdam* (Harmondsworth, Penguin, 1985). This is a revised and updated version of the book first published in 1965. See also the debate in the *New York Review of Books*, 23 October 1980 and 19 February 1981: 'Was the Hiroshima Bomb Necessary?'
2. Alperovitz, pp. 15–16.
3. Michael Mandelbaum, *The Nuclear Question: the United States and Nuclear Weapons 1946–1976* (Cambridge, Cambridge University Press, 1979), p. 19. Mandelbaum is referring to Brodie's 1946 essays in the book he edited on *The Absolute Weapon: Atomic Power and World Order* (New York, Harcourt, Brace and Company, 1946).
4. Robert Gilpin, *American Scientists and Nuclear Weapon Policy*, (Princeton, New Jersey, Princeton University Press, 1962), pp. 42–7.
5. For helpful analyses of the Baruch Plan and Soviet reactions, see Mandelbaum, pp. 23–7, and Daniel Yergin, *Shattered Peace: The Origins of the Cold War and the National Security State* (Harmondsworth, Penguin, 1980), pp. 237–40.
6. See Gilpin, pp. 87–97, for fairly detailed analysis of the Committee Report.
7. A good survey of the nuclear testing debate which started with the Bravo explosion is provided in Robert A. Divine, *Blowing on the Wind: The Nuclear Test Ban Debate 1954–1960* (New York, Oxford University Press, 1978).
8. Gilpin, p. 156.
9. On Eurocommunism see Paolo Filo della Terre, Edward Mortimer and Jonathan Storry, *Eurocommunism: Myth or Reality?* (Harmondsworth, Penguin, 1979).
10. On ICDP see Peggy Duff, *Left, Left, Left* (London, Alison and Busby, 1971), pp. 226–44. On END and its Conventions see Dimitri L. Roussopoulos, *The Coming of World War Three. Volume 1: From Protest to Resistance the International War System* (Montreal, Black Rose Books, 1986), pp. 147–203.
11. There is a large literature on the New Left. On the American New Left see Paul Jacobs and Saul Landau, *The New Radicals* (Harmondsworth, Penguin, 1966). For the British New Left see David Widgery (ed.), *The Left in Britain 1956–1968* (Harmondsworth, Penguin, 1976). See also Nigel Young, *An Infantile Disorder? The Crisis and Decline of the New Left* (London, Routledge & Kegan Paul, 1977).

CHAPTER THREE
The First Nuclear Disarmament Movement: 1957–64

The first wave of protests against nuclear weapons and nuclear testing can accurately be described as a movement. Mass protests in many countries encouraged passionate debates in political parties, trade unions, professional associations and religious bodies, although these debates sometimes preceded public protest. Widespread media coverage of nuclear weapons issues and of demonstrations heightened public awareness of the dangers of radiation and the risks of nuclear war. So governments in the West had to justify policies of nuclear deterrence and respond to public concern about nuclear fall-out.

The first movement against nuclear weapons was genuinely transnational in character. Nuclear fall-out was no respecter of frontiers and a nuclear war would have threatened the future of the whole world, so the need for united action was clear. Moreover, the press, film, radio and the new medium of television ensured that protests could be publicized almost everywhere. The symbol carried on the first march from London to Aldermaston at Easter 1958 rapidly became the world symbol of nuclear disarmament. Contingents from different countries joined in national actions and methods of protest spread by power of example. The independent nuclear disarmament movement was transnational long before it developed its own organizational framework in January 1963. If, however, independent campaigning bodies are distinguished from broader governmental and popular concern about nuclear weapons, significant independent protest took place primarily in North America and Western Europe. The major exception was Japan, where a mass campaign arose in 1954.

Despite the transnational character of the first nuclear disarmament movement, the individual campaigns can best be studied within their national framework. The politics of defence is still largely defined by the political institutions, culture and history of an individual state, and these national factors have determined how far autonomous peace activity is possible, if at all. The organizational basis of campaigns has been primarily national, and even transnational protests have arisen out of the initiative of national groups. So the evolution of the first nuclear disarmament movement can best be examined country by country.

Because movements tend to develop gradually, and often fade away by degrees, precise dating is difficult. As we saw in the previous chapter, scientists raised the alarm about nuclear weapons as early as 1945, and public concern was mobilized by the World Peace Council in the early 1950s. Disquiet about nuclear testing mounted after 1954. However, organized autonomous campaigns against nuclear weapons commanding significant support date in North America and Europe from 1957. The end of the first wave of nuclear disarmament varied between countries, but after the Partial Test Ban Treaty of 1963 there was soon a general reduction in protest.

OPPOSITION TO NUCLEAR TESTING AND WEAPONS IN THE USA

The USA has since 1945 been the dominant economic and political power shaping world politics, the greatest military power and the leader of the West. It was also the first state to develop nuclear weapons. Peace activity within the USA has therefore been particularly important. Because of US great power responsibilities, how ever, and because the Government saw itself as engaged in an ideological crusade against the Soviet Union, peace protest was in the 1950s particularly difficult to mount. The USA is a liberal democracy and governmental decision-making is exceptionally open, making it easier to monitor military policies than in many countries, even when the Administration tries to hide the truth. Numerous constitutional channels for effective protest do, moreover, exist. Tolerance of dissent has, however, varied greatly. During the height of the Cold War any form of dissent, and particularly any criticism of military prep-arations, was reviled as Communist-inspired anti-Americanism.

As scientists and Congressmen began to voice concern about nuclear testing in the mid-1950s (see previous chapter) the long-established peace organizations like the American Friends Service

Committee and the Women's International League for Peace and Freedom issued their own calls for restraint. It was not, however, until the summer of 1957 that they attempted to promote a broader-based campaign. Pacifists then combined with a number of eminent public figures to launch the National Committee for a Sane Nuclear Policy (SANE). Norman Cousins, advocate of world federalism and editor of the *Saturday Review*, played a key role in founding SANE, which was so named on the advice of psychologist Erich Fromm to indicate the insanity of existing policies. SANE had to decide whether to stress the dangers of the arms race as a whole, or to concentrate on the immediate dangers of nuclear fall-out, and whether to engage in quiet lobbying or to mobilize popular support. The group opted for a focus on nuclear testing, while recognizing it was not the only hazard, and appealed for public support through a *New York Times* advertisement. This strategy lost SANE the potential backing of some senior figures formerly part of the nuclear establishment, and some scientists who thought the appeal was too emotional. But the appeal was endorsed by eminent religious, academic and political figures. These included Paul Tillich, the German existentialist theologian, who as a critic of Nazism had to seek asylum in the USA in 1933, and Eleanor Roosevelt, wife of the former President and a noted campaigner for liberal causes in her own right. The appeal drew a response from 1,700 individuals, who in turn helped to create a nation-wide organization, which by mid-1958 claimed 25,000 members and 130 local committees.[1]

SANE did appoint its own Washington lobbyists, but continued to issue open appeals to the Administration and to capitalize on new information about the effects of radioactive fall-out. For example, when it emerged in early 1959 that deposits of strontium 90, which tends to concentrate in children's bones, were twice as high in the New York city area as they were in 1954, SANE ran an information centre in Times Square for four weeks which was visited by an estimated 40,000 people.[2] In May 1960 a mass rally in Madison Square, New York, demonstrated impressive support for SANE's demands for a negotiated test ban treaty, but the organization immediately afterwards faced a major crisis. Senator Thomas Dodd of the Senate Sub-committee on Internal Security attacked SANE in McCarthyist terms, claiming Communists had infiltrated the membership. SANE responded by dismissing the allegedly Communist organizer of the New York rally and passing a resolution which specified that only those judging the USA and USSR by the same standards were welcome as members.[3] Critics in the peace movement argued that SANE had capitulated to anti–Communist witch-hunting, and the student section of SANE disbanded over the issue, many of its members resisting pressure to purge 'pro-Soviet' groups.[4]

SANE did, however, maintain support among its chief constituency: liberal professional and business people. During 1962 SANE joined with Political Action for Peace and Voters for Peace to put the danger of war on the electoral agenda by backing peace candidates in the Congressional primaries that year. California and Massachusetts had the most candidates standing on peace platforms, which included calls for unilateral initiatives to reduce tension. Stuart Hughes, the Harvard history professor who ran as a peace candidate in John Kennedy's former Senate seat, became a co-chairman of SANE in 1963 with Dr Benjamin Spock, the well-known child psychologist.[5] SANE continued to exist throughout the 1960s and later engaged in protests against the Vietnam War, but never managed to become a major movement. Turn Towards Peace, established in 1962 as a coordinating body for existing organizations, tried to create a wider base by 'meeting the public at its level of concern' and did draw in the United Automobile Workers' Union and the Student Christian Federation, but did not pursue specific policies or projects.[6]

A less conventional protest grouping arose in 1961 when a group of Washington housewives decided they must respond to the threat of nuclear fall-out. Women Strike for Peace drew thousands of women onto the streets on 1 November 1961 to call for an end to nuclear testing. It also sent fifty American women to Geneva in April 1962 where they joined fifty other women from around the world to demonstrate and petition the Eighteen Nation Disarmament Committee negotiating on a test ban.[7] Women Strike for Peace had to confront residual McCarthyism when its organizers were summoned before the notorious House Un-American Activities Committee in December 1962. The women responded very differently from SANE, refusing to be intimidated or to try to prevent Communists joining in their activities. Women supporters from around the USA crowded into the hearings and greeted many of the questions – such as 'Did you then . . . have you recently operated a duplicating machine?' – with gales of laughter. The Committee, not the women, emerged discomfited.[8] Women Strike for Peace, with its informal organizational structure, skill in *ad hoc* decision-making and irreverence for established political institutions foreshadowed the feminist peace groups of the 1980s.

SANE prompted the first student peace organization, but even without the dispute over excluding Communists it was not attuned to winning mass student support. The Student Peace Union, set up in 1959, adopted a more militant style and more radical anti-militarist policies, and by 1962 had seventy campus groups. But it disbanded in 1964 and many of its activists entered the New Left Students for a Democratic Society.[9] The priorities for the new generation of student activists, reacting against the conformism of the early 1950s, were the Civil Rights movement, civil liberties and US policy towards Cuba. Southern students began to defy segregation in large numbers in 1960, but many black and white students from the North were then drawn into marches, civil disobedience and voter registration drives, culminating in the Freedom Summer of 1964. The first sign of the new mood of student activism, which led to Students for a Democratic Society, was when California university students demonstrated against a House Un-American Activities Committee hearing in San Francisco in May 1960.[10] Militarism in the USA only became a primary target for student activism after the bombing of North Vietnam and the large-scale committal of troops to South Vietnam.

While civil rights protesters took up the tactics of Gandhian non-violent action to oppose segregation, radical pacifists (some of whom had engaged in non-violent direct action in the South) adopted these methods to highlight the immorality of preparations for nuclear war. Members of the Catholic Worker Group and a few dozen other pacifists were arrested each year from 1955 to 1959 for refusing to take part in compulsory civil defence drills in New York. In 1960 the War Resisters' League promoted a major civil disobedience demonstration against the drill, which brought over 1,000 to protest and 500 to defy police orders to take cover. The following year the number of demonstrators doubled.[11]

Direct protests at nuclear weapon sites began in 1957 when Non-violent Action Against Nuclear Weapons (later the Committee for Non-violent Action) organized a vigil and trespass onto the Nevada nuclear testing site. In the next three years protesters sat in for a week at the Atomic Energy Commission headquarters, obstructed the Omaha missile base (which led to six-month jail sentences for seven activists) and took to small boats to demonstrate against the new Polaris missile submarines. Pacifist dissenters also refused to pay taxes towards arms. The most dramatic protests focused, however, on nuclear tests. The yacht *Golden Rule* tried to sail into the American testing area at Eniwetok in 1958, and when the crew were arrested, another yacht, the *Phoenix*, took up the protest and managed briefly to enter the testing zone.[12] The skipper of the *Phoenix*, an American biologist and anthropologist sailing home from Japan, had attended the trial of *Golden Rule* members in Honolulu.[13] Two more American protest ships, *Everyman I* and *II*, tried to sail from Honolulu for the US testing zone when the USA resumed nuclear testing early in 1962, and an international crew in *Everyman III* left London for Leningrad in the autumn of 1962 to demonstrate opposition to Soviet nuclear testing. After Soviet authorities refused to allow them to land, the crew tried to scuttle their boat to prevent it being towed out of the harbour.[14] These protest voyages achieved widespread publicity and prefigured the environmental and peace protests made regularly by Greenpeace in the 1970s and 1980s.

THE BRITISH MOVEMENT AGAINST NUCLEAR WEAPONS

The movement against nuclear weapons was not the first autonomous peace protest in Britain since the Second World War. The Left had campaigned against German rearmament, while the Peace with China campaign during the Korean War mobilized cross-party support. Peace with China inspired meetings round the country, speeches in Parliament and letters to the press, formation of peace groups in universities and moves to organize doctors and scientists to oppose war.[15] During 1954 Labour MPs and religious groups launched the Hydrogen Bomb National Campaign, which by the end of the year had collected a million signatures to a petition urging negotiated nuclear disarmament – a policy officially endorsed by the Conservative Government itself.

Nevertheless, the campaign that developed in Britain from 1957 became the most significant expression of moral concern and mass protest within the country since 1945. Circumstances in Britain were in fact particularly propitious for a movement for nuclear disarmament. There was a long tradition of liberal dissent and peace protest and established peace bodies to provide experience and supporters. As in the USA a new young generation was ready to assert political idealism, and in the welfare state there were then no overwhelming domestic injustices to confront. Unlike France at that time, Britain was managing to grant independence to its colonies without provoking acute internal crisis, so anti-colonial sentiment could be combined with emphasis on nuclear disarmament. There was a socialist tradition favourable to disarmament and a strong Labour Party which might become a vehicle for anti-nuclear policies. Finally, Britain's international position as a former great power suggested British action would have a significant impact, and the fact that it was the third nuclear weapons state provided a direct target for protest. Stopping the spread of nuclear weapons seemed a possibility, and nuclear disarmers often called for Britain to 'give a moral lead' by renouncing the nuclear bomb. Because prime responsibility for 'the defence of the West' lay on the USA, British campaigners could more easily make radical demands than their American counterparts.

The initial emphasis of British protests was on nuclear testing, and in particular the explosion of the first British H bomb at Christmas Island in the Pacific in the spring of 1957. A number of London groups against nuclear testing came together in February 1957 to form the National Council for the Abolition of Nuclear Weapons Tests, which brought 2,000 women out on a black sash march to Trafalgar Square when the H bomb was tested in May 1957. The National Council was to merge by 1958 into a more prestigious new body with wider aims: the Campaign for Nuclear Disarmament (CND).[16] The direct action wing of the new movement surfaced around the same time, when the *Manchester Guardian* printed an appeal for volunteers to sail into the testing area, and the Emergency Committee for Direct Action Against Nuclear War sent a volunteer to Japan in advance to try to find a Japanese fishing boat for the attempt. The nuclear test took place before he could succeed, but the gesture achieved international publicity.

Two political developments within Britain in 1957 influenced the subsequent campaign against nuclear weapons. The Conservative Government, which had been in office since 1951, decided to reduce its overstretched defence budget by ending conscription and relying heavily on the deterrent value of a British nuclear force, then assumed to be a cheaper option. The 1957 Defence White Paper drew attention to the future role of nuclear weapons in Conservative policy, and also admitted candidly that there was no defence against a nuclear attack. The second event concerned the Labour Party. Although a Labour Government had initiated the British Atomic bomb, rank-and-file opposition was represented by the newly-formed Labour H Bomb Campaign, which held a rally in Trafalgar Square in September 1957. Labour officially favoured some form of non-nuclear zone in Central Europe, but believed a British bomb would give the country independence and weight in disarmament negotiations. At the 1957 Brighton Party Conference the leadership opposed a composite resolution calling for a Labour commitment not to test or produce nuclear weapons. Nye Bevan, the charismatic leader of the Left, had as

Shadow Foreign Secretary to reply to the debate. His famous speech urging the party not to send a British Foreign Secretary 'naked into the Conference Chamber' dismayed the nuclear disarmers. The resolution was resoundingly defeated with the aid of the trade union block vote, then controlled largely by the Labour Right.[17]

After the Brighton Conference public pressure seemed the only way to challenge British policy on nuclear weapons. A group of prominent liberal and left-wing intellectuals came together in January 1958, encouraged by the response to an article about the nuclear threat by novelist and essayist J. B. Priestley in the *New Statesman*, and founded the CND. The meeting selected an Executive Committee, which included Priestley and *New Statesman* editor, Kingsley Martin, and two scientists – Professor Joseph Rotblat, who had worked on the A bomb during the war, and Ritchie Calder, well known for his scientific journalism. Two key members of the National Council for the Abolition of Nuclear Weapons Tests, Sheila Jones – also an atomic physicist – and journalist Arthur Goss, were selected since they handed on the resources of their organization to CND. At this stage the Campaign avoided specific ties to the Labour Party, but Michael Foot, orator and essayist of the Labour Left, who had lost his parliamentary seat in 1955, was on the original Executive.

Membership of CND's Executive Committee changed quite rapidly during 1958, as some members soon resigned and others were coopted, including Priestley's wife, archaeologist Jacquetta Hawkes, who was one of the few women at the top of CND. Two key figures in the launching of CND were, however, to play central role throughout the first wave of the movement: Canon John Collins, who became the Chairman, and Peggy Duff, who became its Secretary. Canon Collins of St Paul's Cathedral had extensive campaigning experience, which included running the South African Treason Trial Fund and Christian Action, and promoting the 1954 Hydrogen Bomb National Campaign. He became a well-known national figure in his cassock and dog-collar between 1958 and 1964 – Christopher Driver records that, at some schools, boys called Collins automatically acquired the nickname 'Canon'. Peggy Duff was also an indefatigable campaigner, who had worked for Save Europe Now after the Second World War and for the National Campaign for the Abolition of Capital Punishment, and was a Labour Party activist until she left the party in the 1960s over the issue of Vietnam. She formed an important link between CND celebrities and a more radical rank and file. The third key figure was the eighty-five year old Bertrand Russell, who had made a famous radio broadcast on 'Man's

Peril' from nuclear war in 1954 and started Pugwash in 1955, who became CND President.

CND was officially launched in February 1958, with a rally of 5,000 in London's Westminster Central Hall, where the audience cheered calls for Britain to abandon the Bomb. The campaign caught a public mood: local CND groups sprang up round the country and held large public meetings addressed by local personalities and national speakers such as the historian A. J. P. Taylor, noted for his skills as a lecturer, who had made a major impression in his speech at the Central Hall. CND's original aim to act as a liberal pressure group was, however, challenged almost immediately, when the Aldermaston march began to transform it into a popular movement flowing out onto the streets.

The Emergency Committe for Direct Action had begun in November 1957 to plan a four-day march at Easter from London to the Aldermaston Atomic Weapons' Research Establishment. It soon enlisted the organizational cooperation of the Labour H Bomb Campaign Committee; and the student New Left grouping, the *Universities and Left Review*, threw its energies behind the March. CND offered its sponsorship to the demonstration, which became the focus of burgeoning anti-nuclear enthusiasm. The march started with a rally of thousands, diminished to hundreds on the second and third days and swelled to perhaps 8,000 at Aldermaston.

CND grew rapidly in the next two years, so that by 1960 there were over 450 local groups.[18] But from Easter 1959 the central CND event, and symbol of its popular support, was the Aldermaston march, which CND had taken over from the Direct Action Committee. The direction of the march was altered to start at the atomic weapons plant and end in London, symbolizing a change of emphasis from protest at the point where the Bomb was developed to protest at the centre of political power. A final rally in London also made mass attendance easier. The 1959 Easter march mustered thousands and culminated in a rally estimated at 20,000; in 1960 estimates of the final rally were as high as 100,000.

Within the broader campaign the Direct Action Committee Against Nuclear War pursued a strategy of protesting where nuclear weapons were produced or deployed, with the aim of arousing local opposition and with an increasing emphasis on trying to secure token strikes and trade union non-cooperation. These campaigns of local agitation ended in a number of instances in acts of Gandhian-style civil disobedience. Two non-violent attempts to obstruct the building of US Thor missile bases in Norfolk in December 1958, the second resulting in brief prison sentences, brought widespread publicity, and sparked off extensive debate about the justification for civil disobedience in a parliamentary democracy. The CND leadership viewed the Direct Action Committee with some alarm, because it was anxious to maintain political control over the movement and worried by the controversial nature of forms of direct action. Most CND supporters, however, welcomed civil disobedience as a complementary tactic; and at a further act of civil disobedience at the Harrington Thor missile base in January 1960, CND organized a legal supporting demonstration.

CND policy evolved over time. When first formed it called for Britain to stop tests and suspend patrol flights of US bombers loaded with nuclear weapons and to delay building of US missile bases pending negotiations. At this point it was able to carry with it the all-party United Nations Association. When CND early on opted for unconditional abandonment of the British Bomb it went too far for the Association. It also went too far at that stage for the Communist Party, which stressed negotiations and opposed unilateralism, though as CND developed into a mass campaign the party made a formal decision in 1960 to support it. CND policy expanded to oppose all US nuclear bases and at its 1960 Conference it voted for a policy of leaving NATO, which was heavily reliant on nuclear weapons. A year later Conference endorsed a policy of 'positive neutralism' which envisaged a Britain out of NATO cooperating with the newly independent Third World states. This policy was morally and politically consistent, but inevitably narrowed potential support, whereas concern about nuclear proliferation and opposition to the British Bomb stretched across a wider political spectrum. According to a 1959 Gallup poll even 20 per cent of Conservative voters favoured giving up the British nuclear force.[19] The Liberal Party voted as early as 1958 for giving up the British nuclear force unconditionally, though it never opposed US bases or NATO.[20]

It was the Labour Party, however, which was the focus of CND's implicit strategy, since Labour could form a new government and there seemed some real prospect of converting it to much of CND policy. The fact that Labour lost the 1959 general election arguably benefited CND, which had more chance of converting the party while it was out of office. During the election CND had to act with great circumspection to avoid alienating any of its diverse supporters, but its failure to make nuclear weapons a major election issue did not really matter as popular support for the movement was still growing.[21] Moreover, during 1959 and 1960 rank-and-file pressure in trade unions forced some reluctant union executives to cast their votes in favour of British unilateralism. A unilateralist resolution was passed at the Labour Party Conference in October 1960, despite impassioned opposition by the Labour leader, Hugh Gaitskell.

In its hour of triumph, however, CND ran into an internal crisis, when plans to set up a body committed to direct action were prematurely publicized. Bertrand Russell, CND President, signed the appeal to many well-known artists and writers to form a Committee of 100, which aimed to launch mass civil disobedience. The Committee was a major organizational and ideological challenge to CND, and the public row resulting was exacerbated by personality conflicts.

Nevertheless, during 1961 both CND and the Committee of 100 apparently flourished. The Easter march continued to grow, with estimates of up to 150,000 at the final rally. The Government's agreement in November 1960 to allow US Polaris nuclear weapon submarines at Holy Loch prompted an upsurge of popular protest on Clydeside, where a long tradition of socialist militancy combined with Scottish national consciousness. The Direct Action Committee and later the Committee of 100 relied on this local opposition to back civil disobedience at Holy Loch in 1961.

The Committee of 100 demonstration, in which Russell led over a thousand to sit down peacefully outside the Ministry of Defence in February 1961, was followed by a protest in Parliament Square in April when 800 were arrested and fined. Real confrontation with the state took place in September. The Committee planned a sit-down in Trafalgar Square on 17th September, but police arrested about a third of the Committee in advance and magistrates sent those who refused to be bound over to keep the peace to prison for a month. Photographs flashed round the world of Earl Russell, then eighty-nine years old, as he attended the London magistrates court. The planned demonstration went ahead. Advance publicity ensured mass attendance, and when the government invoked the Defence of the Realm Act to prevent it, the occasion turned into a civil liberties issue. Canon Collins, who came to observe, was accidentally arrested, and police arrested over 1,300 of the 12,000 who sat down in the Square. A simultaneous protest at Holy Loch resulted in 300 arrests.

Encouraged by the extent of its support, the Committee planned an ambitious set of demonstrations for December at three USAF bases, with the aim of invading the bases and blocking the planes, and in four different cities. Six Committee organizers (none of them well-known personalities) were arrested and charged under the Official Secrets Act. The December demonstrations went ahead at the bases and mobilized 4,000 supporters, whose impact was dissipated by being dispersed. Only 850 were arrested. The trial of the six organizers in February 1962 allowed them to challenge the morality of nuclear policies and prompted legal debate about government claims to equate official defence policy with 'the security of the state'. But the six were convicted, and the sentences of 18 months on the five men, and one year for the sole woman, were clearly intended to deter. They arguably had some success.

Certainly the Committee of 100 began to lose momentum, although it organized a series of demonstrations both in London and at bases during 1962. It also devoted a good deal of its energies to internal reorganization into a set of provincial committees, a move consistent with belief in participatory democracy but promoting fragmentation. Russell resigned in November and set up his own Peace Foundation, and other celebrities moved away from the Committee. The range of activities diversified during 1962 and included attempts to promote industrial action against nuclear weapons, especially among dockers where the Committee had direct contacts. This strategy produced some lively docks meetings, and the blacking of a specific consignment to Aldermaston, but no more. Proposals to encourage support in the armed forces provoked internal controversy over the wisdom of promoting 'sedition'. A number of young servicemen had in fact independently demonstrated public sympathy with CND, and two RAF members proposed forming a Forces CND Group. Publication of their letter in *Peace News* prompted a court martial.[22]

The Committee achieved publicity in 1963 over two highly contentious actions. A small group within it, 'Spies for Peace', issued detailed information about the secret regional seats of government, to be administrative headquarters after a nuclear attack. Breakaway demonstrations at these newly revealed sites disrupted the 1963 Aldermaston march. The Committee then protested against the visit of Queen Frederika of Greece in July 1963, out of solidarity with nuclear disarmers in Greece facing repression (see later) and in opposition to an authoritarian right-wing regime. Because the demonstration was reported as anti-royalist and suggested the Committee had become identified with wider left-wing goals, many commentators at the time, and retrospectively, saw it as damaging to the nuclear disarmament movement as a whole, especially as CND had also (despite strong reservations) staged a less provocative protest.

The Committee continued in being for some years after 1963 and held further demonstrations, but it ceased to have any political impact on the nuclear weapons issue. As the policy goals of the Committee broadened it organized direct action on domestic social issues, most successfully in protests against homelessness, which led to the campaign of squatting in empty council properties and office blocks. The Committee had failed in the explicit aim of swamping the jails with thousands of protesters. It did promote direct action as a form of popular protest and promoted a view of protest more anarchistic in style than that associated with the Direct Action Committee.

The Committee was most effective in 1961, a crucial year for CND when the struggle to maintain a unilateralist policy was taking place in the Labour Party. Some commentators have argued that the Committee's civil disobedience protests reduced sympathy for CND among the public.[23] Given disapproval of any demonstrations among sections of opinion, this is quite plausible, although the media reported the February and April demonstrations and the arrest of Russell and other celebrities in September sympathetically. Whether the publicity from demonstrations was on balance helpful (showing the strength and commitment of campaigners) or counter-productive (suggesting the demonstrators were socially disreputable and irres-ponsible), remained a tactical problem for the nuclear disarmament campaign. Similar questions would apply to the Aldermaston marches.

CND had suffered a major political setback in October 1961, when its strategy of working through the Labour Party to implement unilateralism had been defeated at the Party Conference. Hugh Gaitskell won a resounding victory when, after an effective campaign within the party, he overturned the previous year's unilateralist resolution, and his status as party leader rose in the opinion polls.[24] Nevertheless, CND maintained its internal momentum into 1962, when the Easter march was estimated by many to be bigger than ever before. Soviet and then American nuclear testing resumed in 1961 and 1962, prompting further protests outside both embassies. The major international event of 1962, the Cuban Missile Crisis in October, had a more negative effect. The crisis, which brought the world to the brink of nuclear war, showed that nuclear disarmers were correct to fear war by miscalculation, but also demonstrated that they were helpless in a crisis. Bertrand Russell did try to intervene by sending a series of cables to both Kennedy and Khrushchev, but the overall impact on many campaigners was demoralizing.

The 1963 Easter march indicated some falling off of support: *Peace News* estimated that there were 70,000 at the final rally. There had been internal splits over policy and tactics in the previous year, and the Easter demonstration brought CND and the Committee of 100 into conflict again over the breakaway action at regional sites of government. A year later CND was in decline. Canon Collins resigned after the 1964 Easter march only mustered 20,000 in London on a one-day demonstration; other well-known personalities had already left.

The election of a Labour Government in October 1964 was another significant factor in CND's decline. Many Labour MPs and rank-and-file activists ceased to oppose the party leadership now in power; and when the new Labour Government under Harold Wilson decided, despite its previous pledges, to continue developing the new Polaris submarine force, there was no significant internal protest. Many CND activists, after years of exhausting campaigning, retreated into private life, while others turned their attention to the Vietnam War. CND ceased to be a newsworthy or fashionable cause, and the new student generation focused on Vietnam.[25]

THE CHARACTER OF THE BRITISH CAMPAIGN

The group who launched CND had envisaged a brief campaign along standard pressure group lines: public meetings, petitions, parliamentary lobbying and sufficient media coverage to influence public opinion and have an impact on policy-makers. In practice they soon found themselves at the head of a popular movement more radical both in its policies and tactics than they had intended. There was therefore a built-in friction between the self-appointed élite of the CND Executive and many members of the wider movement. The campaign did not adopt a formal constitution and hold elections for its National Council and officers until 1961, although the annual national CND Conference had voted on policy issues in earlier years.

The organizational structure of CND reflected the extent of support throughout the country. At its peak in 1961 it claimed over 800 local groups, organized in six regions – each with its own full-time regional organizer – and a staff of over twenty in its national office. There were CND sections for Women, Students and Youth and a Christian CND, and professional groups, such as scientists and architects, formed to offer their support. The CND monthly newspaper *Sanity* reached a circulation of 45,000.[26] (Individual CND membership was not introduced until 1966, when local groups were disintegrating.)

Many who wore a CND badge, initiated resolutions on unilateralism within their own organizations or joined the Aldermaston march may, however, have had no formal links with CND. It is impossible, therefore, to make any accurate assessment of the total number of active supporters of British nuclear disarmament.

Support for CND came from all parts of England and opposition to nuclear weapons was strong in both Wales and Scotland – indeed local resistance to nuclear bases had deep roots in Scotland, where campaigning revived in the early 1970s, when elsewhere CND was at a very low ebb. CND also drew on people of all ages, though Christopher Driver stresses that the thirty-five to fifty-five age group, whose politics had been decisively shaped by the experience of the Second World War, were less evident on protests, and an informal survey of a women's organization against the Bomb confirmed this perception.[27] Students were active from the outset of the movement in 1958 and played a major role in promoting debate and information and in demonstrations. CND also attracted large numbers of teenagers, and the Aldermaston marches became a focus for the youth culture which had emerged during the 1950s, and for the music which transcended class differences among its fans. Jeff Nuttall in his evocation of this anti-establishment culture remembers the beatniks 'in their grime and tatters' and with their banjos, guitars 'antiquated cornets and sousaphones' and comments that although – contrary to the impression created by the press – teenagers were a minority on the marches 'they nevertheless made each march into a carnival of optimism'.[28]

The position of women in the campaign reflected their wider position in society. They played a very important role in running local groups, but despite a number of women scientists, novelists and actors, who were prominent among CND speakers and sponsors, the CND leadership was male-dominated. Women also played a secondary role in the Committee of 100, with its initial array of playwrights, poets and painters. Women were more central in the small, earlier, direct action protests. Some of them were also atypical, including former suffragettes, pacifists and ex-Communists. Many women who went on the Aldermaston marches stressed their concern as mothers for the health and future of their children, and this constituency was tapped by two new groups which sprang up in 1961 in response to renewed nuclear testing and the Berlin crisis: Women Against the Bomb in London and Voice of Women which attracted 1,000 readers of the *Guardian*'s Women's Page.[29] These groups did show some awareness of the advantages of women organizing separately, but women in CND were not at this stage explicitly feminist – the new feminism was not launched in Britain until 1968.

A common criticism of CND has been that it failed to attract much working-class support, and the first sociological survey of CND by Frank Parkin described it as 'middle-class radicalism'. This point can be exaggerated. Parkin's own random sample suggested a third counted as working class,[30] and trade union activists brought their banners on the Aldermaston marches and influenced union policy. Aside from those already involved in politics, however, CND did draw primarily on highly educated professionals. This was true of the women as well as the men, though given the much smaller proportion of women then who had been to university, Parkin found education levels among his sample somewhat lower, and many women who joined CND did so as young mothers and housewives.

The nuclear disarmament movement drew on a number of ideological groupings. The left wing of the Labour Party was central to CND throughout the period 1958–63. Former Communists who resigned over Hungary in 1956 and launched the New Left, gave momentum to early campaigning and later helped to shape CND policy, developing for example the idea of 'positive neutralism'. The student New Left generated lively debate in the *Universities and Left Review* Club, and some of them were influential in later policy analysis. Many pacifists supported CND, although the Peace Pledge Union officially refused to compromise by focusing on the Bomb instead of opposing all weapons. Anarchists were hostile to the CND leadership, but anarchist ideas gained ground within the Committee of 100. Communists had given some qualified support to CND before 1960, but after their official change of policy in favour of unilateralism Communists became more prominent in the organization.[31]

CND's early impact depended however on its ability to attract thousands not previously involved in political activity and to draw on the liberal centre ground. When by 1961 the nuclear disarmament movement was seen as more 'extreme' it became easier for its critics to discount it as a serious political force, despite the large numbers involved.[32]

ASSESSING THE BRITISH MOVEMENT

The most obvious measure of the success of a campaign is its direct impact on the Government. The Prime Minister, Harold Macmillan, did respond to public concern about nuclear weapons and testing, and was diplomatically active in promoting the test ban negotiations. His diaries do suggest that in 1959 he was aware nuclear weapons could surface as an election issue,[33] but in general he claims quite convincingly to have been motivated primarily by a desire for world security. Although some Conservative voters initially had sympathy with CND there was no question of a challenge from inside the party to government defence policy. Conservative speakers periodically tried to discredit nuclear campaigners as ill-informed, naive or Communist-inspired. Research into government documents at the Public Records Office (opened after thirty years) has revealed that the government was worried by the growing movement and that Macmillan asked the Chancellor of the Duchy of Lancaster to direct a campaign against CND in March 1958. Available documents show that the government tried to prompt churchmen, scientists and intellectuals to express their support for official defence policy. The government also had some success in using the lobby system for journalists to persuade the press to play down a petition by 618 British scientists against nuclear tests. The records so far made public do not disclose whether the authorities engaged in surveillance of campaigners or infiltrated *agents provocateurs*, although it seems virtually certain in the light of protesters' own experiences that Special Branch and the security services did adopt counter-measures. American historian Lawrence Wittner notes that: 'the official document list for the period to 1959 shows that the folder which produced most of the information . . . is followed, sequentially, by four others marked "Closed for the next 100 years" '.[34]

CND did have support in opposition parties: the Liberal Party votes for the abandonment of the British Bomb – although in the context of loyalty to NATO – have already been noted. The Welsh Nationalists had always supported British unilateral nuclear disarmament, and the Scottish Nationalists evolved from opposing nuclear bases in the early 1960s to opposing NATO by the end of the decade.[35] During the heyday of the two-party system in Britain, however, the policies of these small parties could not influence government policy. The real fight had to be in the Labour Party, and here CND did have considerable impact. Support in the parliamentary party was indicated by the fact that in March 1960 forty-three Labour MPs refused to vote for a Labour motion on defence.[36] The unilateralist vote at the 1960 Party Conference was however a pyrrhic victory for CND, resting on a trade union block vote which swung the other way in 1961.[37] Both the 1960 and the 1961 votes were linked to other internal party issues – controversy over the party's commitment to nationalize the economy and over Gaitskell's leadership. Gaitskell forced the issue of whether opposition to US bases meant leaving NATO, benefiting from the fact that many in the Labour Party stopped short of voting for 'neutralism'. Despite mounting evidence after the government scrapped the Blue Streak missile, early in 1960, that the 'independent deterrent' was heavily dependent on the USA, CND was not able to make political capital out of this fact.[38]

CND also failed to bring about a major change in the views of the wider society. The churches might have been expected to be most receptive to the moral arguments for unilateralism, but only the Methodists endorsed it; and they had been calling for an unconditional end to testing as early as 1957. The Church of England continued to back government policy, although a dozen bishops identified themselves as unilateralists.[39] Poll evidence shows that between 19 and 33 per cent of the respondents supported giving up the British Bomb unconditionally. Support did appear to grow between 1958 and 1960, slipped back in 1961 until December that year when 31 per cent again supported unilateralism, but tailed off in 1962.[40] So there was no lasting shift in public attitudes. People may well have become accustomed to Britain having the H bomb, and by 1964 – when both France and China had become nuclear weapons states – the case for Britain giving a lead to prevent proliferation looked less persuasive.

It is true to say that, at the very least, the British nuclear disarmament movement was instrumental in keeping the issue of nuclear weapons squarely on the political agenda for five years, and its demonstrations prompted campaigns in a number of other countries. CND also played a key role in founding the European Federation Against Nuclear Arms in January 1959 and the International Confederation for Disarmament and Peace in January 1963.

WEST GERMANY

The campaign against nuclear weapons in West Germany appeared much stronger in 1958 than its British counterpart, but was losing momentum by 1960 because the Social Democratic Party (SPD) had ceased to support it. The new Easter March Committee began in 1960 with a small demonstration but in the next four years built up to Aldermaston proportions, despite SPD hostility. The Easter March Committee was independent of all political parties. West Germany's political position in the front line of the Cold War was in many ways unfavourable to peace activity, but there were factors precipitating anxiety about nuclear weapons and NATO policy.

The developing Cold War in the late 1940s had meant the merging of American-, British- and French-occupied zones of Germany into a new West German state tied to the West, while the Communist-dominated Socialist Unity Party began to create a Soviet-style system in what became the German Democratic Republic. As West Germany recovered from the war, NATO began to look to West German manpower and technology to help defend this critical border. German rearmament was still a sensitive issue, especially in France, but in 1955 NATO governments secured West German entry into the Alliance. German rearmament, and commitment to the Western bloc, was highly controversial within West Germany itself. While the Christian Democratic Government, led by Konrad Adenauer, was committed to the Atlantic Alliance, the SPD and the trade unions were against membership, as were many Protestant groupings. Widespread but brief public agitation against joining NATO swept the country early in 1955.

Entry into NATO seemed to sever irrevocably links with East Germany and the possibility of creating a united neutral Germany. Social Democrats lost a region where they had traditionally been strong, and had to give up hope of a democratic, socialist and non-militarist Germany. The protestant denominations were especially anguished over the division of Germany because four-fifths of the population of East Germany were Protestants, and they constituted over 40 per cent of all German Protestants.[41] Although the Protestant Synod (representing the Lutheran Churches of the Länder and the United Church) was divided on rearmament, prominent Protestant pastors campaigned against it. The most respected voice was that of Pastor Martin Niemöller, former First World War U-boat commander, who had preached eloquently against Nazism from his Berlin church after 1933 and spent the years 1937–45 in Sachsenhausen and Dachau concentration camps. (Niemöller remained a leading figure in the peace movement into the 1960s). The Catholic Church, which had few members in the East and was adamantly opposed to *rapprochement* with a Communist regime, backed rearmament. Dissenting Catholics did, however, join peace protests.

Other reasons for opposing rearmament were anxiety about reviving German militarism, especially as the Government maintained its claim to Germany's pre-1939 borders, and worry about Germany being devastated in any central European war. Both these concerns were intensified when proposals were made to arm West Germany with atomic weapons. Public opinion had been alerted to the hazards of NATO plans for fighting a 'limited' nuclear war in Germany by a NATO exercise in 1955. 'Carte Blanche' assumed 355 bombs were exploded and calculated that this would leave 1.7 million West Germans dead and 3.5 million wounded by the immediate effects of blast and fall-out.[42]

Therefore, when the NATO Council decided early in 1958 that West German forces should be armed with US nuclear weapons, there was a long and impassioned debate in the Bundestag. The SPD lost the parliamentary vote and immediately appealed to the country to reverse the Government's decision; the party also tried to introduce a Bill requiring a referendum. The group of Free Democratic Party (FDP) MPs had failed to reach agreement on the issue (in the Bundestag debate one voted with the Government, one with the SPD and all the rest abstained), but subsequently issued a joint statement with the Trade Union Federation noting public opposition and calling for a referendum. Union resistance to arming the *Bundeswehr* with nuclear weapons was expressed both at the top and by the rank and file. The leadership backed mass demonstrations and promised support to individuals who refused to build missile sites, while brief protest strikes took place at the Hamburg docks and at Volkswagen works in two towns at the end of March. A poll in March 1958 showed that 83 per cent of the whole sample were against government policy.[43]

The SPD and the unions gave specific support to the organization Struggle Against Atomic Death, which had issued an appeal on 10 March calling for a nuclear-weapons-free zone in Central Europe. Whether West Germany should endorse the Polish Rapacki Plan for such a zone was a key issue in the Bundestag debate. Prominent party and union officials joined the Struggle Against Atomic Death Committee. A parallel group – the Campaign Against Atomic Weapons – arose in Bavaria under the chairmanship of author Hans Werner Richter, but was somewhat less dependent upon the SPD.[44]

Intellectual dissent from plans to give German forces atomic weapons had been expressed a year earlier, when in April 1957 eighteen very distinguished West German physicists signed a declaration stating their deep concern.[45] Scientists, artists and academics expressed widespread opposition during 1958: for example '936 Doctors of Hamburg' signed a collective protest in March, and in May 103 professors made an appeal to the churches. Physicist Max Born was among seventy professors endorsing a call for popular demonstrations. The Protestant Church initiative Action Reconciliation, designed to send volunteers abroad to atone for German war guilt through constructive action, also backed protests. Student demonstrations erupted at the same time in many universities.

The SPD began to reduce support for the Struggle Against Atomic Death later in 1958 in response to setbacks in *Länder* elections and a Federal Constitutional Court ban on *Länder* plesbiscites on nuclear weapons.[46] At the party's 1959 Bad Godesberg Conference, the new programme showed that the SPD was adjusting socialism to a flourishing capitalism to win back electoral support. The party did, however, reiterate opposition to West Germany acquiring its own Bomb, and maintained a policy favouring disengagement in Central Europe until 1960.

Forthcoming elections in 1961 persuaded the SPD leadership to abandon their independent defence and foreign policy and to distance themselves even further from the protests against nuclear weapons. Some Social Democrats, especially from the SPD youth section, and rank-and-file trade unionists defied party warnings and joined in the growing Easter march movement. The Socialist German Student League, which broke away from the party after Bad Godesberg, also endorsed the March policy.

The Easter marches were launched by a group of pacifists and gained the official backing of all the independent peace groups. The policy called for a nuclear-weapons-free zone in Central Europe, cuts in conventional forces and an end to nuclear testing. Only 1,000 attended the final rally in 1960, but numbers grew steadily. Its strength as the focus of a growing extra-parliamentary opposition was indicated by the fact that in 1964 there were 65,000 marchers and 100,000 at the final rally. The march appeal was endorsed by over a thousand ministers of religion, hundreds of academics, writers, artists and jurists, and by trade unionists and town councillors. The Easter march organization took pains to preserve strict non-alignment, but the SPD leadership alleged that it was under Communist influence.[47]

Despite surges of opposition to rearmament and to nuclear weapons the political environment in West Germany was hostile to peace activity. The Communist Party was banned in 1956 and not allowed to organize legally again until 1968. Peace groups were suspected of acting as vehicles for the banned party, and some, like the German Peace Union party founded in 1960, could with some degree of truth be placed in this category. Independent peace groups had to walk a tightrope, keeping open the possibility of reconciliation with the GDR while opposing its government's policies, and maintaining credibility with the West German public while avoiding surrender to rabid anti-Communism. The sensitivity to any suspicion of links with the Soviet bloc created a crisis in the European Federation Against Nuclear Arms in 1960, when Canon Collins proposed a meeting with representatives from the East after consulting with World Peace Council members. The SPD deputy representing the Struggle Against Atomic Death opposed such a meeting, and the Chairman of the Bavarian Campaign sought to postpone it.[48]

SWITZERLAND AND SWEDEN

Apart from West Germany and Britain, the two most significant European campaigns against nuclear weapons in 1958 were in Switzerland and Sweden, where governments were seriously considering developing their own tactical atomic forces. The Swiss Movement Against Nuclear Rearmament and the Swedish Action Group Against a Swedish Atom Bomb were among the founder members of the European Federation. Indeed the Federation's first plan, which proved over-ambitious, was to mobilize pressure on the Swiss Government to convene the International Red Cross to discuss banning nuclear weapons.[49]

The Swiss Movement decided to make use of its country's participatory democracy to call for a referendum to change the Constitution to forbid acquisition of nuclear weapons. The organizers made public their aim of collecting the necessary 50,000 signatures in May 1958, and in 1959 handed in a petition signed by 73,000 men (women could not vote). At that stage, however, the Swiss Society of Officers was debating the case for and against using atomic weapons in a limited war more vehemently than the wider public. The Government organized a referendum, as required, in April 1962, when the Movement failed to secure a majority of the male popular vote for a change in the Constitution: of the 54.9 per cent of the electorate who voted, there were 286,858 votes for and 587,387 votes against, with strong support for the proposal in French-speaking areas.[50] Nevertheless, the Government decided, partly on military and economic grounds, against acquiring any kind of nuclear force as an extension of its armed neutrality.[51]

A campaign against nuclear weapons arose in Sweden in the mid-1950s, when the Swedish airforce, backed by the Defence Council, was arguing strongly the advantages of strengthening its general policy of military deterrence with atomic bombs.[52] Sweden even had its own uranium. Public opposition was initiated by a group of about thirty intellectuals, who launched the Swedish Action Group, which held debates, rallies and demonstrations.[53] This debate took place against a background of Swedish neutrality in both world wars and a strong tradition of peace activity stretching back to the mid-nineteenth century. The Swedish Social Democratic Government suspended funding on research for a nuclear force at the end of 1959. This decision was, as in Switzerland, influenced partly by military calculations which cast doubt on the strategic sense of preparing for possible atomic war. Sweden was also very aware of the political importance of its role in Scandinavia in helping to maintain the more precarious neutrality of Finland and as a buffer enabling Norway and Denmark to avoid total integration into NATO's nuclear policies. Public protest raising moral issues may, however, have had some impact: Alva Myrdal claims that the campaign by the Social Democrat Women's Organization in particular did influence the outcome.[54] Certainly Sweden engaged in active diplomacy to promote a nuclear test ban treaty from 1962, and helped to launch the negotiations which culminated in the 1968 Non-Proliferation Treaty. It was revealed in the 1980s that the Swedish Government had in great secrecy continued nuclear weapon research as a hedge against changing military circumstances, but by then Sweden had publicly helped to create a non-proliferation regime.

DENMARK AND NORWAY

Despite the links between Sweden and its Scandinavian neighbours (Norway had only become independent from Sweden in 1905) the campaigns in both Denmark and Norway were sparked off by the British Aldermaston marches rather than the Swedish protests. Both countries had after their experience of occupation in the Second World War joined NATO in 1949, but chose this option in preference to a possible Nordic security arrangement only after some hesitation and in the face of internal opposition. Domestic pressures also contributed to both countries refusing to accept foreign troops in 1953 and rejecting the stationing on their territories of nuclear weapons in 1957. Danish public opinion in particular remained sceptical about the value of military defence; an anti-militarist wing existed in the Socialist Party and the neutralist Socialist People's Party was founded in late 1958, winning eleven out of 174 seats in the 1960 election.[55] The Danish CND did not, however, surface until October 1960, when young Danes who had joined in the Aldermaston marches organized their own march. Over the next three years the predominantly youthful Campaign Against Nuclear Weapons flourished. Numbers on the four-day Easter marches from Holback to Copenhagen reached a maximum of 20,000 in 1961.[56] Denmark had its own non-violent direct action wing: the Danish Section of the War Resisters' International (WRI), which had initiated action against nuclear weapons in 1960 with a protest against the unloading of Nike and Honest John missiles for NATO. Danish WRI also supported international radical protests such as the San Francisco to Moscow March in 1961 and the sending of the *Everyman III* protest ship to Leningrad in 1962.[57]

A number of Norwegians involved in the first Danish march against nuclear weapons in turn launched their own Protest Against Nuclear Weapons at a rally in November 1960. This campaign was known as 'The 13' after the original signatories to an anti-nuclear appeal. The aim of 'The 13' was to ensure Norway's policy of refusing to have nuclear bases was maintained and the campaigners collected about 225,000 signatures to a petition. When the governing Labour Party reiterated in December 1961 its commitment not to allow nuclear weapons into Norway in peace-time, 'The 13' declared their aim had been achieved and disbanded. More radical members of this grouping then set up their own Campaign Against Nuclear Weapons and organized their first Easter march in 1962, which was supported by soldiers in uniform who joined the 2,500 demonstrators. But this body disbanded after the Partial Test Ban Treaty.[58] A new left-wing Socialist People's Party with an anti-nuclear policy, and also opposed to Norway's membership of NATO, contested the 1961 elections and won two seats, thus holding the balance of power between the Labour Party and the Conservative opposition groups. The party had been founded by Labour dissidents, but won some Liberal support.[59]

FRANCE

In France the governments of the mid-1950s had begun the French nuclear weapons programme, but the Fourth Republic avoided public debate on the issue.[60] France publicly became the fourth nuclear weapon state in 1960 when de Gaulle's Government announced plans to test its first atom bomb in the Sahara. Despite this clear focus for protest, in the context of an international campaign against nuclear weapons, and despite a French tendency to engage in mass demonstrations and vigorous resistance on many other political issues, no movement comparable to those in Britain or West Germany arose at this stage. The French Federation Against Nuclear Weapons, founded in April 1959, held a public meeting in May and launched a national appeal against the tests in November, but proceeded very cautiously and had limited support.

The most obvious reason for the silence of much of the Left was that their energies were engaged in resistance to the Algerian War and the related threat from domestic right-wing terrorism. Indeed it was only after the war ended in 1962 that a more significant independent grouping, the Movement Against Nuclear Weapons, emerged. A secondary reason was that the Communist-dominated Movement for Peace was agitating against nuclear weapons, but unable to lead a broad-based movement. France did not suffer from the anti-Communist paranoia to be found in West Germany and the USA (the Communist Party could still poll 3.9 million votes in 1958), but the rest of the Left was in competition with the Communists and unwilling to collaborate. A third factor was that French socialists, unlike the British Labour Party, did not encompass a strong anti-war tradition; instead the French Left glorified the wartime armed resistance and associated pacifism with collaboration. The opposition parties had of course when in government sanctioned the Bomb, but so had the British Labour Party.

There was, however, some evidence of concern about the development of the French Bomb outside the ranks of the Communist Party. A group of eighty-two pacifists staged a sit-in at the Marcoule atomic research laboratory in April 1958 and refused to leave until granted an interview with the Assistant Director, and several pacifists also agreed to appear on the platform of the Movement for Peace rally about nuclear weapons that same month.[61] When the first French tests took place, and a Bill to authorize the nuclear force was introduced in Parliament in the autumn of 1960, opposition was voiced in the Radical Party, the Popular Radical Movement (MRP) and the Socialist Party, and censure votes were passed in Parliament. The *force de frappe* was denounced as strategically unsound and a manifestation of a *folie de grandeur*.[62] However, no protests took place in France.

Nevertheless, by 1963 the left-wing socialist, Claude Bourdet, who had maintained personal links with West European nuclear disarmament bodies since 1958, was able to set up the Movement Against Nuclear Weapons. (Bourdet was a prominent intellectual figure on the French Left, with a record in the Resistance, publisher of the daily *Combat* and later of the weekly *France Observateur*. He had always advocated neutralism in the Cold War, and became well known in the international opposition to nuclear weapons both in the 1960s and again in the 1980s.) The Movement, which later became the Movement for Disarmament, Peace and Liberty, had the backing of the United Socialist Party (PSU), which was itself a coalition of small left-wing groups but included some authoritative figures. Left-wing Catholics in the Catholic trade union body (CFDT) also backed the movement.[63] It never achieved a strong popular organization, but it did promote interest through a series of rallies and stimulated for a time a complementary campaign run by socialists and Communists against the French nuclear force. During the 1965 elections the parties of the Left denounced the wastefulness and folly of the French Bomb in much the same terms as they had initially in 1960, and declared their commitment to abandon it.[64] Popular protest, however, died down after 1965. When de Gaulle took France out of NATO's integrated military command structure in 1966, and improved relations with Moscow, the French Communist Party reduced active opposition to the *force de frappe*. Nevertheless, as late as 1972, when the Socialist and Communist Parties endorsed a Common Programme, their policy called for 'renunciation of the strategic nuclear strike force in any form'. Both parties performed a volte-face and announced support for the French force when they split in 1977.

GREECE

The anti-Americanism which inspired Gaullist foreign policy and the *force de frappe* was in other parts of Europe one element in campaigns against nuclear weapons, especially when the focus was US nuclear bases. The most dramatic events in the first wave of the nuclear disarmament movement in Europe took place in Greece, which was of strategic importance to NATO, had a large number of American military bases and installations under the 1953 Agreement with the USA, and had since 1958 accepted US nuclear weapons. The USA intervened more openly in Greek politics than in other European countries; in the early 1950s the American Embassy (implementing a change of policy inside Washington) helped the electoral victory of the Right over the previous centrist coalition. The CIA was active, and extensive American economic aid, initiated under the Marshall Plan, provided another lever on the Greek Government.[65]

American influence in Greece stemmed, however, from the nature of internal Greek politics. The USA took over from Britain the great power role of backing the Right against the Communists in the bitter civil war that erupted in Greece at the end of the German occupation. After the Communist defeat Greece acquired formal democratic institutions, but it was a system in which a strong army combined with the security services and an interventionist monarchy to keep a grip on power behind the facade of prime minister and Parliament. The USA backed and worked with the military. The Communist Party was banned and many of its members were in exile or in prison for extended periods. Party front organizations were tolerated, however, including a World Peace Council branch set up in 1955.

The new Bertrand Russell Committee, founded in 1962 by students aided by older activists, was a non-aligned body, avoiding the stereotyped anti-Americanism of pro-Soviet propaganda. This was one reason why the Committee opposed nuclear bases in Greece but did not oppose NATO. It had strong support among musicians and actors, and was influenced by the youthful idealism and protest style of the British CND and Committee of 100.[66] Given the authoritarian context in which it grew, the Bertrand Russell Committee did, however, espouse a wider programme, calling for the right of democratic dissent and protest. It also got caught up in the developing internal struggle between right-wing forces and the centre Left. By the early 1960s the liberal politician, George Papandreou, who was a contender for the premiership in the next elections, was mobilizing the urban and rural poor with his populist oratory. When the Bertrand Russell Committee planned a peace march from Marathon to Athens in April 1963, the Conservative Karamanlis Government, which was already repressing a wave of strikes and demonstrations, saw this as a dangerous focus for radical opposition.[67] The Government banned the march, police arrested and beat up over a thousand demonstrators, and contingents of the British Committee of 100 travelling to join the march were barred from entering Greece. Grigoris Lambrakis, a popular member of the United Democratic Left Party in Parliament, and well known as a former athlete and gold medallist in the Balkan games, undertook the Marathon March alone. He had already marched from Aldermaston at Easter 1963, and as a deputy he could not be arrested.

The extreme Right responded to the challenge posed by the new peace campaign by assassinating Lambrakis a month later, when a car ran him down in Salonika as he emerged from a public meeting. His funeral drew a crowd of half a million and was attended by representatives from peace movements abroad; the Bertrand Russell Committee carried the CND symbol in the funeral procession, and many mourners delivered wreaths in the shape of the nuclear disarmament symbol.[68] Despite attempts at a cover-up, journalists' enquiries and the persistence of an examining magistrate revealed in due course that the Salonika police had connived at the murder. The Government was shaken by the death of Lambrakis, and the Palace forced Karamanlis out of office, just before the royal visit to London in July 1963, which evoked Committee of 100 and CND demonstrations.

The November elections brought a Centre Left Government under George Papandreou to power. The Bertrand Russell Committee, which had gained in support, stepped up its campaign and held further Marathon marches in the more favourable political conditions created by the Papandreou Government. The Second Marathon to Athens march in May 1964 gathered 500,000 people at Marathon in memory of Lambrakis, in a legal demonstration which was not disrupted by the police. The Right was, however, increasingly alarmed by the apparently leftist and neutralist trend of the Government, in particular by the role of George's son, Andreas, who wished to curb American influence and proposed a trip to Moscow. So Papandreou in turn was forced out of office in 1965. A period of uncertainty ended with the Colonels' coup of 1967, which also brought to an end peace marches, together with all forms of democratic protest, for seven years.

Fifty members of the Committee of 100 came together under the banner of 'Save Greece Now' and staged a non-violent invasion of the Greek Embassy in London at the end of April 1967 to protest against the coup, and three were jailed as a result.[69] British peace activists were not only expressing solidarity with fellow campaigners against nuclear weapons in their 1963 and 1967 demonstrations, but their commitment to the cause of democracy and freedom in Greece. Lambrakis had himself linked these issues when towards the end of the 1963 Aldermaston march he laid a wreath at the statue of Byron, the poet who had identified himself with the Greek struggle for independence from the Ottoman Empire in the 1830s.

NUCLEAR DISARMAMENT MOVEMENTS OUTSIDE EUROPE: CANADA, AUSTRALIA AND NEW ZEALAND

British connections with the two former dominions of Canada and Australia were extensive, and it is not surprising that CND and Committee of 100 demonstrations found an echo in both countries; though as usual national circumstances shaped the campaigns. The relationship of both countries with the USA was also of considerable importance. Canada was economically dominated by American companies and tied to the USA through NATO. But despite this, Canadian governments tended to adopt a mediatory role in arms control negotiations in the 1950s and 1960s, distancing themselves from rigid NATO positions. Canada had early on decided against developing its own nuclear force and was active in promoting the Test Ban and then the Non-Proliferation Treaty. The key issue for Canadian peace groups was the equipping of Canadian forces with US nuclear weapons to be deployed in Canada or by NATO units in Europe. Australia was linked to the USA through the ANZUS treaty of 1951 and in SEATO, signed in 1954. It had US monitoring stations and it offered port facilities to the US fleet. Because of the fear of being isolated, especially against Communist China, Australia has been a staunch American ally, sending contingents to fight not only in Korea but in Vietnam. During the 1950s the Australian Government promoted its own form of McCarthyism, though a proposal to ban the Communist Party was defeated in a referendum.

The Canadian nuclear disarmament campaign began, as in Britain and the USA, as an expression of public concern about the effects of nuclear tests. The Committee for the Control of Radiation Hazards, set up in Edmonton in 1958, had developed by the following year into a country-wide campaign with support from well-known personalities calling for an end to nuclear testing. When the Conservative Diefenbaker Government announced during 1959 that Canadian forces would accept US Bomarc anti-aircraft missiles, which would be nuclear-tipped, it stimulated a new stage of protest among students, who set up a Combined Universities CND on the British model to oppose the missiles. The students' initiative began in Montreal, but spread across the country, and gained support for a petition and a Christmas Day demonstration in Ottawa. The students tended to remain at the forefront of the protest in the next three years, setting up their own CND paper, *Sanity*, and a theoretical quarterly *Our Generation Against Nuclear War*. Other social groups, however, also joined the campaign.

Voice of Women was founded in Toronto in 1960, while prominent individuals questioned Canada's role in NATO. The Committee for the Control of Radiation Hazards broadened its policy to oppose nuclear weapons for Canada and collected about 150,000 signatures to a petition in 1961. It became the Canadian CND in 1962.[70]

The developing public protests reached a political climax when the Progressive Conservative Government under Diefenbaker, re-elected in 1962, split on the defence issue early in 1963. The Government was still engaged in protracted negotiations with the USA about accepting nuclear warheads. Diefenbaker was then arguing that the strategic position had changed since the original 1959 agreement, and resisted storage of US warheads under US control in Canada on grounds of national sovereignty. The Defence Minister resigned in protest against the Government's unwillingness to fulfil NATO obligations, while the retiring Supreme Commander of NATO and the US Administration exerted public pressure on Diefenbaker. Lester Pearson, leader of the main opposition party, the Liberals, seized the opportunity to support the American position and castigate the Government for hypocrisy. Parliament dissolved after two votes of no confidence in February 1963. Although budgetary issues and the defection of the Conservatives' coalition partner, the Social Credit Party, played a role in the crisis, the subsequent elections were fought largely on the issue of nuclear weapons. The Liberals under Pearson won the April 1963 elections with 129 seats to 95 for the Conservatives, with the help of strongly pro-Liberal preference of voters in the armed services. The Bomarc missiles and US warheads were installed in Ontario and Quebec.[71]

Disillusioned peace activists, who believed earlier that they had won the support of the Liberals, turned to non-violent direct action in Quebec by organizing a blockade of the Bomarc base near Montreal. Although the growing nationalist movement in Quebec was very critical of American economic dominance it did not take up the struggle against the missiles. Individuals in British Columbia mounted a carefully organized campaign of civil disobedience in 1965, without gaining widespread support from peace groups. They did, however, resuscitate sit-down protests in 1971, when the USA launched a nuclear test programme at Amchitka, Alaska, and together with groups in Ontario and Quebec demonstrated at the border with the USA. After 1963, however, both Voice of Women and student activists had extended their protests to encompass issues of domestic injustice and then to the Vietnam War. So the Canadian CND lost impetus.

Australia, like Canada, is a vast country, its diversity reflected in a federation in which the constituent states exercise some political autonomy and have varying political cultures. In both countries campaigns tend to start in particular cities, and movements reflect decentralization and local differences. The established peace organizations, the Women's International League for Peace and Freedom, War Resisters' International and the Quakers were all represented in Australia. But nuclear disarmament only came to the fore after 1960, when CND groups grew up in major cities drawing on young people. Renewed US nuclear testing in the Pacific in 1962 activated large protests in Melbourne and Sydney in May, and Easter marches took place in both cities in 1963. The newly formed West Australian CND also marched to Perth.[72] The numerically stonger Australian Peace Council, hindered by its reputation for being Communist-dominated and its reliance on left-wing unions, adopted a low-key role, stressing use of petitions. Only limited public concern about nuclear tests and nuclear weapons surfaced in New Zealand in this period. A small New Zealand CND marched to Wellington at Easter in 1961, 1962 and 1963, mustering 800 at the final rally in the latter years. The theme of the 1963 protest was a call for a nuclear-free zone in the Southern hemisphere.[73]

JAPAN

By far the largest movement against nuclear weapons arose across the Pacific, in Japan. This movement developed well before big campaigns in the West, and maintained its momentum much longer, though internal divisions disrupted it in the early 1960s. Japan had renounced any claim for reparations for the atomic bombs dropped on Hiroshima and Nagasaki in its Peace Treaty with the USA, and was occupied by the United States until 1952, so the authorities discouraged any publicity about the effects of the bombs. Indeed the survivors of Hiroshima and Nagasaki were given little assistance and their plight was not openly discussed. Various forms of peace activity were allowed – especially in the later 1940s, before the Korean War hardened attitudes, many dissenting groups were able to organize and there was a demonstration against nuclear weapons in Hiroshima in 1948. But the campaign against nuclear weapons dates from 1954. The catalyst was, as noted in the previous chapter, the irradiation of the crew of the *Lucky Dragon*.[74]

Housewives and students in Tokyo and Hiroshima took the lead in organizing a petition against nuclear testing, which was signed by over thirty million people. A World Conference Against Atomic and Hydrogen Bombs was held in Hiroshima on 6 August 1955, ten years after the destruction of the city. Gensuikyo, the Japanese Council Against A and H Bombs, was founded the same year with a programme calling for general and nuclear disarmament. A wide range of political, trade union and religious groups affiliated to it. Gensuikyo became one of the key groups in coordinating the annual conferences in Hiroshima and sent frequent delegations abroad to lobby and protest. Despite the Council's initially non-aligned stance, by the later 1950s American and European peace groups had reservations about the Communist influence within it.[75]

Opposition to nuclear testing united Japanese opinion. When the USA resumed nuclear testing in the Pacific in the spring of 1956, the Japanese Diet called for a halt, and there were official and unofficial protests over Soviet nuclear tests early in 1957. When Britain announced its H Bomb tests in the Pacific for early 1957, the Japanese prime minister asked Britain to desist, and over 350 Japanese physicists signed an appeal to British scientists. Thousands of students demonstrated against the tests in May 1957.[76]

Political opinion was more sharply divided over the Security Treaty with the USA signed in 1951, but a campaign against US military bases and Japanese subservience to American military policy was launched on the second anniversary of the outbreak of the Korean War. The principle of relying heavily on the USA for defence, and in return providing it with military bases and port facilities, was enshrined in the 1957 Basic Policy for National Defence. The American presence appeared to left opposition parties, however, as a source of danger rather than enhanced security, and when the 1951 Treaty was due for renewal in 1960 the ruling Liberal Democrats rushed the Treaty through the Diet, evoking mass protests from trade unionists. Disgust at the Government's political tactics prompted widespread calls for new elections, and this issue overlapped with the more fundamental opposition to the Treaty itself. President Eisenhower was due to visit Japan, but the storm of public protest persuaded the Government to call off the visit. The Student Federation, Zengakuren, twice invaded the grounds of the Diet, and inaugurated a militant phase of New Left tactics distinct from the more pacific protests of the peace movement.[77] Zengakuren, previously the student branch of Gensuikyo, was expelled in 1961, because, the students claimed, they opposed Soviet nuclear tests. Gensuikyo claimed that Zengakuren had become too violent.[78]

Sentiment against nuclear weapons in Japan has not only been widespread but has also had a variety of ideological and organizational bases. A number of Buddhist sects have been influential in promoting peace activities. One with several million adherents is Rissho Kosei Kai (the Society for the Establishment of Righteousness and Friendly Intercourse) founded in the 1930s and based on the teachings of Nicheren, a thirteenth-century Japanese Buddhist monk. A less numerous but dedicated pacifist Buddhist organization was inspired by Maha Thera Nittatu Fujii, who also drew on the teachings of Nicheren but in addition spent ten years working in India with Gandhi, before returning to Japan in 1935 to promote non-violence. After 1945 he prompted the building of a number of peace pagodas and in April 1954 held a world pacifist congress in Japan attended by Buddhists, Hindus, Moslems and Christians. His followers, the Fujii Nittatsu, dressed in yellow robes led the peace march to Hiroshima and have frequently sent delegations on marches in other countries.[79]

Nevertheless, political parties played a very important role in the Japanese movement against nuclear weapons, in particular the Socialist and Communist Parties. The Socialists and their trade union allies were for example behind the 'Anti-Bases Struggle' of the 1950s which resisted government acquisition of land for military purposes and organized the July 1957 demonstration to trespass onto the Tachikawa base at Sunakawa. Campaigners used the 'Pacifist Clause' in the Constitution to appeal against a conviction for trespass, a plea backed by a Tokyo District Court, but turned down by the Supreme Court.[80] (Article Nine of the 1947 Constitution stated that the Japanese people renounced war and the maintenance of armed forces.)

Although Gensuikyo began as an all-party grouping, by 1963 the Socialists alleged that it was dominated by the Communists and so had ceased to oppose all nuclear weapons and tests impartially. The Japanese Communists effectively supported the Chinese in the Sino-Soviet conflict (although they remained nominally neutral between Moscow and Peking) and hence were sympathetic to the Chinese arguments for an 'anti-imperialist' bomb. The Socialist Party and their trade union organization broke away in 1963 to form Gensuikin (Congress Against A and H Bombs), which maintained opposition to all nuclear weapons, leaving Gensuikyo as the recognized organ of the Communist Party. The split between the two anti-Bomb bodies continued until 1977, when they began to cooperate again in supporting the World Congress Against A and H Bombs. Anti-nuclear sentiment in Japan remained strong, however, and in 1967 Prime Minister Sato enunciated the 'Three Non-Nuclear Principles': not to produce or own nuclear weapons and not to allow them to be brought into Japan.[81]

TRANSNATIONAL ACTION AND NON-ALIGNED GOVERNMENTS

The non-aligned peace movement and non-aligned governments shared opposition to superpower military policies and in particular to nuclear testing, and in the early 1960s both direct action groups and European CND organizations cooperated with the Ghanaian Government to pursue their ends.

Radical pacifists in the USA and Britain took the lead in organizing joint transnational protests, because close personal links already existed between pacifists round the American monthly *Liberation* and the London-based weekly *Peace News*. They also shared adherence to the Gandhian tradition of non-violent resistance, commitment to non-alignment in the Cold War and belief in stimulating popular protest round the world against military policies. So the Committee for Non-Violent Action and the Direct Action Committee cooperated in transnational actions such as the San Francisco to Moscow march in 1961, which involved a selected team of Americans and West Europeans in the final part of the walk through West and East Europe.

The most important transnational protest was the linking of Western peace groups with the concerns of African countries through the plan for an international team to travel by jeep from Accra to the French nuclear testing site in the Sahara. The newly formed Ghanaian Council for Nuclear Disarmament sponsored the protest, and the team included eleven Ghanaians, one Nigerian and the President of the Basutoland National Congress. Two French citizens took part, but did not represent any French peace organizations, which feared protests by foreigners would be counterproductive in France. French peace organizations were then operating in a repressive environment in which the authorities regularly banned issues of the opposition press, controlled the radio and TV and tried to suppress all news of opposition to the tests. The participation of the Reverend Michael Scott, then well known in Africa for pleading the cause of the Herero nation in South-West Africa before the United Nations, gave legitimacy to the British involvement. The team made several unsuccessful attempts to get through the French-controlled West African territories. Their presence had stimulated numerous demonstrations against the French tests, but they failed to evoke any opposition to the tests within French West Africa.[82]

The team was inevitably dependent upon the political backing, and to a large extent the unofficial financial support, of the Ghanaian Government. Subsequently, President Nkrumah played a more direct role, calling in 1961 a special conference to coordinate pan-African opposition to French tests. But the conference illustrated the problems of joint action at a political party and government level, encompassed the struggles in Algeria and South Africa, and did not achieve much beyond resolutions. The Ghanaian Government did take some steps to set up a centre for training in non-violence, but this evolved into an institute for the governing Convention People's Party. The experiment illustrated both the possibilities of cooperation between radical activists and a non-aligned government, and some of the inevitable conflicts of interest and aims.

Diversity of aims also created problems when Nkrumah agreed to cooperate with the European Federation Against Nuclear Arms in organizing an Assembly in Accra on the theme 'The World Without the Bomb'. The British CND had by then adopted a policy of 'positive neutralism', which envisaged working with non-aligned Third World states to promote disarmament. Yugoslavia agreed to host a meeting of the Preparatory Commission, which included some Third World representatives, but most of the organization devolved on the Ghanaian and London CNDs. The Assembly met in June 1962 with a number of World Peace Council representatives from the USSR and Eastern Europe as observers. While the proceedings of the Conference Commissions and plenary debates were quite impressive, there was a behind-the-scenes struggle about the role of CND. When the Assembly agreed to set up a Continuing Committee with a secretariat in Accra, the Ghanaian Government made clear it would be under their control. The secretariat continued to exist, and its head attended international peace movement conferences, until Nkrumah was overthrown.[83] But it was apparent that autonomous peace activity was likely to be almost as difficult in new African states as in the Soviet bloc.

TRANSNATIONAL ORGANIZATION AND THE WORLD PEACE COUNCIL

The diverse national and ideological groups that arose to combat nuclear weapons did not immediately coordinate their policies or activities through a formal international organization. The European Federation Against Nuclear Arms represented the first attempt to combine CND bodies and reflected the position in Europe in 1958. The Swedish and Swiss campaigns, the West German SPD-inspired nuclear disarmament organizations, and the Dutch Anti-Atom Bomb movement, founded at the end of 1957, combined with the British CND to set up the Federation in 1959.

This first nuclear disarmament international was, however, soon overtaken by the changing movement. New Easter march organizations grew up (as already indicated) in West Germany in 1960, and then in The Netherlands in 1961, when they mustered 2,000 in Amsterdam; while in Sweden a new Campaign Against Atomic Weapons marched to Stockholm at Whitsun 1962 in support of the Unden Plan for a nuclear-free Nordic zone. The Youth section of the Swiss Movement Against Atomic Armaments took the initiative in holding Easter marches in 1963 and 1964. The Committee of 100 also inspired the creation of civil disobedience groups in other countries, for example the Norwegian Action Committee of Ten, which planned a protest against a NATO Council meeting in Oslo in 1961.[84]

The movement was not only taking new forms but extending to an increasing number of countries, such as Ireland and Austria.[85] It even found some support in conditions generally unfavourable to autonomous peace activity, as in Italy. Despite US bases and battle-field nuclear weapons in Italy, there was virtually no public debate about defence matters. When deputies voiced protests about the Government decision to deploy US Jupiter missiles in 1959 they engaged in what was only the second major parliamentary debate on defence since 1945.[86] Protest in Italy had been linked to political parties, and the parties of the Left had their own domestic preoccupations and did not make nuclear weapons a central issue. Nevertheless, the Italian Committee for Nuclear Disarmament was formed, held a march in Milan in November 1961 and mustered 5,000 at Easter 1962. It claimed support from the Socialist and Communist Parties, Trade Unions and Catholics.[87] Nuclear disarmament protests proved to be short-lived, though broader anti-militarist campaigns began to develop in the early 1960s. The Radical Party, whose left-wing activists had taken over from a more orthodox liberal leadership in 1963, became one of the key groups in initiating campaigns on peace, feminism and other progressive causes up into the 1980s.[88]

The European Federation did not readily adapt to the expanding movement of the 1960s. It was intended to exclude those who embraced direct action as a tactic or pacifism as a policy – the constitution limited membership from each country to two organizations. Its presidents were also wary of encouraging new bodies to join. Although the Federation did extend a welcome to the Yugoslav League for Peace, a meeting designed to bring in new Scandinavian campaigns failed to secure their admission.

Under increasing pressure from American peace organizations and the Canadian Student CND, and from inside Europe, the Federation agreed in 1962 to convene a conference to set up a new International. The meeting in Oxford in January 1963 brought together about eighty delegates from forty-four non-aligned nuclear disarmament and peace organizations. The Conference succeeded in linking both groups with limited policies stressing negotiations to end tests and groups calling for unilateral disarmament by adopting a rather general and long-range set of goals. It also embraced organizations pursuing a variety of tactics from lobbying to civil disobedience. The greatest difficulties revolved round its non-aligned status in terms of relations with the World Peace Council.[89]

The Presidents of the Federation had, without advance consultation, invited ten observers from the World Peace Council to attend the Oxford Conference. Many delegates were worried about the extra political complications of a World Peace Council presence while they were trying to resolve their own policy differences, and define what a non-aligned international would mean. The proposed World Peace Council attendance was therefore extremely divisive. Most non-aligned peace organizations were not opposed in principle to dialogue with the World Peace Council and the official Soviet and East European Peace Committees. Indeed many had attended a July 1962 World Peace Council Conference in Moscow, where they took the opportunity to present their own position, especially in the working groups, to distribute leaflets in Russian to delegates, and to issue their own minority report. (The Committee of 100 also used the occasion to defy the Soviet authorities and demonstrate with a banner and leaflets in Red Square.) The majority of those attending the Oxford Conference remained opposed, however, to admitting the World Peace Council delegates to the founding of a new non-aligned peace international. This resulted in the World Peace Council delegation, including the distinguished Soviet novelist Ilya Ehrenburg (author of *The Thaw*), sitting for days in a London hotel waiting to hear if they could attend the Oxford Conference, and finally being refused.[90]

The International Confederation for Disarmament and Peace nevertheless came into being, and went on to hold a follow-up conference in Sweden in January 1964. The nuclear disarmament movement which had led to the creation of the Confederation waned rapidly, but under Peggy Duff, who became its Secretary in 1967, it focused instead on promoting world-wide opposition to the Vietnam War.

CONCLUSION

As this survey has shown, the scale and persistence of campaigns varied considerably between different countries and the protesters had different goals, so it is difficult to generalize about the total impact of the first wave of the transnational nuclear disarmament movement. Where popular pressure had most success, in Sweden and Switzerland where governments decided against developing nuclear forces, the campaigners' aims meshed with foreign policy and defence assessments by powerful sections of the governing parties and state organs. Where a strong grass-roots movement ultimately had very little effect in terms of government or even opposition policy – notably Britain – the protesters were pitted against prevailing defence and foreign policy orthodoxy. In West Germany, where the shape of future defence policy looked more open-ended in the 1950s, the opposition to basing tactical atomic weapons in Germany was undermined by the rightward swing of the Social Democrats, faced with a strongly entrenched Christian Democratic government in a booming capitalist economy. Whether any German government could have resisted US and NATO nuclear weapons strategy in this period is questionable, though the possibility of a Central European nuclear-free zone was being seriously debated in the late 1950s.

Two treaties were signed in the 1960s which indicated governmental concern about nuclear weapons. The Partial Test Ban Treaty of 1963 did not curb further development of nuclear weapons because it permitted underground testing. But it did halt atmospheric testing by the signatories (which did not include France or China) and so meant a reduction in the nuclear fall-out which had caused worldwide concern. The 1968 Non-Proliferation Treaty allowed the existing nuclear-weapons states who signed – the USA, USSR and UK –

to keep their nuclear forces, but pledged all other signatories to refrain from acquiring the Bomb. Did the campaigns between 1957 and 1964 make a significant contribution to either of these agreements?

The Test Ban depended upon the decisions of the US and Soviet Governments. Britain was a party to the talks throughout, but played a secondary if quite constructive role. When the negotiations were transferred to the Eighteen Nation Disarmament Committee in 1962, the eight non-aligned states, especially Sweden, tried hard but unsuccessfully to promote agreement. The final negotiations in Moscow (in 1963) depended very largely on the personal interest of both Khrushchev and Kennedy in an agreement and their diplomatic and political skill in circumventing strong internal opposition. Pressure from Third World governments and growing popular anxiety about nuclear testing helped to bring the USA and USSR to the conference table in 1958 (see Chapter 2), and encouraged them to continue talks, even after apparent breakdown at the end of 1961 and resumption of testing by both. Since Kennedy faced strong opposition from his military and a section of the Senate, public pressure could have assisted him in 1963 by strengthening the support of liberal senators and convincing waverers, to ensure ratification of the treaty by the two-thirds of the Senate required. Kennedy achieved ratification by astute lobbying and by concessions to his hawks on related issues, but the American peace groups opposed to testing did not have the breadth of support to influence Congress. Moreover, they had already lost their initial momentum. Important backing for a test ban did, however, come from a number of atomic scientists.

The Non-Proliferation Treaty was not signed until several years after the nuclear disarmament movement had faded away, and was prompted partly by the efforts of a number of governments – Ireland, Canada and Sweden – to start serious negotiations. The USA and USSR had strong strategic and political incentives to limit a potentially destabilizing spread of nuclear weapons, and these were conclusive. Nevertheless, in the 1950s experts were predicting twenty or thirty nuclear-weapons states by the 1970s, and heightened awareness of the dangers of nuclear weapons, together with the Swiss and Swedish decisions to forgo the nuclear-weapons option, arguably created a context favourable to limiting the spread of nuclear weapons.

Indeed, one obvious claim to make for the nuclear disarmament campaigns is that they altered consciousness about nuclear tests and weapons, raised the level of public knowledge and marked out nuclear weapons as especially horrendous. At a time when production of smaller warheads and early experiments in minimizing fall-out from 'clean bombs' was tending to make nuclear weapons seem simply an extension of the armoury of conventional weapons, the public protests may have strengthened inhibitions against using nuclear bombs. It is hard to prove the influence of protests on public consciousness. One problem is that organized campaigns themselves reflect a shift in awareness of certain issues, and we saw in Chapter 2 that growing concern about nuclear tests and weapons preceded the growth of protest in the West. This groundswell of unease was expressed in fiction – for example Nevil Shute's *On the Beach*, and in science fiction, Walter Miller's *Canticle for Leibowitz* – and also in a growing scientific and polemical literature on nuclear issues. Nevertheless, campaigners did directly inform their supporters through public meetings, films, leaflets and pamphlets, and helped create a market for publishing on the nuclear threat. Protesters also illustrated the depth of feeling about nuclear weapons and directly prompted debate in the media. So it is reasonable to conclude that the movement intensified awareness and concern.

A movement with long-term goals may also achieve some intermediate success if it lays the foundations for more effective action in the future. The first wave of nuclear disarmament campaigns left behind many of its organizations, which continued to act as a focus for anti-war protest, and had politicized a generation of young people. In addition, the academic study of peace and conflict began in the 1960s – starting in Norway, The Netherlands, Canada and Britain. By 1964 the International Peace Research Association was founded and peace research spread from independent institutes to universities, creating alternative sources of research and expertise to balance the generally more 'realist' emphasis of international relations departments and strategic studies institutes. When a new movement against nuclear weapons arose in the 1980s it built on these foundations.

NOTES AND REFERENCES

1. R. A. Divine, *Blowing on the Wind* (New York, Oxford University Press, 1985), pp. 163–8.
2. Divine, pp. 262–8.
3. Lawrence S. Wittner, *Rebels Against War: the American Peace Movement, 1941–1960* (New York, Columbia University Press, 1969), pp. 258–9.
4. Nigel Young, *An Infantile Disorder? The Crisis and Decline of the New Left* (London, Routledge & Kegan Paul, 1977), pp. 298–9. For a somewhat

different emphasis see Philip Altbach, 'Concern in the Midst of Apathy', *Fellowship*, November 1965, p. 27.

5. Godfrey Hodgson, *In Our Time: America from World War II to Nixon* (London, Macmillan, 1979) pp. 276–7; Sanford Gottlieb, 'Campaigning for Peace', *Bulletin of the Atomic Scientists*, **28**, 9, November 1962, p. 38.

6. Altbach, p. 28.

7. Catherine Foster, *Women for All Seasons: the Story of the Women's International League for Peace and Freedom* (Athens, Georgia, The University of Georgia Press, 1989), pp. 27–8 looks at rise of Women Strike for Peace and role of women from the more orthodox and bureaucratic WILPF. On the Geneva lobby see Anne Eaton, 'Women in Geneva', *Bulletin of the Atomic Scientists*, **18**, 7, September 1962, pp. 47–8.

8. Barbara Deming, 'Letter to WISP' *Liberation*, April 1963, pp. 18–19. See also A. Swerdlow, 'Ladies' Day at the Capitol; Women Strike for Peace vs HUAC', *Feminist Studies*, **8**, Fall 1982, pp. 493–520.

9. Hodgson, pp. 277–8 and Young, p. 34.

10. Paul Jacobs and Saul Landau, *The New Radicals* (Harmondsworth, Penguin, 1967), p. 21.

11. David McReynolds, 'Compulsory Air Raid Drills of New York', *War Resistance*, **2**, 21, 1967, p. 21.

12. Peter Brock, *Twentieth Century Pacifism* (New York, Van Nostrand Reinhold, 1970) pp. 250–2; Albert Bigelow, *The Voyage of the Golden Rule* (New York, Doubleday, 1959).

13. Earle Reynolds, *The Forbidden Voyage* (London, Cassell, 1962).

14. For the *Everyman I* and *II* voyages see *Peace News*, 20 April 1962, p. 8; 1 June 1962, p. 6; 15 June 1962, p. 9; 13 July 1962, p. 12. For *Everyman III*, see *Peace News*, 14 September 1962, p. 1; and Barbara Deming, 'Earle Reynolds: Stranger in this Country', *Liberation*, March 1963, pp. 26–7.

15. For 'Peace with China' campaign see *Peace News*, January–November 1951.

16. The background to CND and the Direct Action Committee, and the subsequent evolution of the nuclear disarmament movement in Britain from 1957 to 1964 are covered most thoroughly by Christopher Driver, *The Disarmers: a Study in Protest* (London, Hodder and Stoughton, 1964) and Richard Taylor, *Against the Bomb: The British Peace Movement 1958–1965* (Oxford, Clarendon Press, 1988). James Hinton, *Protests and Visions: Peace Politics in 20th Century Britain* (London, Hutchinson, 1989) places CND in historical context. Relevant memoirs include: L. John Collins, *Faith Under Fire* (London, Leslie Frewin, 1966); Bertrand Russell, *The Autobiography of Bertrand Russell, Vol. 3: 1944–1967* (London, Allen and Unwin, 1969).

17. Michael Foot, *Aneurin Bevan 1945–1960* (London, Paladin, 1975), pp. 564–76; John Campbell, *Nye Bevan and the Mirage of British Socialism* (London Weidenfeld and Nicolson, 1987), pp. 330–9.

18. John Minnion and Philip Bolsover (eds.), *The CND Story: the First 25 Years of CND in the Words of the People Involved* (London, Alison and Busby, 1983), p. 25.

19. Driver, p. 70.

20. A. J. R. Groom, *British Thinking about Nuclear Weapons* (London, Frances Pinter, 1974) p. 231. See also pp. 145–6, 492–3 and 497 for the Liberal

position in 1957 and 1960 and 1962. In 1958 the Party Assembly urged NATO control of US nuclear weapons assigned to NATO and opposed fixed-site missile bases.

21. Attempts by students and by the Direct Action Committee to promote a 'Voters' Veto' of all parliamentary candidates opposed to unilateralism were divisive and not noticeably effective. A later more positive initiative to put up unilateralist candidates in selected constituencies was also controversial. For details on the latter see Taylor pp. 81–8.
22. *Peace News*, February 1963, p. 11; 22 February 1963, p. 1.
23. See for example Frank Parkin, *Middle-Class Radicalism: the Social Bases of the British Campaign for Nuclear Disarmament* (Manchester, Manchester University Press, 1966), pp. 4–5.
24. Philip Williams, *Hugh Gaitskell* (Oxford, Oxford University Press, 1982). Chapter 21 gives Gaitskell's view of the struggle. See also Philip Williams (ed.), *The Diary of Hugh Gaitskell* (London, Jonathan Cape, 1983).
25. John Cox, *Overkill: the Story of Modern Weapons* (Harmondsworth, Penguin, 1981, 3rd edn.) includes a final chapter on CND up to the 1970s.
26. Minnion and Bolsover, p. 25.
27. Driver, pp. 127–8.
28. Jeff Nuttall, *Bomb Culture* (London, Paladin, 1970), p. 47.
29. Driver, pp. 127–8 and Taylor, pp. 79–80 and 232–4.
30. Parkin, p. 166.
31. Richard Taylor, 'The Marxist Left and the British Peace Movement since the War' in Richard Taylor and Nigel Young, *Campaigns for Peace* (Manchester, Manchester University Press), pp. 163–8.
32. See for example, Williams, p. 375. *The Economist*, 8 April 1961 commented on the more prominent role of Communists on the Aldermaston March and made comparisons with the growing role of the Communist Party in the Japanese anti-nuclear movement. Those who had always opposed CND were beginning to perceive it as less of a threat.
33. Harold Macmillan, *Pointing The Way 1959–1961* (London, Macmillan, 1972), p. 86.
34. Lawrence Wittner, 'The Misuse of the High-minded: The British Government's First Campaign Against CND', *New Blackfriars*, 72, no. 846, February 1991, p. 59. Driver, p. 37, cites attacks by Selwyn Lloyd and Lord Cherwell on anti-test agitation in 1957, referring respectively to Communist inspiration and 'hysteria'.
35. Isobel Lindsay, 'CND and the Nationalist Parties' in Minnion and Bolsover, pp. 134–6.
36. Williams, p. 336.
37. Williams, pp. 359–60; Richard Taylor, 'The Labour Party and CND: 1957–1984', in Taylor and Young, pp. 112–15.
38. The British Government decided to buy the US Skybolt missile. When the USA cancelled Skybolt in 1962 Britain had to switch to a submarine-launched missile and buy Polaris instead. For a history of the British nuclear force see Lawrence Freedman, *Britain and Nuclear Weapons* (London, Macmillan, 1980); John Simpson, *The Independent Nuclear State: Britain, the United States and the Military Atom* (London, Macmillan, 1983).

39. Driver, pp. 200–1.
40. Driver, pp. 98–9. The dip in support during most of 1961 is often ascribed to the counter-productive impact of the Committee of 100, but there are other possible reasons, in particular the intransigent behaviour of the USSR over Berlin and its resumption of nuclear tests.
41. Alfred Grosser, *Germany In Our Time* (Harmondsworth, Penguin, 1974), p. 369.
42. For 'Carte Blanche' see Lawrence Freedman, *The Evolution of Nuclear Strategy* (London, Macmillan, 1981), pp. 109–10 (though he does not specify the date).
43. See *Keesings' Contemporary Archives*, 24 April–3 May 1958, pp. 16141–4.
44. Theodor Michaltscheff, 'German Federal Republic', *War Resistance*, **2**, No. 12, 1965, p. 14; *Keesings*, 1958, p. 16144; Peggy Duff, *Left, Left, Left: a Personal Account of Six Protest Campaigns 1945–65* (London, Alison and Busby, 1971), pp. 226–9.
45. For text of Declaration and signatures see *Bulletin of the Atomic Scientists*, **13**, No. 5, May 1957, p. 228.
46. Joyce Marie Mushaben, 'Cycles of Peace Protest in West Germany: Experiences from Three Decades', *West European Politics*, **8**, 1, January 1985, p. 28.
47. Andrew Trasler, 'Official Attitudes to the Easter Marches', *War Resistance*, **2**, No. 10, 1964, p. 13; Herbert Stubenrauch, 'The Peace Movement in Germany', *War Resistance*, **11**, No. 4, 1963, p. 8.
48. Duff, pp. 229–31.
49. Duff, p. 229.
50. *The War Resister*, **80**, 1958, p. 4; Ralph Hegnauer, 'Atomic Armaments Referendum', *The War Resister*, **84**, 1959, p. 14; *Peace News*, 30 March 1962, p. 11; 13 April 1962, p. 3.
51. Adam Roberts, *Nations in Arms: the Theory and Practice of Territorial Defence* (London, Chatto and Windus, 1976), pp. 52–3.
52. Roberts, pp. 98–9.
53. Jan Andersson and Kent Lindkvist, 'The Peace Movement in Sweden', in Werner Kaltefleiter and Robert L. Pfaltzgraff (eds.), *The Peace Movements in Europe and the United States* (London, Croom Helm, 1985), p. 12.
54. Alva Myrdal, *The Game of Disarmament: How the United States and Russia Run the Arms Race* (Nottingham, Spokesman Books, 1980), pp. 86–7.
55. Erling Bjol, *Nordic Security*, Adelphi Paper No. 181 (London, IISS, 1983); *Keesings*, 1959, p. 16718 and 1964, p. 20371.
56. *Peace News*, 31 March 1961, p. 6; 7 April 1961, p. 1.
57. *War Resistance*, **2**, 6, 1963, p. 29.
58. Sten Sparre Nilson, 'The Peace Movement in Norway', in Kaltefleiter and Pfaltzgraff, p. 36. See also *Peace News*, 18 May 1962.
59. *Peace News*, 20 October 1961, p. 3.
60. Wolf Mendl, *Deterrence and Persuasion: French Nuclear Armament in the Context of National Policy, 1945–1969* (London, Faber and Faber, 1970) p. 164.
61. *War Resistance*, **80**, 1958, p. 5.
62. See Dorothy Pickles, *The Fifth French Republic: Institutions and Politics* (London, Methuen, 1964), pp. 191–2.

63. 'An Interview with Claude Bourdet', *European Nuclear Disarmament Bulletin*, **6**, Autumn 1981, pp. 5–6.
64. Diana Johnstone, *The Politics of Euromissiles: Europe's Role in America's World* (London, Verso, 1984), pp. 87–8.
65. Thanos Veremis, *Greek Security: Issues and Politics*, Adelphi Paper 179 (London, IISS, 1982).
66. Adam Roberts, 'The New Peace Movement in Greece', *Peace News*, 20 September 1963, pp. 6–7.
67. Constantine Tsoukalis, *The Greek Tragedy* (Harmondsworth, Penguin, 1969), especially pp. 174–8, for political context.
68. For an account of the events of 1963 see Duff, pp. 245–8; and *Peace News*, 7 June 1963, pp. 1, 3.
69. *War Resistance*, **2**, No. 22, 1967, on the second Marathon March see *From Protest to Resistance*, Peace News Pamphlet, No. 2, 1981, p. 57.
70. See Dimitrios L. Roussopoulos, *The Coming of World War Three, Vol. I 'From Protest to Resistance: the International War System'* (Montreal, Black Rose Books, 1986).
71. *Keesings*, 1963, pp. 19285, 19413, 19615.
72. *Peace News*, 4 May 1962, p. 12; 26 April 1963, p. 9.
73. *Peace News*, 14 April 1961, p. 5; 27 April 1962, p. 8; 26 April 1963, p. 9.
74. Caroline Moorehead, *Troublesome People: Enemies of War 1916–1986* (London, Hamish Hamilton, 1987), Chapter 9: and N. Bamba, 'Peace Movement at a Standstill: Roots of the Crisis', *Bulletin of Peace Proposals*, **13**, 1, 1982, pp. 39–48.
75. Homer A. Jack, 'The Tokyo Conference and Beyond', *Bulletin of the Atomic Scientists*, **14**, 2, February 1958, p. 91.
76. Divine, pp. 75, 119–20; *Bulletin of the Atomic Scientists*, **13**, 5, May 1957, p. 178.
77. Fred Halliday, 'Students of the World Unite' in Alexander Cockburn and Robin Blackburn (eds.), *Student Power: Problems, Diagnosis, Action* (Harmondsworth, Penguin, 1969), pp. 296–8.
78. Earle Reynolds, 'To Our Great Regret: a Report on the Peace Movement in Japan', *Peace News*, 24 August 1962, p. 5.
79. See Moorehead, pp. 246–9; and Alfred Tucker, 'Pacifism in Japan', *War Resister*, **65**, Summer 1954.
80. D. C. S. Sissons, 'The Pacifist Clause of the Japanese Constitution: legal and political problems of interpretation', *International Affairs*, **37**, January 1961, pp. 54–9.
81. Yukio Satoh, *The Evolution of Japanese Security Policy*, Adlephi Paper No. 178 (London, IISS, 1982, p. 3).
82. A. J. Muste, 'Africa Against the Bomb' and 'Africa Against the Bomb (II)', *Liberation*, January 1960, pp. 4–7; February 1960, pp. 11–14; April Carter, 'The Sahara Protest Team', in A. Paul Hare and Herbert H. Blumberg (eds.), *Liberation Without Violence*.
83. Duff, pp. 233–7. For a more detached report see Wayland Young, 'Mosquitoes in Accra', *Bulletin of the Atomic Scientists*, **18**, 7, September 1962, p. 45.
84. *Peace News*, 7 April 1961, p. 1 and 22 December 1961, p. 8 on Netherlands; 25 May 1962, p. 4 on Sweden; and 26 April 1963, p. 9 and 24 April 1964, p. 9 on Switzerland. *Peace News*, 21 April 1961, p. 1

covers Norwegian Committee of Ten and 17 November 1961, p. 12 also reports the setting up of a Committee of 100 in Amsterdam.

85. See for example, *Peace News*, 10 March 1961, p. 5 on Irish student Ban the Bomb march and 26 April 1963, p. 9 on Austrian Easter demonstration. Belgium was one country where no strictly autonomous CND group developed, though Young Socialists drew 7,000 on an anti-militarist March against NATO in 1961 (*Peace News*, 27 October 1961). The May 8 Movement promoted a national fifteen-minute token strike against nuclear weapons in 1962 (*Peace News*, 18 May 1962) and the National Federation of Institutes for a Belgian Contribution to International Cooperation organized a march of 1,500 and a rally of 4,000 at Antwerp at Easter 1960. Youth organizations with political party and religious groups affiliating, held a big march in Brussels in March 1963 under a strictly multilateralist slogan, and tried to prevent use of the CND symbol, which was, however carried by some Belgians and by foreign contingents on the demonstration (*Peace News*, 29 March 1963). Belgium was a predominantly Catholic country and its politics increasingly dominated by the split between the Flemings and Walloons in the early 1960s, but neither of these factors explains why World Peace Council influence remained stronger in peace protests than in most other West European countries. See Arno Hamers, 'Painful Progress in Belgium', *Peace News* 17 May 1963, p. 6.

86. Marco De Andreis, 'The Nuclear Debate in Italy', *Survival*, May–June, 1986, pp. 195–7.

87. *Peace News*, 27 April 1962, p. 8.

88. 'Partito Radicale: Between Revolution and Reform', *Peace News*, 25 January, 1980, p. 8.

89. Duff, pp. 227–44, covers the European Federation, Moscow Conference and the founding of the International Confederation. She moved in 1967 from being CND Secretary to being ICDP Secretary up until the early 1980s.

90. For other perspectives on the Oxford Conference see Homer Jack, 'Oxford Conference: Organizing the Non-Aligned', *Bulletin of the Atomic Scientists*, **19**, 6, June 1963, pp. 38–40; and A. J. Muste, 'The Oxford Conference', *Liberation*, March 1963, pp. 23–4.

CHAPTER FOUR

The Movement against the Vietnam War and its Impact

INTRODUCTION

As support for the nuclear disarmament campaign ebbed in 1964, the movement against the Vietnam War began to gain momentum. Both movements mobilized large numbers of demonstrators, made news and had an impact on public opinion. Both also promoted a culture of protest in the West. There were however important differences between the nuclear disarmament and Vietnam movements. Activists against the Vietnam War tended to reject utterly the USA's world role since 1945, as an extension of their resistance to the Vietnam War and American anti-Communist ideology, and they also attacked domestic American politics and values. Their rhetoric was more violent than that of the protesters against nuclear weapons and their methods more militant. Although sections of the liberal American establishment moved from support for the war to organized opposition, the Vietnam movement created a profound division between the demonstrators and the millions of older, white, conservative citizens who comprised Middle America. The switch from liberal beliefs and non-violent protest, which characterized the nuclear disarmament campaigns, to a more revolutionary rhetoric and espousal of violent resistance was evident in the transnational campaign against the war as well as in the USA itself. Sections of the movement also aligned themselves with the National Liberation Front in South Vietnam and with Ho Chi Minh's government in the North, hoping for victory over the American forces.

The Vietnam movement acquired more radical ideas, a bitter tone and a sense of desperation, largely because of the increasing horror and destructiveness of the war itself and its potent images on the television screen. The Vietnam War became for the protesters a symbol of American imperialism employing its technological might to destroy an Asian peasant society. Conversely, the endurance, ingenuity and effectiveness of the Vietnamese guerrillas evoked admiration and encouraged a largely rhetorical call to bring guerrilla tactics into the struggle to stop the war and to overthrow capitalism inside America.

The movement against the Vietnam War was also strongly influenced by the wider protest culture of which it became a part. The period 1964–70 saw a series of student campaigns against the administration and ethos of their universities and against the politics and culture of Western societies. The student movement began with the Free Speech Movement in Berkeley, and led towards the end of the 1960s to student strikes and occupation of their universities throughout the United States and Western Europe. The most politically significant student rebellion erupted in May 1968 in France, where de Gaulle's regime was seriously shaken. The student protesters concerned themselves only intermittently with Vietnam, but the movements inevitably overlapped, especially of course in the USA where the draft confronted all male students. University involvement with defence establishments through research contracts and graduate recruitment was also an issue for student radicals in the USA and Britain. The growth of hippy culture in the 1960s was another important influence on protesters, associating protest with 'dropping out' of middle-class society into alternative life-styles projected in music, dress and drugs. Hippy influence imported a gentler and more imaginative strand into protest demonstrations, promoting the imagery of flower-power rather than the power flowing from the barrel of a gun, and was reflected in some of the demonstrations, such as the 'levitation' of the Pentagon staged in 1967. But smoking pot and growing long hair alienated working-class and middle-class Americans from the protesters almost as much as throwing stones or brandishing the 'Vietcong' flag. The third movement which specifically influenced the American Vietnam protests was the evolution of the Civil Rights campaign into Black Power, with its rejection of the white liberal establishment and the Democratic Party.

The Vietnam movement was, like the nuclear disarmament campaign, a transnational movement, with demonstrations taking place in many parts of the world at US embassies. But the central opposition to the war naturally grew up in the USA itself. Apart from South Korea, the only US ally sending significant numbers of troops to Vietnam was Australia, and Japan feared being drawn into the war through the US bases on its territory. So there were major protests in both countries. In Europe pacifists encouraged opposition among American troops stationed abroad, networks sprang up to help American deserters and Sweden offered them asylum. So opposition to the Vietnam War outside the USA went beyond protests in the streets, and included attempts in Britain to run anti-Vietnam War candidates to raise the issue in domestic elections. The USA could, however, rely on its allies not to press criticisms of American conduct of the war. The only factors that really mattered were the military and political developments in South Vietnam and public opinion in the USA. How far the growing movement against the war in the USA directly influenced public opinion and US Administration policy is examined below. The question raises wider issues about the effectiveness of peace movements.

PEACE GROUPS START TO PROTEST ABOUT VIETNAM

When France withdrew from Vietnam, after military defeat by the Vietminh at Dien Bien Phu in 1954, the USA took over its role as Western protector of the anti-Communist regime in South Vietnam. The Ngo Dinh Diem regime in the South refused to accept elections to create a united Vietnam in 1956 – as laid down by the 1954 Geneva Accords – and as the regime became more oppressive in the late 1950s internal opposition grew. The National Liberation Front, combining Communists and some non-Communist opposition groups, was set up at the end of 1960 to wage guerrilla war. The Front had the political backing of Hanoi, but the extent of direct North Vietnamese involvement was for some years limited and much disputed in the growing debate on Vietnam. President Kennedy increased the number of US military advisers to the South from 4,000 to 16,000 to combat the Front. The Diem regime was, however, condemned by international opinion after troops fired on a Buddhist demonstration in Hue in May 1963, and several Buddhist monks subsequently set fire to themselves to protest against discrimination against Buddhism by the Catholic Diem. The US Administration found Diem's government increasingly embarrassing and connived at his overthrow in November 1963 in the first of many military coups.[1]

During 1964 the National Liberation Front stepped up its attacks, killing a number of American servicemen. When in August of that year, President Johnson claimed North Vietnam had fired on an American warship in neutral waters, Congress invested the President with open-ended military powers in South-East Asia in the 'Tonkin Gulf Resolution'.[2] Johnson was, however, fighting the 1964 Presidential election and beat the right-wing Republican candidate, Barry Goldwater, partly by arousing widespread popular fears that Goldwater would lead the USA into war. It was in February 1965 that Washington accepted the argument of many in Saigon that the war in the South could only be won by attacking the North, and the USA launched its first bombing raid against North Vietnam. During 1965 the USA also committed itself to fighting the Liberation Front on the ground and by the end of the year had sent 200,000 troops to Vietnam.

The movement against the Vietnam War took off in 1965. Before then concern about developments in a far-away Asian country was limited to a few informed intellectuals and to established peace groups. The Student Peace Union, for example, held a rally at the University of Wisconsin in autumn 1963 against the growing American military role in Vietnam.[3] SANE switched its attention from nuclear testing in 1963 to hold two demonstrations outside the White House against American support for the Diem dictatorship, and went on in 1964 to initiate a petition calling for both halves of Vietnam to be neutralized. As soon as news broke about the American bombing of North Vietnam SANE sent a telegram of protest signed by its co-chairmen, Professor Stuart Hughes and Dr Benjamin Spock. Over the next two years SANE became increasingly committed to the Vietnam movement: for example it coordinated a March on Washington for Peace in November 1965, which drew 40,000. SANE also became increasingly associated with support for draft resistance through Dr Spock. The man renowned for advising millions of middle-class parents on how to bring up their children now urged the young to rebel over the Vietnam War. The SANE leadership split in 1967 on this issue.[4]

The pacifist War Resisters' League claimed to be the first group to demonstrate against the Vietnam War in 1963, and in 1964 it combined with the Committee for Non-violent Action to hold a vigil of several hundred people outside the Democratic Party Convention. The two organizations sponsored another vigil outside the White House in August 1965 and in October 1965 the League cooperated in calling for the Fifth Avenue Parade for Peace in Vietnam in New York, which mustered 25,000. The most important role played by the War Resisters' League, however, was to begin a campaign of draft resistance, when twelve young men burned their draft cards at a rally in May 1964.[5]

The USA did not practise universal conscription, but had a system of selective service which required all young men of draft age to register and to be available for call-up if required, as increasing numbers were from 1965. The legislation did provide for conscientious objectors (COs), but only those with religious objection to all war. The Supreme Court decided to give a liberal interpretation to the requirement that COs must believe in a 'Supreme Being' in a 1965 test case, and thereafter applicants for CO status had only to show a sincere and consistent personal commitment to pacifism. The court ruled out 'essentially political, sociological or philosophical views' which made it impossible to claim CO exemption because of specific objections to the Vietnam War.[6] Some objectors apparently stretched their moral grounds for refusing to serve in Vietnam to encompass a pacifist stance. The growing proportion of COs to men inducted into the forces in the late 1960s suggests this tendency.

Many young men, however, decided to demonstrate their total resistance to the Vietnam War by refusing to register at all, and burned their draft cards or posted them to the Justice Department. Draft refusal could carry a five-year prison sentence. Some pacifists who could qualify as COs, or had already done so, decided to opt for total resistance, arguing that conscientious objection for a small and educated minority acted as a safety valve, and that it was a form of cooperation with the draft.[7] Public defiance would, they believed, promote wider resistance to the war. Between mid-1964 and mid-1965 there were 380 prosecutions of draft resisters.[8]

The Fellowship of Reconciliation initiated another form of civil disobedience when it sponsored a group of twelve who announced publicly that they would pay no taxes on their 1964 income and prompted the creation early in 1965 of the No Tax for War in Vietnam Committee. The Fellowship also began to mobilize opposition to the war in the religious community in 1965 and set up the Clergymen's Emergency Committee for Vietnam, which sponsored an advertisement in the *New York Times* under the heading 'Mr President, In the Name of God Stop It'. Twelve American Clergymen visited Vietnam and published another advertisement 'We Have Seen the Anguish of Vietnam'. The Committee then solicited international support from religious leaders.[9] The war brought increased support for the Fellowship from the churches, especially Catholic monks and nuns.

The Women's International League for Peace and Freedom was

slower to take action against the war, but after its 1965 International Congress celebrating its fiftieth year the League organized an Appeal to American Women, delivered to the President's wife and to a hundred women's organizations early in 1966. The League also ran an advertisement in the *New York Times* in April 1966, and through its world-wide branches organized international demonstrations. The League maintained a respectable profile and moderate policy calling for an 'honourable peace', though many individual members in the USA and many branches abroad favoured unconditional American withdrawal of its troops from Vietnam. One individual League member, Alice Herz, an eighty-two year-old refugee from Nazism living in Michigan, took more desperate action to appeal to young Americans to resist the war. She followed the example of the Buddhist monks in Vietnam and set herself on fire in March 1965, dying ten days later.[10] As the war continued two other Americans, Quaker Norman Morrison and a Catholic, Roger LaPorte, burned themselves to death to protest against what their government was doing in Vietnam.

MOUNTING PROTEST AGAINST THE WAR

The bombing of North Vietnam in February 1965 prompted opposition to the war outside established peace groups. The first to respond were the staff and students at the major American universities, but over the next three years increasing numbers from varied social circles engaged in active protest and public opinion began to swing against American military involvement.

Academics at the University of Michigan invented a new form of public protest and debate when they held a 'teach-in' on Vietnam on 24 March: 216 faculty members signed a statement declaring their anxiety about the war and inviting students to a night of lectures, seminars, informal debate and a protest rally. The teach-in had been substituted for a more controversial one-day strike to avoid confrontation with the state government and the university authorities.[11] It proved to be an ideal method of raising consciousness about the war in universities, combining the academic activity of disseminating information on a still obscure topic and the airing of a range of views (supporters of the Administration policy were invited to address teach-ins), with the sense of concern and involvement and solidarity generated by campaign meetings. The teach-ins brought in moderates among staff and students, and at the same time helped create a constituency for future campaigns. In the following weeks teach-ins spread to many campuses and they reached a climax in a televised teach-in held in Washington. The Washington event did however reveal the gap between intellectuals such as international relations theorist, Hans Morgenthau, who opposed the American involvement in Vietnam on the grounds that it was opposed to a *realpolitik* view of the national interest, and the moral indignation and leftist views of some academics and students involved in the teach-ins. There was also some inevitable tension between the academic and political aims of a national teach-in.[12]

Political protest soon predominated. A student march on Washington in April 1965 attracted 20,000 and Vietnam Day rallies, organized by Vietnam Day Committees, took place in many universities in October 1965. At Berkeley the Vietnam Committee directed the energies of students previously radicalized by the Free Speech Movement into opposing the war. The most important strand in student protest became resisting the draft. 'We Won't Go' unions on élite university campuses organized draft card burnings (for example 175 Cornell students burned their cards on 15 April 1967) and sit-ins at draft boards. Many resisters publicized their reasons for refusing to fight. The Justice Department in mid-1968 announced 3,305 prosecutions in twelve months for defying draft registration. Dr Spock, a Yale chaplain and three other intellectuals were put on trial in 1968 for publicly encouraging draft resistance. Many students who could not claim CO status, and were not willing to accept a prison sentence, chose to evade the draft and crossed the border into Canada. A poll of Harvard graduates in February 1968 indicated that 40 per cent would either resist or evade the draft.[13]

Students were active in the draft resistance campaign for a number of reasons: they were well informed about Vietnam by the mid-1960s; they belonged to a generation already politicized by the Civil Rights movements and the wave of campus protests and with a belief in their own political power; and they had a strong sense of social guilt as a privileged élite. Students were well placed to secure deferment if called-up, poor white men and in particular most blacks could not. It soon became evident that a disproportionate number of blacks were being drafted to Vietnam, and were dying when they got there. Many young men from the ghettoes did manage to evade the draft and were not pursued by the authorities, who were perhaps unwilling to provoke further trouble in a period which saw a growing number of violent urban riots in the black ghettoes. But the number of blacks drafted to Vietnam roused increasing anger and was taken up by black leaders.

Martin Luther King, the leading figure in the non-violent civil rights movement, voiced his personal opposition to the Vietnam War in January 1966. He did not, however, throw his full weight behind the anti-war campaign until a sermon in April 1967, which called passionately on America to stop the war, both in the name of the Vietnamese and of the poor of America. Moderate civil rights leaders were still hesitating in 1967 to oppose the Johnson Administration, which had significantly advanced their own cause, over the controversial issue of Vietnam. The much more radical Student Non-Violent Coordinating Committee had attacked the 'aggressive policy' of the USA in Vietnam early in 1966, and six of its members were jailed for invading a draft induction centre in Atlanta. When the high-profile heavyweight boxer, Muhammed Ali (Cassius Clay), declared publicly that he would not fight in Vietnam, his stand attracted widespread publicity. Ali, who had converted to the Black Muslims, lost his right to the world heavyweight title as a result of his opposition to the draft, although he was never sent to prison.

A more unexpected source of radical protest against the war was the Catholic Church. Priests, nuns and lay members of the Church began a series of raids on draft board offices in late 1967, entering the offices, covering the records with blood, or destroying them. The best-known case was that of the Catonsville nine, who had invaded a draft office in Maryland and were jailed for several years. They included the brothers Daniel and Philip Berrigan, both priests, who were to be prominent in anti-war protest into the 1980s and advocates of uncompromising personal resistance. Protestants and Jews also took part in these actions, but Catholics predominated.

Protestant clergy were at the forefront of debate and orthodox protests against the war, although there were significant differences in attitude between denominations. A 1968 survey of clergy in California found that 82 per cent of the fundamentalist Southern Baptists favoured military escalation and 15 per cent the less hawkish position of continued bombing. On the other hand clergy from the United Church of Christ and the Methodists overwhelmingly opposed both these options and supported either a halt to the bombing, withdrawal of US forces to enclaves or (40 per cent in each case) total withdrawal of American troops. Other denominations (Lutherans, Presbyterians, American Baptists and the Episcopalians) fell in between. One very interesting finding was that although almost all the clergy in the sample raised the war with their parishoners, and a significant number made their views public, those who supported the scaling down of the war or total withdrawal were one and a half times as likely to have preached sermons, made public statements or petitioned public officials on the issue. Almost half of those choosing the two most 'doveish' options had been to protest meetings and nearly a fifth favouring complete withdrawal had been on a protest march. The Protestant clergy were on average more opposed to the war than the total population, but in addition the anti-war ministers were especially active, thus creating the general impression that the Protestant clergy were part of the movement against the war.[14]

Protests by the clergy helped to make opposition to the war respectable, and to draw in the liberal establishment. Senator Eugene McCarthy recalls as significant one protest meeting sponsored by 'clergy and others' at which he and Senator Morse both spoke. During 1967 leading liberal intellectuals decided that they had to break with the Democratic Administration and come out against continuing the war. John Kenneth Galbraith, well known for his writings on the American economy and for his castigation of a society which combined private wealth and public squalor, had spoken against the war 'in a low key' for some time. Galbraith became chairman of Americans for Democratic Action in 1967 and together with Arthur Schlesinger, the respected historian of the New Deal and the Kennedy Administration, and other intellectuals swung the association against the war.[15]

The Senate Foreign Relations Committee under the liberal Senator William Fulbright had held important televised hearings in February 1966, which had raised serious doubts about the prosecution of the war. At the end of 1967 many liberal Democrats decided that the time had come to take a call for peace in Vietnam into the elections for the Presidency. Robert Kennedy, who had the glamour and the connections of the Kennedy name, and who had in addition identified himself with the causes of civil rights and economic support for the poor, was the obvious candidate. But he hesitated to challenge President Johnson in the primaries. Eugene McCarthy then agreed to stand against the President in the New Hampshire primary.

During 1968 there seemed to be a real possibility of the movement against the Vietnam War having an impact on the established political process. Disillusionment with the Johnson Administration had alienated many protesters from the political system. Some had worked for his election in 1964 only to see him escalate the war, using as authority the Tonkin Gulf Resolution. The protesters did not trust any Administration statements about the war – one of the slogans associated with the movement was 'Tell me lies about Vietnam'. However, when McCarthy decided to stand against Johnson many anti-war activists, including a large number of students, flocked to work for him. Despite the fact that he was challenging an established president on a controversial anti-war platform, McCarthy created a sensation by wining 42 per cent of the vote in the New Hampshire primary. Kennedy almost immediately declared he would enter the contest, creating great bitterness in the McCarthy camp, but increasing the pressure on Johnson. As it became clear that Johnson would do badly in the Wisconsin primary, he announced he would withdraw from the presidential contest, just before (on 2nd April) McCarthy won 56 per cent of the primary vote.[16]

McCarthy's candidacy represented a coalition between liberal Democrats and a section of the protest movement, but his remarkably good showing reflected the wider public mood. Public opinion had gradually been moving against American involvement in the war. In answer to the same Gallup question, only 24 per cent thought sending troops to Vietnam was a mistake in August 1965, whereas 47 per cent thought it was a mistake by October 1967.[17] But most commentators agree that the Tet Offensive by the Communist-led forces in Vietnam had a major impact on American attitudes. As Kennedy noted, in a bitter speech immediately after the 1968 New Year offensive, half a million US troops and total control of the air did not enable the USA to hold a single South Vietnamese city against the National Liberation Front. Although the immediate public reaction to Tet was to endorse further US bombing, the longer-term reaction was to doubt whether more American lives should be lost in an unwinnable war.[18] The Tet offensive gave a new dynamism to McCarthy's campaign in New Hampshire.

Despite the bitterness between McCarthy and Kennedy in the campaigns in the succeeding primaries, which divided opponents of the war, prospects for a Democrat presidential candidate committed to ending the war looked increasingly promising. Then Robert Kennedy was shot just after he had won the California primary. That August the Democratic Party Convention met in Chicago where an old-style machine politician, Mayor Daley, manipulated the Convention to ensure election of Humphrey, then Vice-President, and his police launched a violent, pre-planned, attack on 100,000 demonstrators outside the Convention Hall.[19] The third disaster for the anti-war movement was the election of Nixon to the White House on the basis of his successful appeal to white, conservative Middle America. Although in retrospect it is clear that 1968 was a turning point in the war – the Administration rejected military requests for a further 200,000 troops in Vietnam and opened negotiations with the National Liberation Front – the next three years saw further escalation of the war in South-East Asia and an even greater polarization of American society.

THE MOVEMENT'S FINAL PHASE: 1969–72

The movement against the war gathered momentum and support as evidence piled up of the suffering of the Vietnamese people caught up in the war and the corruption of American soldiers engaged in fighting it. The revelation of the My Lai massacre in February 1970, in which an American platoon searching for 'Vietcong' forced hundreds of villagers into a ditch and shot them, dramatized the horror of the war. The number of CO applications rose steadily: by 1970 there was one CO exemption for every four men inducted.[20] Draft resistance and evasion also increased dramatically. At one induction centre in Northern California in 1969 2,400 out of 4,400 due to report for registration failed to do so, and 11 per cent of those who did report then refused to serve in the armed forces.[21] Veterans returning from Vietnam gave significant support to the anti-war cause. Veterans for Peace arose in the mid-1960s, and Vietnam Veterans Against the War in 1970. A third organization for Veterans and Reservists to End the War in Vietnam was the most willing to defy the law.[22] Veterans could speak with authority about what was happening in Vietnam: a wounded and disfigured veteran left his hospital bed to speak at an anti-war rally on the eve of Nixon's inauguration, and veterans gave public testimony at a 1970 demonstration about crimes they had seen troops commit. Veterans could also make powerful symbolic gestures to show revulsion against the war: over a thousand threw their Vietnam medals away at the Capitol in April 1971.[23]

The greatest challenge to the Administration was growing disaffection within the armed forces. At first a few individuals openly opposed the war and were court-martialled. They included an army doctor who refused to help train the special Green Beret forces, a navy nurse who dropped anti-war leaflets from a plane, and two black marines who urged resistance to the war. By 1970 debates about the war and underground papers promoted opposition in military bases both in the USA and Europe, encouraged by coffee shops and bookshops set up by peace activists near bases in America and by widespread distribution of anti-war leaflets by pacifists in Europe. Twenty-eight officers openly launched the Concerned Officers' Movement in June 1970, and a thousand US servicemen in Britain signed a petition against the war in 1971.[24] GI opposition was dramatized by the case of the Fort Jackson Eight, jailed for demonstrating against the war in March 1970. They were members of GIs United Against the War in Vietnam, which coordinated protests.[25] Even in Vietnam itself troops wore armbands to show solidarity with a mass demonstration in Washington in October 1969. Alongside principled opposition to the war there was widespread demoralization among servicemen in Vietnam, demonstrated by extensive use of drugs and by a growth in 'fragging', which meant killing their officers. Thousands of GIs deserted both in North America and Europe.

Students played an increasingly significant role in demonstrations. A Student Mobilization Committee to End the War in Vietnam was formed in 1968 in parallel to the National Mobilization Committee. But student protests became most intense and spread to more colleges than ever before when Nixon invaded Cambodia with US and South Vietnamese forces in late April 1970. Some demonstrations erupted into violence, which turned into tragedy at Kent State University, Ohio, where National Guardsmen opened fire, killing four students and wounding others.

Despite increasing militancy among sections of the anti-war movement, liberal and middle-ground support for ending the war grew between 1969 and 1971. The nation-wide Moratorium demonstrations in October 1969 brought out two million across the country, and in November half a million mustered to protest in Washington. A thousand lawyers urged immediate withdrawal from Indo-China in May 1970. Former members of the Johnson Administration began to air public doubts about the conduct of the war and Congress also began to signal increasing disquiet about the unchecked use of presidential power in the prosecution of the war.

Then one Defence Department intellectual, Daniel Ellsberg, changed his mind about the war and decided in 1971 to make a huge collection of Defence Department documents available to the *New York Times* for publication. The *Pentagon Papers* had been assembled in 1967 on the orders of Defence Secretary McNamara to throw light on the evolution of policy over Vietnam. Reading the papers persuaded Ellsberg himself that the USA should never have involved itself in Vietnam in the first place and had no right to be there. While working at the Rand Corporation he was able to photocopy the entire collection and pass them on to Fulbright as the basis for Senate Committee hearings. When Fulbright felt unable to make use of them, and when Nixon stepped up the bombing of Laos and North Vietnam, bombed Cambodia and then invaded Cambodia and later Laos, Ellsberg decided to risk prosecution and seek publication. The *New York Times*, the widely respected and most national of American papers, had assisted the anti-war movement by its excellent reporting from Vietnam throughout the 1960s, and decided to publish a book based on the papers.[26] The Administration tried to quash publication, but was overruled by the Supreme Court. Ellsberg escaped prosecution, but was added to Nixon's personal black list of subversives, and post-Watergate revelations showed that Nixon ordered the burgling of Ellsberg's psychiatrist. The *Pentagon Papers* provided further information for opponents of the war.

By 1972, however, Nixon and Kissinger were engaged in intensive negotiations with the North Vietnamese and close to agreement towards the end of the year. The Administration had for some time been withdrawing American troops – thus reassuring that section of public opinion primarily concerned about American boys dying in Vietnam – and in 1972 Nixon ended the system of registration for the draft. After a final, exceptionally heavy, series of bombing raids against Hanoi late in 1972, to force the hand of the North Vietnamese in the negotiations, a peace accord was signed in 1973.[27]

ASSESSING THE AMERICAN MOVEMENT AGAINST THE WAR

The impressive scope of the movement against the Vietnam War, and the scale of the resistance to the draft, suggest that the movement played a major role in ending the war. There are, however, good reasons to question this simple conclusion. One is that the Nixon Administration, which negotiated the withdrawal from Vietnam, was primarily concerned with maintaining the great power status of the USA. Although *realpolitik* arguments might have suggested that after a major investment of lives, money and prestige the USA had to win, realism also dictated avoiding the risk of Soviet or Chinese intervention (which invasion of the North or use of nuclear weapons might have provoked). Military and economic calculations therefore pointed to a face-saving negotiated withdrawal. The Americans could not win the war on the ground in the South, and expenditure on the war was fuelling inflation, which in turn did grave damage to US exports and the balance of payments. So depleting gold reserves undermined the international role of the dollar and the USA had to suspend convertibility of the dollar into gold in 1971.

Secondly, although US administrations are certainly constrained by public opinion, which feeds into Congressional and Presidential elections, the impact of the anti-war movement on wider public attitudes to Vietnam is itself debatable. American public opinion had swung against the war by 1968, and so limited Presidential options; but it is not clear that this was directly in response to the peace movement. One study suggests that in both the Korean and Vietnam Wars the key factor influencing the American public was the casualty rate for American soldiers, that only liberal intellectuals made a sharp distinction between the different international contexts of the two wars, and that the frequent TV images of the horrors of the Vietnam War did not influence general attitudes until the casualty rate rose sharply.[28] Godfrey Hodgson deploys poll evidence to argue strongly that the peace movement and the wider opposition to the war were quite distinct, that the former stressed what the USA was doing in Vietnam and the latter the cost to the USA, and that many in favour of ending the war were also extremely hostile to the peace movement. Even members of the public in favour of the radical call for immediate US withdrawal often reacted strongly against peace protesters.[29]

Public attitudes to the movement were influenced by the highly provocative tactics of a section of protesters, such as burning the American flag and identification with the Vietnamese 'enemy', and by media images which tended to screen out respectable middle-class demonstrators and focus on those representing the 'counter-culture'. In addition the peace movement suffered from the fact that even 'respectable' liberal intellectuals from the top universities (who made up a large part of the opposition to the war) tended to rouse hostility among many 'average Americans'.[30]

The simplifications produced by most opinion polls and generalizations about class attitudes both need, however, to be treated with ∠ care. For example, although an AFL–CIO poll of its members in 1967 found about a third backed Johnson's handling of the war, and the next largest group advocated escalation of the war, a number did favour an immediate end to the war. By 1969 several unions were willing to back the Moratorium demonstrations, and two unions (of the clothing workers and of state and local government employees) opposed Nixon's Indo-China policies in May 1970.[31] So working-class and union attitudes were not monolithic. Nor, indeed, did all the highly educated or student generation support the protest movement, as Hodgson notes.[32] The active opposition to the war was also divided into a variety of social and ideological grouping with differing motives. Many draft evaders, activist veterans, deserters and GIs protesting against the war probably felt angry both about American casualties and the suffering of the Vietnamese. Black Power militants opposed the war partly because it demanded disproportionate sacrifices by the black community and because they did not see why, when they were denied democratic rights at home, they should fight for the USA in Asia. While, at the other end of the spectrum, the remarkable existence after 1967 of groups of businessmen publicly opposing the war probably reflected a mix of moral, political and economic concerns.[33]

Even if there was a gap between much passive public opinion and many peace movement activists, the protesters had an important role in articulating and demonstrating the existence of opposition, both to the public and to Congress and the Administration. The liberal intellectuals and the students also created the channels for public opposition to the war to surface in the McCarthy candidacy. It does, moreover, appear that Nixon was influenced by the mass Moratorium demonstrations in October 1969 when deciding whether to escalate the war, for example by invading North Vietnam or blockading Haiphong. Although Nixon went on television soon after the demonstrations to appeal to the 'silent majority' against the demonstrators, in his memoirs he does suggest that he feared escalation would divide public opinion too sharply, though he gives other foreign policy reasons for not escalating the war.[34]

One index of the seriousness with which both the Johnson and the Nixon Administrations viewed the anti-war movement might be the extent of police and intelligence service activity against it. Peace groups had, like other dissenting circles, been natural targets for surveillance by the FBI – which found it necessary to bug the rooms even of Martin Luther King – and both the CIA and Army Intelligence also gathered intelligence on internal opposition. Moreover, the FBI had a long established Counter-Intelligence Programme, which was designed to smear radical leaders, spread disinformation, foster ideological divisions and sabotage demonstrations. As the movement against the Vietnam War gained momentum in 1967 and 1968 FBI efforts to create confusion also increased and agents sometimes tried to incite violence.

Nevertheless, a concerted campaign to crush the anti-war movement only came when Nixon gained the Presidency and his Attorney-General authorized extensive harassment of the anti-war protesters, including numerous legal charges which tied down the activists, even though many of the charges were eventually overthrown by the courts. (The most dramatic example of this approach occurred when thousands converged on Washington in May 1971 with the stated goal of 'stopping the government'. Police backed by troops seized 13,400 people – including innocent bystanders – over four days and filled the jails, ignoring normal arrest procedures. The courts later ruled that the methods of arrest were illegal.) John Dean testified in the Watergate Hearings that the White House constantly sought intelligence information to discredit anti-war demonstrators and their leaders. Although pressure on the anti-war movement was part of a wider drive against all anti-establishment activists, and was influenced by the paranoid style of Nixon's politics, which led to Watergate, it did indicate that the Nixon Administration saw the opposition to the war as a threat to his own policies and position.[35]

THE TRANSNATIONAL MOVEMENT

Outside the USA the movement which came closest to having a real political impact grew up in Australia. Despite the fairly limited support for the campaign against nuclear weapons and nuclear testing in the early 1960s, when the Australian Government decided in 1965 that SEATO membership required sending Australians to fight with the Americans in Vietnam, the peace movement gathered momentum. Several groups were formed specifically to oppose conscription and sending troops to Vietnam. The campaign against the Vietnam War drew on the young, on the universities, on women – for example in the organization Save Our Sons – and on ex-servicemen. It also gained respectability from backing by the clergy, who formed the Committee for the Canberra Vigil. In Sydney the Association for International Control and Disarmanent (created in 1964 out of the former New South Wales Peace Committee) had already gained some high-level Anglican support. The anti-war groups engaged in vigils and marches and began to experiment with civil disobedience – over fifty were arrested for sitting down in the street at a Vietnam Action Committee protest in Sydney in October 1965. Demonstrations multiplied in 1966 and 20,000 protested when President Johnson visited Australia.

The main focus for the anti-war campaign in 1966, however, was provided by the 1966 election, and the most important political support for the campaign came from the Australian Labour Party. Left-wing Labour MPs actively endorsed the opposition to the war and addressed protest meetings. More significantly, the Labour leadership was specifically opposed to sending troops to Vietnam. Ralph Summy, historian of the Australian peace movement, notes that for the first time since 1945 'the peace dissenters felt they were spearheading a popular protest where the outcome *might* be favourable'.[36] Their hopes were crushed by Labour's resounding defeat in the November 1966 elections, and by the party's subsequent decision to abandon its commitment to withdraw troops from Vietnam. Since the polls showed that half of Labour voters (and three-quarters who backed the government) supported Australian involvement in Vietnam between 1966 and 1969, the protesters were in a clear minority.[37]

The opposition to the war received partial endorsement from the churches in 1967 when Roman Catholic bishops in Australia urged peace in Vietnam and the Anglican Primate appealed for an end to the escalation of the war. Opposition to the draft was signalled by a growing number of COs. But the movement against the war became increasingly polarized between the moderate peace groups, responsive to strong criticism from press and politicians of the militancy of the movement's demonstrations, and young radicals who moved further to the Left. The latter set up Vietnam Solidarity Committees openly backing the National Liberation Front, and arguing for socialist revolution at home. This wing of the Australian movement was comparable to the Trotskyist-led Vietnam Solidarity Committee in Britain, which organized demonstrations in 1967 and 1968.

The most radical wing of the Japanese opposition to the Vietnam War was represented by the Zengakuren students' union, which by 1968 had adopted overtly violent tactics involving pitched battles with the police and attacks on US bases.[38] There was also a broader-based Peace for Vietnam Committee, drawing on citizens' groups, women's organizations and trade unions which could call on over a million supporters; and both the Communist and Socialist Parties were against the US role in the war and the use of US bases in Japan to prosecute it.[39]

Ideas for action spread by power of example from the USA: teach-ins for example were organized at universities in Britain and Canada. The flow of draft evaders over the Canadian border prompted the creation of groups in several cities to give practical aid, and deserting

GIs found support in Europe. There were, in addition, a number of initiatives to demonstrate international outrage at American conduct of the war. Potentially the most influential was the Bertrand Russell War Crimes Tribunal, which brought together international celebrities to examine evidence of American and South Vietnamese atrocities. The Tribunal was convened in late 1966 and held hearings in Paris in 1967. Russell's own unqualified condemnation of the USA and backing for the National Liberation Front, combined with the clearly committed views of the Tribunal members (which included Jean-Paul Sartre) made it a focus for anti-war campaigning, but limited its influence on middle-ground opinion.[40]

Non-aligned opposition to the bombing of North Vietnam was represented by a visit to the North by a team including an Anglican bishop, a Canadian rabbi, Pastor Martin Niemöller and the American pacifist, A. J. Muste. The original aim had been to send an international team to share the dangers of the bombing, but the North Vietnamese were unwilling to accept a large team or expose them to danger. After negotiations through the Paris-based North Vietnamese delegation, the Government agreed to accept a team of four international observers composed of four venerable figures, ages ranging from sixty-seven to eighty-two, sponsored by the International Confederation for Disarmament and Peace and the War Resisters' International.[41] A group of British peace activists, including the Reverend Michael Scott and Welsh Nationalist MP Gwynfor Evans, made another attempt to go to Hanoi to show solidarity with its citizens under attack. In 1968 they did manage to visit the Cambodian border area under attack from South Vietnam, but were not allowed to stay in the danger zone. Prince Sihanouk's Government showed some ambivalence about the team, but used their presence to make a diplomatic point about recognition of Cambodia's frontiers. The group split up after leaving Cambodia, several being arrested after staging a protest at a US base in Thailand.[42]

In countries not directly involved in the Vietnam War the debate about it tended to be polarized between Left and Right. Despite increasing doubts, Western governments and establishments hesitated to criticize the USA publicly – the British Labour Government was especially loath to do so. The Right also reacted against the rhetoric and style of the protests against the war, which often uncritically endorsed the National Liberation Front. Communists and other Marxists were prominent in the movement against the Vietnam War; but, in addition, the pacifist and liberal peace organizations had difficulties in projecting independent and non-aligned policies. In part this hesitancy reflected the view that whatever criticisms could be made of the North Vietnamese Government and of the Front, the USA was waging an illegitimate war and inflicting untold damage on the Vietnamese people. Secondly, although Western pacifists looked hopefully to the Vietnamese Buddhists as a possible third force in the South, and CND in demonstrations against the Vietnam War sometimes gave them a platform, there was no really credible long-term alternative government to the Vietnamese Communists, once the USA withdrew. Space for a third force narrowed as the war escalated and the North sent troops to the South.

Nevertheless, the Buddhists did provide an important opposition to the American-backed military regimes in South Vietnam in the mid-1960s, and formed the basis of a growing anti-war movement within Vietnam itself. The Buddhists reorganized themselves early in 1964, drawing together two different traditions within Buddhism to form the United Buddhist Church of Vietnam, which had both spiritual and secular organizational wings. The Buddhists called for a cease-fire, free elections in the South and negotiations to end the war (though nuances of policy varied with the shifting politics inside the South and between Buddhist leaders). The Buddhists' protests against the war and the South Vietnamese Government were actively supported by students, and even by South Vietnamese army units in March 1966. The Buddhists also argued strongly that the creation of a democratic government committed to social reform would erode much of the popular support gained by the National Front. Once the USA had entered direct negotiations with the Front and with Hanoi, the Buddhists had been relegated to the sidelines, but the United Church established its own peace delegation in Paris in May 1969.[43] The Buddhists did receive support from some peace organizations in the USA, for example the Fellowship of Reconciliation, but the ideological divisions within the American and Western movements against the war precluded really significant linkage with the Buddhists. The variety of peace proposals put forward by liberal political organizations, churches, unions and peace bodies tended to stress negotiations between governments plus the National Liberation Front, although they did usually include a call for supervised elections in the South.[44]

CONCLUSION

The experience of the Vietnam War had a major impact on American political attitudes. It created a widespread distrust of the role of the military and secret services, concern about the scope of arbitrary presidential power in foreign and defence policy, opposition to US military action overseas, and greater scepticism about American values and institutions. These attitudes were not only held by intellectuals and students on the liberal–left axis of political opinion, but were reflected in a significant segment of Congress after 1968. These sentiments prompted resistance to enormous military expenditure, put pressure on the Nixon Administration to agree to SALT I and Anti-Ballistic Missile Treaty in 1972 and led to the passing of the 1973 War Powers Act, which required the President to consult with Congress early in an international crisis. The strength of these attitudes continued to inhibit the Carter Administration, but were for a while overridden when President Reagan came to power.

It is difficult to determine how far changed attitudes were due to the disillusioning developments of the war itself, and how far the peace movement directly influenced people through its protests and through its attacks on official misrepresentation. At a minimum the movement created the context which fostered radical journalism – for example the exposés by the Berkeley-based *Ramparts* magazine – and which encouraged leaks from within the political establishment – notably the *Pentagon Papers*. The campaign among Vietnam veterans also ensured the publicizing of atrocities committed in the course of the fighting.

The movement against the Vietnam War had a lasting influence upon those who were engaged in it – especially the student generation called upon to resist the draft. It also left a legacy of organizational experience and tactical possibilities, which were reflected in the new wave of protest against nuclear weapons which arose in the 1980s.

NOTES AND REFERENCES

1. The position in both Saigon and Washington in late 1963 was complex, with several different coups being planned. See: David Halberstam, *The Making of a Quagmire* (London, Bodley Head, 1964); Jean Lacouture, *Vietnam: between Two Truces* (London, Secker and Warburg, 1965); and the *New York Times, The Pentagon Papers* (Toronto, Bantam Books, 1971), Chapter 4.

2. Congress did not understand the significance of the Resolution at the time, according to Fulbright, then Chairman of the Senate Foreign Relations Committee. See Michael Charlton and Anthony Moncrieff (eds), *Many Reasons Why: the American Involvement in Vietnam* (London, Scolar Press, 1978), pp. 111–12

3. Paul Boyer, 'From Activism to Apathy: the American People and Nuclear Weapons, 1963–1980', *Journal of American History*, **70**, March 1984, p. 837.

4. Boyer, pp. 836–7; Godfrey Hodgson, *In Our Time: America from World War II to Nixon* (London, Macmillan, 1976), p. 285.

5. *War Resistance*, **2**, 16, 1st Quarter 1966, pp. 10–11.

6. Peter Brock, *Twentieth-Century Pacifism* (New York, Van Nostrand Reinhold Co., 1970), pp. 256–8. When the length of military service was extended in 1967 the reference to a Supreme Being was dropped.

7. See for example Richard M. Boardman, 'Letter to Local Board No. 114', in Hugo Adam Bedau (ed.), *Civil Disobedience: Theory and Practice* (Indianapolis, Pegasus, 1969), pp. 178–86.

8. Howard Zinn, *Postwar America: 1945–1971* (Indianapolis, Bobbs Merrill Co., 1973), p. 221.

9. *Fellowship*, March 1965 (Insert on Vietnam Protest) and April 1965, p. 1; *War Resistance* 1st Quarter 1966, p. 12.

10. Catherine Foster, *Women for All Seasons: The Story of the Women's International League for Peace and Freedom* (Athens, Georgia, University of Georgia Press, 1989), pp. 31, 33–7.

11. Hodgson, pp. 285–7

12. Marvin E. Gettleman, *Vietnam* (Harmondsworth, Penguin, 1966), pp. 408–26 includes extracts from the 15th May national teach-in; Irving Kristol, 'Teaching In, Speaking Out', *Encounter*, **25**, August 1965, pp. 65–9 gives a critical view of the teach-ins.

13. Zinn, p. 221. *War Resistance*, **2**, 21, 2nd Quarter 1967, pp. 12–31; Paul Jacobs and Saul Landau, *The New Radicals* (Harmondsworth, Penguin, 1967), pp. 73–7. See also Alice Lynd, *We Won't go* (Boston, Mass., Beacon Press, 1968).

14. Harold E. Quinley, 'The Protestant Clergy and the War in Vietnam', *Public Opinion Quarterly*, **34**, 1, Spring 1970, pp. 43–52.

15. Charlton and Moncrieff, pp. 161–2 and 164–5 for views of Galbraith and McCarthy.

16. Arthur M. Schlesinger, Jr, *Robert Kennedy and His Times* (London, Future, 1979), pp. 911 and 933 give primary percentages.

17. J. E. Mueller, 'Trends in Popular Support for the Wars in Korea and Vietnam', *American Political Science Review*, **33**, June 1971, pp. 358–71.

18. Schlesinger, p. 905 on Kennedy's speech and Gallup poll showing 70 per cent wanted to continue the bombing.

19. The Democratic Chicago Convention became notorious. For a detailed account see Norman Mailer, *Miami and the Siege of Chicago* (Harmondsworth, Penguin, 1969).

20. William Worthy, 'Draft Resistance and US History', *Peace News*, 1 October 1986, p. 8 (interview with Stephen Kohn, author of *Jailed for Peace: the History of American Draft Law Violators, 1658–1985* (Westport, Conn., Greenwood Press, 1986).

21. Zinn, p. 221.
22. Irving Louis Horowitz, *Ideology and Utopia in the United States, 1956–1976* (London, Oxford University Press, 1977), p. 348, essay on 'Organization and Ideology in the Antiwar Movement'.
23. Zinn, p. 230; David Dellinger, 'The Bread is Rising', in Michael Albert and David Dellinger, *Beyond Survival* (Boston, Mass. Southend Press, 1983), p. 14.
24. Zinn, pp. 229–30.
25. Roger Lewis, *Outlaws of America: the Underground Press and its Context* (Harmondsworth, Penguin, 1972), pp. 130–4 includes a list of GI papers. See also Fred Halstead, *GIs Speak Out Against the War: the Case of the Fort Jackson Eight* (New York, Pathfinder Press, 1971).
26. *The Pentagon Papers.*
27. For Kissinger's version see Henry Kissinger, *The White House Years*, (Boston, Mass., Little Brown, 1979).
28. Mueller, p. 365.
29. Hodgson, pp. 384–98.
30. Populist politicians have often exploited this tendency in American society, and Nixon himself did so.
31. Thomas R. Brooks, *Toil and Trouble: A History of American Labor* (New York, Dell Publishing Co., 1971, 2nd rev. ed), pp. 373–4.
32. Hodgson, p. 387.
33. See McCarthy's comments, Charlton and Moncrieff, p. 165 and Horowitz, p. 349 notes that Business Executives for Vietnam Peace, mostly representing managers and owners of medium-sized companies, was set up in September 1967.
34. Richard Nixon, *The Memoirs of Richard Nixon* (London, Sidgwick and Jackson, 1978), pp. 392–5 and 399–404.
35. For detailed examples of FBI attempts to damage the anti-war campaign see Dellinger, pp. 34–6; Cathy Perkus, (ed.), *COINTELPRO: the FBI's Secret War on Political Freedom* (New York, Monad Press, 1975), pp. 111–36. On Nixon's policies, see John Dean, *Blind Ambition: the White House Years* (London, W.H. Allen, 1977), pp. 42–4 covering Dean's role in collecting 'anti-war intelligence' and on May 1971 demonstration, Cal McCrystal, Lewis Chester, Stephen Aris and William Shawcross, *Watergate: The Full Inside Story* (London, André Deutsch, 1973), pp. 32–4 elaborate on the May 1971 events.
36. Ralph V. Summy, 'Militancy and the Australian Peace Movement, 1960–67', *Politics*, **5**, 2, November 1970, p. 154.
37. J.D.B. Miller, 'Australia in Vietnam', *Round Table*, **60**, July 1970, p. 299.
38. Fred Halliday, 'Students of the World Unite', in Alexander Cockburn and Robin Blackburn (eds), *Student Power* (Harmondsworth, Penguin, 1969), p. 298.
39. N. Bamba, 'Peace Movement at a Standstill: Roots of the Crisis', *Bulletin of Peace Proposals*, **13**, 1, 1982, p. 41.
40. See Bertrand Russell, *War Crimes in Vietnam* (London, Allen and Unwin, 1967) for his views and a brief account of the War Crimes Tribunal. Alan Ryan, *Bertrand Russell: a Political Life* (London, Allen Lane 1988), pp. 202–6 discusses Russell's position on Vietnam.

41. Michael Randle, 'Volunteers for Peace in Vietnam', *War Resistance*, **2**, 20 1st Quarter 1967, pp. 11–14.
42. Pat Arrowsmith (ed.), *To Asia in Peace* (London, Sidgwick and Jackson, 1972).
43. The Buddhist case was put by Trich Nhat Hanh, *Lotus in a Sea of Fire* (New York, Hill and Wang, 1967). Seventy academics from South Vietnamese universities endorsed proposals for an interim government in the South to be created which could negotiate with both the USA and the National Liberation Front. Adam Roberts, 'The Buddhists, the War and the Vietcong', *World Today*, May 1966, pp. 214–22 assessed the political potential of the Buddhists.
44. See for example United Nations Association, *Vietnam: a Plea for Self-Determination* (London, June 1966; and World Without War Council, *Vietnam Peace Proposals* (Berkeley, California, 1967).

CHAPTER FIVE

Nuclear Disarmament: the Second Wave in Europe, 1979–87

INTRODUCTION

The second wave of the nuclear disarmament movement brought in more countries than the first, and evoked more intensive support within these countries. Campaigns in different parts of the world were quite closely linked, but had their own regional priorities. This chapter concentrates on the movement which brought thousands of protesters onto the streets throughout almost all of Western Europe in the early 1980s.

Why was there such a strong groundswell of public opposition to nuclear weapons after a period of apparent apathy towards the dangers of nuclear arsenals? One answer lies in the growing environmental concerns of the 1970s, which created a consciousness and campaigning experience which fed into the peace movement of the next decade. The new protests against nuclear weapons were, however, precipitated by the breakdown of detente, and given specific impetus by NATO's 1979 decision to deploy new land-based cruise and Pershing nuclear missiles in Europe. In order to understand the mounting opposition to these missiles it is also necessary to look at the preliminary campaign which arose in 1977–78 against President Carter's abortive proposal to arm NATO troops in Europe with neutron bombs.

THE INFLUENCE OF THE GREENS AND FEMINISM

The most direct link between the new Green movement and campaigners against nuclear weapons has been concern about the dangers of nuclear power. Whereas in the 1950s both governments and peace groups tended to draw a sharp distinction between the military and peaceful uses of nuclear power, by the 1970s there was widespread concern that possession of nuclear reactors made development of nuclear bombs easy.[1] So nuclear disarmament organizations, like CND in Britain, found it natural to extend their policy to criticize building new reactors.[2] Worry about the effects of radioactivity also linked the Greens and the nuclear disarmers. The Greens raised a range of issues, for example the mining and transport of uranium, the undemocratic nature of nuclear power decisions and the civil liberties implications of a society highly dependent upon nuclear power, all of which had relevance for campaigners against nuclear weapons.

Environmentalist protests against nuclear reactors both created a constituency of political activists sympathetic to a reinvigorated peace movement and a fund of campaigning experience. Environmentalist campaigns made skilful use of scientific expertise to strengthen their case, turned to the courts to argue legal points and mobilized local communities and local governments against proposed reactors. In addition they engaged in mass direct action at the designated sites.[3] Although some of these protests in France and West Germany erupted into violent confrontation with the police, others (notably the 1977 Seabrook Campaign in the USA) became models of how to organize to ensure non-violent demonstrations.[4] The 1980s campaigners drew on this tactical legacy.

The Greens tended to assimilate the values associated with the other major movement of the 1970s – feminism. The 1980s peace campaigns also owed a debt to feminism, which had helped to draw women into radical politics and raised the issue of force and domination in both private and public life. The experience of Women's Liberation activism also popularized informal modes of organization, and 'networking' was to prove very effective in bringing out women for peace protests. In addition feminism tended to challenge the romantic image of the guerrilla fighter popular in the 1960s (although a few women's groups had accepted this kind of imagery), so the general effect of feminist theory and action was to reject violent confrontation and strengthen a culture of non-violent protest appropriate to peace activity.[5]

THE SECOND COLD WAR AND INF

Despite the continuities between the 1980s peace movement and earlier anti-nuclear power protest, international factors precipitated the new wave of peace campaigning. Polls in Western Europe showed that fear of war increased between 1977 and 1980.[6] After the détente of the early 1970s, which included the first SALT accords (the ABM Treaty curbing anti-missile defences, and a freeze on strategic land and sea-based missiles), Western strategic circles became concerned about the build-up of Soviet military power and extension of Soviet influence in Africa. The West German Chancellor, Helmut Schmidt, also voiced anxiety about deployment of Soviet SS20 missiles in Europe in December 1977. Negotiations for SALT II were impeded by powerful right-wing pressure groups in the USA, who claimed the USSR was acquiring strategic superiority, and when Carter and Brezhnev signed the Treaty in June 1979 it was already clear that the Senate was unlikely to ratify it. The subsequent Soviet invasion of Afghanistan in December 1979 and election of Ronald Reagan to the Presidency in November 1980 promoted extreme hostility between the USA and USSR not experienced since the 1950s.[7]

The 'Second Cold War' was the context of the revived nuclear disarmament movement; the NATO 1979 decision to deploy a new generation of land-based nuclear missiles in Europe the central focus for protest, especially in the five countries due to take the missiles: the UK, West Germany, Italy, the Netherlands and Belgium. Plans for cruise and Pershing II missile deployment highlighted the uncertainties created by NATO's heavy reliance on nuclear weapons. While most Western governments wished to commit the USA to using its nuclear forces in Europe in the event of a European war, there was some popular suspicion that the USA might plan to fight a nuclear war limited to Europe. Both the new Soviet missiles and NATO deployment plans awakened public fears that Europe would be destroyed in a nuclear war.

President Reagan's commitment to an unprecedented build-up of US nuclear and conventional forces, his opposition to arms control and his anti-Communist rhetoric dismayed millions of Europeans who joined or sympathized with the new peace movement, and caused some concern in most European circles. Even Margaret Thatcher's Government (elected in 1979), which enthusiastically endorsed Reagan's free-market and anti-Communist ideologies, as well as his policy of promoting Western military superiority, did not want to break off the economic links with the Soviet Union and Eastern

110

Europe which had been created during the era of détente. When the Polish army, under the influence of Moscow, crushed the Solidarity movement in December 1981, and the USA called for economic sanctions, West European governments refused to follow suit. West European governments were also anxious that the USA should fulfil both parts of the 1979 'dual-track' decision relating to missile deployment: to enter into negotiations on reducing intermediate-range nuclear forces (INF) with the USSR at the same time as pressing ahead with planned production and deployment of the missiles. So the Reagan Administration found itself, contrary to its own philosophy of avoiding arms control talks, committed to starting INF negotiations by the end of 1981.[8]

The new Cold War alerted a new generation to the possibility of a nuclear holocaust, while the developing missile technology created the strategic conditions for a first strike against nuclear bases on the other side, as missiles now had the accuracy to achieve this mission. American strategic planning altered in the 1970s to envisage a possible 'counterforce' strike. So many feared that a crisis anywhere in the world, where both superpowers were involved, could lead to one side becoming convinced that it was rational to strike first. Moreover, the short flight times of missiles, which could not be recalled, and the reliance on computers, raised the spectre of war due to computer failure. In 1983 Reagan launched with great fanfare his 'Star Wars' plan to build a space shield against missiles. Although most experts were sceptical about the technical feasibility of the plan, it looked as though the USA and USSR might become engaged in a new arms race in space. It also looked as though success in achieving even a very partial defence against missiles would increase the temptation to strike first in order to 'win' a nuclear war.

The Second Cold War differed, however, in important ways from the original Cold War. Despite alarm created by the Soviet invasion of Afghanistan, and by the build up of the powerful intermediate-range SS20 missiles in the early 1980s, most in the West did not fear deliberate Soviet aggression. Moreover, the Soviet Union under Brezhnev and his two brief successors – Andropov and Chernenko – might be inefficient economically and politically repressive, but it had altered considerably since the Stalin era. Minority dissent continued to surface, despite KGB harassment. Moreover, there was considerable diversity among East European regimes: Hungary had initiated a degree of economic reform and political liberalization; Poland was with difficulty trying to conciliate or repress mass resistance to old-style party rule; East Germany partially tolerated limited expressions of dissent; while Czechoslovakia was overtly repressive but could not totally suppress organized opposition. Indeed during the early 1980s an unprecedented development took place: independent peace groups emerged in a number of East European countries, and in Czechoslovakia Charter 77 gradually began to link demands for disarmament and détente to its insistence on human rights and democratic reform. A tiny independent peace group, calling for trust and reconciliation, even emerged in Moscow and gained some adherents in other parts of the Soviet Union. The Western peace organizations could for the first time look to similar groups in the Soviet bloc, and did not have to rely for all contact upon the official party-sponsored peace committees.

THE NEUTRON BOMB CAMPAIGN

The neutron bomb episode of 1977–78 set the scene for the later campaign against the missiles. The plan for NATO to be armed with enhanced radiation weapons (neutron bombs), which would maximize emission of deadly radiation but minimize blast damage and long-term fall-out, became public in 1977. The neutron bomb became popularly known as the weapon which killed people but preserved property and so it was dubbed by some left-wing opponents 'the ultimate capitalist weapon'. When President Carter pressed European countries to deploy the neutron bomb, he helped to put nuclear weapons on the public agenda again, and to arouse a campaign against them.[9]

A prominent part in the protests against the neutron bomb was played by the Dutch Interchurch Peace Council (IKV), set up in 1966 to promote debate on peace issues within the churches. IKV campaigned alongside a Communist-initiated Stop the Neutron Bomb group, and they secured over a million signatures to a petition against the new weapon. The extent of the opposition was indicated when the Minister of Defence resigned in March 1978 over proposed NATO deployment of neutron weapons.[10] IKV policy was not, however, simply directed against the neutron bomb. Its aim was to promote a movement to 'rid the world of nuclear weapons', and to start by removing all nuclear weapons from The Netherlands.[11]

The campaign against the neutron bomb, after gathering momentum in The Netherlands and in Denmark, took off in Norway in January 1978. Established peace bodies began the protests, but won support from the youth sections of almost all the political parties. The Norwegian Government's Committee for Arms Control and Disarmament had produced a critical assessment of the implications of the bomb in late 1977 and the Norwegian bishops issued a statement about the dangers of the nuclear arms race in the spring of 1978. So the Norwegian campaign had weighty backing for its argument that the neutron bomb was a threat to arms control.[12] In West Germany Chancellor Helmut Schmidt met strong resistance from within the Social Democratic Party to deploying neutron weapons.

Disputes over deployment of the neutron bomb in Europe were therefore a significant prologue to the much more important struggle over the 1979 NATO decision to deploy cruise and Pershing II missiles. The neutron bomb created tension between Bonn and Washington, since President Carter insisted that Schmidt and other European leaders should publicly ask for neutron weapons, which Schmidt did reluctantly. The Chancellor was even angrier when Carter then changed his mind and decided against immediate production of the neutron bomb. American officials on the other hand became even more determined that European governments should shoulder NATO commitments and exerted pressure to secure the 1979 NATO decision.

Washington tended to see the neutron bomb campaign as evidence of Soviet ability to manipulate sections of West European opinion, and as a 'defeat' for NATO plans which must not be repeated. Hence as popular resistance mounted, and some European governments wavered, the American government saw missile deployment as a test of NATO unity and firmness. Ironically many members of the Reagan Administration did not believe the cruise and Pershing II deployments to be strategically necessary, but keeping to the deployment timetable became essential to inflict political defeat on the peace movement.[13]

The campaigns that sprang up during or after 1979 were therefore to some extent trapped by a 'bloc logic' which they were aiming to transcend. On the one hand the Soviet Union clearly did hope the peace movements would prevent the NATO deployments, which it saw as threatening, without the USSR having to make major concessions in the Geneva INF talks. On the other hand Washington and some right-wing European parties and groups were determined to defeat 'the enemy within'. Although the peace movement raised many issues beyond the cruise and Pershing missiles, these were at the centre of the mass European protests.

THE EXTENT OF THE EUROPEAN NUCLEAR DISARMAMENT MOVEMENT

The NATO decision in December 1979 to deploy intermediate-range nuclear forces with a deadline of December 1983 for starting deployment, stimulated active opposition in all five countries designated to receive the missiles. Protests took place not only in West Germany, The Netherlands and Britain, where a history of nuclear disarmament campaigns stretched back to 1958, but also in Belgium and Italy, where there had been little previous interest in nuclear weapons. Citizens in other NATO countries, though not directly involved with the deployments, joined in campaigning against the missiles, which they viewed as a threat to Europe and a symbol of the nuclear arms race. Peace activists in neutral countries also responded to renewed anxieties about nuclear war and backed calls for a loosening of military and political blocs.

The campaigns against the missiles which won most domestic support were those in Belgium and The Netherlands; protests started in 1979 in both countries and continued until 1985. The Belgian Government hedged its final acceptance of the missiles with conditions, but only the Dutch peace movement persuaded its government to delay the NATO deployment schedule. The movement in West Germany began rather later, but mobilized the most demonstrators in terms of absolute numbers, and because of West German's strategic position was the most significant of the anti-missile protests. The campaign brought considerable pressure to bear on the SPD Government, headed by Schmidt. But after Schmidt had lost power in October 1982, due to the defection of the small coalition party, the Free Democrats, and the CDU won the 1983 election, the missile deployment in West Germany was assured.

The decision to set up a base for cruise missiles at Comiso in Sicily had a remarkable effect on Italian politics. For the first time defence and arms control figured prominently in the media and in Parliament, where deputies asked numerous questions about nuclear weapons. The resistance to cruise began in rural and impoverished Sicily and then spread to other parts of Italy. Local opposition declined in 1982 after the Mafia (believed to be involved in building contracts for the missile base) murdered the regional Communist Party Secretary who had been a leader of the campaign against the base. National and international peace activists, however, joined the protests against the Comiso missiles, and the Italian movement against cruise reached a climax in November and December 1983, just before deployment.[14]

CND became the basis for a new mass movement in Britain against the NATO missiles and Britain's own nuclear force. Between 1980 and 1983 nuclear weapons were a central political issue, and although CND's importance began to decline after Mrs Thatcher's re-election and the beginning of cruise deployment, it retained impressive support up to 1987. In June 1987 Mrs Thatcher was re-elected for her third term, but then nuclear disarmers were able to celebrate the signing of the INF Treaty in December. Despite CND's prominence in domestic politics, two quite different groupings had more impact on the transnational movement. The women's peace camp at Greenham Common symbolized the special role women could play, the links between feminism and peace activism, and a style of inventive and indomitable resistance. The European Nuclear Disarmament (END) Appeal launched in 1980 from Britain brought a specific political and intellectual stance to the emerging European movement. The appeal, which called for no cruise and Pershings and no SS20s, envisaged a nuclear-free Europe from Poland to Portugal, independent of both Washington and Moscow. END also aimed from the outset to gain support from individuals and autonomous groups in Eastern Europe and the USSR itself.

Scandinavian peace groups were active early on in opposing both the NATO and the Soviet missiles and in calling for elimination of nuclear weapons from Europe. The Norwegian campaign No To Nuclear Weapons began in October 1979 and consolidated its organization and policy goals early in 1980. Both the Norwegian group and its Danish counterpart, with the same name, gave priority to the goal of a Nordic nuclear-weapons-free zone as a first step.[15] Public unrest about nuclear weapons policies spread to neutral Finland, where peace organization dating from the previous nuclear disarmament wave – the non-aligned Committee of 100 – cooperated with the Finnish branch of the World Peace Council in demonstrations calling for a nuclear-free Northern Europe and featuring END slogans against nuclear weapons in both East and West.[16] The ruling Social Democratic Party in Sweden was quite favourable to the idea of a nuclear-free Nordic zone, but heightened commitment to disarmament issues among rank-and-file party members and unionists was demonstrated by the setting up of a Labour Peace Forum in 1981. The oldest and largest Swedish peace body, the Swedish Peace and Arbitration Society, cooperated with the new European nuclear disarmament movement, and Women for Peace founded in 1978 campaigned for a nuclear-free zone, against the new missiles in Europe, and to promote détente between people by personal contacts across the East–West divide.[17] In Iceland the Campaign Against Military Bases brought out 5,000 in a march from the US base at Keflavik to Reykjavik in June 1981.[18]

The campaign against the missiles had reverberations in the southern NATO countries, Greece and Turkey, which both had numerous American military bases and American nuclear weapons on their territory. The 1980 END Appeal was signed by Andreas Papandreou, leader of the Panhellenic Socialist Party which had been in opposition since the overthrow of the military junta in 1974. The non-Communist Greek peace movement was closely linked to the Socialist Party (both the Communists and weaker Eurocommunists also had their own peace bodies), so when the Socialists won the 1981 elections the movement looked as though it could achieve its immediate aims. Papandreou had promised in the elections to remove American bases and to leave NATO, and had publicly endorsed the idea of seeking a Balkan nuclear-free zone.[19] However, it gradually became clear that negotiations with the USA would not mean rapid withdrawal of the bases. An agreement with the USA in 1983 leased the bases to the Americans until 1988, when the position was to be reviewed.[20]

Greece's neighbour and traditional enemy, Turkey, had its own independent peace organization, the Turkish Peace Association, but it faced repression, as the Greek peace movement had done twenty years earlier. Founded in 1977, during one of the more democratic periods in Turkish politics, the Turkish Peace Association had the backing of women's and youth organizations and the second largest trade union federation. The Executive included Social Democratic MPs, scientists, artists and academics, the President of the Istanbul Bar Association and the President of the Turkish Medical Association. Its President was former ambassador Mahmut Dikerdem. The Association was cautious in its policy aims, stressing debate and public education on the Helsinki principles and nuclear disarmament, and settlement of the dispute with Greece. It did, however, also call for an end to secret military treaties with the USA.

After a military junta seized power in 1980 the military prosecutor called for the arrest of the Peace Association Executive, but was twice overruled by a higher military court for lack of evidence of any crime. Then the entire Executive was arrested at midnight on 26 February, 1982. The military authorities accused the Executive of opposing NATO and military bases, and at the trial charges included spreading Communist propaganda and damaging the interests of the Turkish state abroad.[21] Just before Christmas 1982 Dikerdem, then sixty-six years old and ill with cancer, and twenty-three of his companions were released on bail in response to international pressure from peace organizations and Western liberals. But after prolonged trials in which the main evidence came from a political prisoner under torture (and was later withdrawn) eighteen Peace Association leaders were sentenced in late 1983 to periods between five and ten years in prison and internal exile. Another forty-eight Association members were charged in September 1984.[22] Suppression of the Association was linked to moves against trade uionists.

The END slogan was for a nuclear-free Europe from Poland to Portugal, but Portugal was emerging from military dictatorship followed by a period of revolutionary upheaval in the mid-1970s, and did not have an established peace constituency. Nevertheless, individual political personalities and municipal assemblies began to express support for European nuclear disarmament in 1980.[23] The most powerful peace campaigns in the Iberian Peninsula, however, developed in Spain, sometimes in association with the Portuguese, but the massive anti-NATO campaign focused solely on Spanish government policy.

The 1980s movement for nuclear disarmament affected almost all European countries. In neutral Switzerland and Austria activists joined in demonstrations of solidarity, and Ireland had its own active CND, committed to oppose Irish membership of NATO. The new movement was also a more self-consciously transnational movement than its predecessor, and this awareness was represented by early moves to create a basis for European cooperation and to formulate all-European policies.

END AND TRANSNATIONAL ORGANIZATION

The END Appeal launched in April 1980 came at an early stage of the protests and gave a name and an idea to the new Europe-wide campaign. It is, however, important to understand that END never represented a European organization and that the END strategy of making links with opposition groups and individuals in the USSR and Eastern Europe was a source of controversy.

The group which drafted and publicized the END Appeal included Edward (E.P.) Thompson, historian of the Labour movement and a theorist of the original New Left grouping in Britain, Mary Kaldor, a peace researcher, and Zhores Medvedev, the exiled Soviet biologist whose twin brother, Roy Medvedev, a dissident historian still living in Moscow, signed the appeal. The group worked with the Bertrand Russell Peace Foundation based in Nottingham, which had extensive international contacts in Socialist and revisionist Communist circles. Later the END Committee set up its own London office and built up a group of supporters in Britain, and published the *END Journal* (previously produced in Nottingham). END never tried to become a rival to CND in Britain (although a few END groups arose spontaneously in 1980), and the London office was never the headquarters of a European campaign. END had a Europe-wide presence through the personal influence and contacts of key personalities, and through linking up with strong national bodies sympathetic to END aims, of which the most important was the Dutch IKV. END maintained a high profile and helped to consolidate the European campaign through holding annual END Conventions, beginning in Brussels in 1982. An END Liaison Committee was responsible for organizing the Conventions, but did not have any other role.

Indeed the organizational structure of the transnational movement was somewhat confused. The Secretariat of Dutch IKV, headed by Jan Mient Faber, the best-known figure of the Dutch campaign against the missiles, became the centre for the International Peace Communications and Coordination network set up in 1981 to link the new European campaigns. The International Confederation for Disarmament and Peace (created in 1963) still existed in 1980, and its Secretary, Peggy Duff, helped with the launching of the END Appeal shortly before she died of cancer. The Confederation continued until 1984, though largely moribund, when it merged with the almost century-old International Peace Bureau.[24]

The variety of international organizations created some irritation and duplication of effort – for example sometimes holding meetings on dates that clashed. But any tightly knit structure would have been at odds with diversity and spontaneity of the movement, and much transnational activity took place through joint demonstrations, personal contacts and meetings with like-minded groups in other countries or specialized conferences. By the mid-1980s the END Convention had emerged as the focus for not only European campaigns but for a world-wide movement against nuclear weapons. The second Convention in West Berlin in 1983 drew over 2,500 people, and the 1984 Perugia Convention, though attended by only 1,000 had an even wider geographical spread.[25]

The Conventions reflected the ideological range of the new movement as well as its territorial diversity. The problems of combining pacifists and nuclear disarmers, which had loomed large at the founding of the Confederation twenty years earlier, had already been resolved by national campaigns. So had relations between middle-ground lobbying groups and direct action protesters. The 1980s campaign also encompassed Eurocommunist Parties, notably the Italian PCI, without fear of damaging its non-aligned stance between NATO and the Warsaw Pact. There was, however, some continuing tension within the END Liaison Committee about the balance of representation between political parties and trade unions, which had the advantage of political experience and continuity, and the new campaigning bodies which expressed the dynamism of the new movement. Perhaps the most crucial disagreements occurred in relation to the always difficult question of whether representatives from the official Soviet and East European peace committees should be invited to Conventions, and if so in what capacity. The varying policies adopted for different Conventions are discussed in more detail below. Opposition and autonomous peace groups in Eastern Europe sympathetic to the END objective of a Europe without nuclear missiles or military blocs received regular invitations, but for the most part never obtained visas from their governments to attend, until the 1990 END Convention celebrated the end of the Cold War.

THE MASS PETITIONS AND DEMONSTRATIONS

A crude but important measurement of the strength of a movement is the number of signatures on a petition and the size of marches and rallies – after making allowances for the widely divergent estimates of numbers on any demonstration. Large protests can make news and prompt debate; they may also have repercussions on party politics. Certainly the size of demonstrations against the new missiles in Europe alarmed NATO. Issues of *NATO Review*, for example, had pictures of the peace demonstrations together with analyses of public opinion, or even of the churches' position on deterrence.[26]

The first signs of opposition to the planned NATO missiles appeared late in 1979 before the NATO Council met to reach a final decision. The Norwegian campaign, which sprang up in October 1979 to oppose new nuclear weapons in both halves of Europe, collected 69,000 signatures in six weeks to urge the Norwegian Government to oppose NATO deployment.[27] The well-organized Dutch IKV combined with other religious and political groups to

119

hold a march of 20,000 in Utrecht in November, while the crucial NATO Council meeting in Brussels in December 1979 was reminded of popular unrest by 50,000 to 70,000 Belgians, joined by international contingents, demonstrating outside.[28]

After the NATO decision the campaign began to gather momentum in Britain. Local groups against the missiles protested in Oxford and Cambridge in March 1980 and the Labour Party brought out 20,000 at a London rally in June. The potential of the new movement became clear in October 1980, when 80,000 marched in a CND demonstration to Trafalgar Square.[29]

The West German campaign against the cruise and Pershing II missiles to be deployed in their country took off in November 1980, when a group which included well-known Green Party representative Petra Kelly, and recently retired General Gert Bastian, launched the 'Krefeld Appeal' against the missiles. Protests mounted in the first half of 1981: 25,000 demonstrated against a NATO meeting in Bonn in April; 20,000 marched in Frankfurt in May; and thirty organizations backed a peace forum in Marburg the same month. The first mass expression of opposition to nuclear weapon policies took place in June 1981 in Hamburg. A Congress of the Protestant Churches on the theme 'Fear Not' attracted a breakaway rally on the danger of nuclear war, using the slogan 'Have Fear – Atomic Death Threatens Us All'. Estimates of the protesters ranged from 80,000 to 130,000. A Dortmund meeting of 13,000 in November 1981 marked the first anniversary of the Krefeld Appeal, which by then had around two million signatures.[30]

Transnational demonstrations to dramatize the theme of a nuclear-weapons-free Europe began in 1981 with a march from Copenhagen to Paris. A core of Scandinavian women marched the whole way, and up to 10,000 joined a rally on 21st June to send them off.[31] A year later a Scandinavian women's peace march passed through the Soviet Union.

By the autumn of 1981 extensive debate about nuclear weapons had helped to rouse public opinion, and President Reagan's record in the White House was confirming the fears aroused by his election campaign. The United Nations had declared 24th–31st October Disarmament Week, and this became the focus for mass demonstrations of strength. Between 250,000 and 350,000 took to the streets in Bonn on 10th October. Rallies of 120,000–250,000 in Brussels, 150,000–250,000 in London and 10,000 in Oslo took place on the last weekend in October. Even more dramatically, the new Italian peace movement displayed its strength that weekend with 30,000 gathering at Comiso and between 400,000 and 500,000 in Rome. On 28th October a total of about 120,000 demonstrated in several Finnish cities. The Dutch campaign drew up to 400,000 on a march through Amsterdam on 21st November and on 5th December Copenhagen saw the largest protest – up to 100,000 – since the Second World War. The same day 30,000–40,000 turned out in Bern, Switzerland.[32]

President Reagan's visit to Europe in June 1982 stimulated large demonstrations in Bonn, Rome and London, and smaller protests in Spain, Ireland, Austria and Sweden.[33] In December marches from Milan and Catania converged on Comiso, and 30,000 women from Britain, West Germany, The Netherlands and Sweden 'embraced the Base' in a human chain at Greenham Common cruise base.[34] Protesters did not, however, congregate in huge numbers again until December 1983, just before cruise deployment began in West Germany, Italy and Britain, when up to a million demonstrated across West Germany, 600,000 in Rome and 300,000–400,000 in London. Both Brussels and the Hague saw protests of up to half a million. Major supporting actions took place in Norway, Denmark, Sweden, Finland and Spain. In Paris the Committee for Nuclear Disarmament (CODENE), the confederation of independent peace groups, sponsored a human chain between the American and Soviet Embassies. A similar chain in Vienna included at least 50,000. among them the Socialist Minister of Education and a bishop.[35]

After 1983 varied and committed campaigns continued in most countries, but the hope of victory in stopping the missiles remained only in The Netherlands and Belgium. Dutch campaigners achieved a fifteen-minute general strike involving several hundred thousand workers in May 1984. Cruise deployment did not begin until March 1985 in Belgium and this event brought up to 150,000 protesters to Brussels.[36]

PERSONALITIES AND LEADERSHIP

The 1980s peace movement grew out of a culture of protest often distrustful of centralized organization and of individual leaders. Feminist groups in particular stressed group decision-making and were hostile to élitism, and the more orthodox campaigning bodies like CND were partially influenced by these attitudes.

Nevertheless, a number of well-known personalities did emerge and had considerable influence on the movement. Edward Thompson became a central figure, especially during 1980–81, not only for promoting the idea of a nuclear-weapons-free Europe, East and West, but also for his pamphleteering skills, his analytical writings and his eloquence as a speaker. Mary Kaldor was also respected as a theorist in Britain and in the wider European movement, where she gained a reputation for her writings and her contributions to international conferences. Others became prominent national figures through holding a key post in a large campaigning organization: Jan Mient Faber, for example, was as IKV General Secretary the voice of IKV in The Netherlands.

Several factors encouraged the emergence of peace movement personalities. One was the constant need for speakers at meetings. More fundamentally, many rank-and-file campaigners did still look for inspiration and leadership from respected figures. In addition the major campaigning bodies were well aware of the need to promote representatives who presented a favourable image to the public and could perform well on radio and television. CND, for example, re-elected Joan Ruddock as chairperson from 1981 to 1985 both because of her tact and skill in the chair and because she could present the CND case well to the media. Journalists themselves played an important role in building up personalities, because they tend to turn to known spokespersons for quick comment, and because the media often personalize stories and project images of leaders. Although the German Green Party repudiated the principle of national leaders, in practice some individuals became nationally and internationally known, and Petra Kelly in particular received considerable media coverage, well before she was elected to the Bundestag in 1983.

There were, however, differences in the type of leaders who came to the fore in the 1980s compared with the 1950s. Whereas CND was founded by a group of celebrities who gave their prestige to the campaign, in the 1980s the key CND personalities became widely known through the campaign. Joan Ruddock had previously been working at a Citizens' Advice Bureau and had stood as a Labour parliamentary candidate in the 1979 general election. Bruce Kent, who was CND's General Secretary in the early 1980s and then its Chairperson until 1990, was a Catholic priest until he left the priesthood in 1987 under increasing pressure over his role as a turbulent priest. Throughout the decade Bruce Kent personified CND in the media.

Nevertheless, the internally created leaders still prompted controversy over their role. In particular the representatives of major campaigns come into conflict with their more radical members on issues of policy and tactics. Bruce Kent and the CND Executive hesitated to endorse the anti-NATO policy repeatedly passed at CND annual conference and tried to plan demonstrations which would not alienate centre ground opinion. Jan Mient Faber of IKV was also criticized for leaning too far to meet the middle ground in some of his policy statements during the complex manoeuvres over cruise deployment in the Netherlands.[37]

To see the second wave of the nuclear disarmament movement primarily in terms of individual leaders would, however, be profoundly misleading. It encompassed literally hundreds of independent initiatives and organizations, and this diversity was the source of its strength.

FORMS OF ORGANIZATION

The pattern of organization varied considerably between countries, though new groups sprang up almost everywhere to challenge the missiles, and most peace movements had some overarching coordinating body. For the sake of simplicity this section concentrates on the five countries due to deploy INF.

Britain had the most centralized campaign, since CND was mainly responsible for organizing national demonstrations and presenting the nuclear disarmament case to the public. Many other professional, research and campaigning groups grew up, but most affiliated to CND or cooperated with it. CND itself had an established structure of local groups attached to regions, an annual conference and national council of elected and regional representatives. Local CND groups springing up after 1979 fitted easily into this structure. A national membership scheme dating from the mid-1960s allowed individuals to join and subsidize CND without necessarily joining local groups. Individual membership grew from 50,000 by 1982 to 110,000 by 1985, when CND also claimed 1,000 local groups.[38] The great majority of CND supporters joined a local group and did not become national members.

The West German movement was the least centralized, and was made up of several thousand diverse local groups, which came together in peace 'initiatives' in the larger cities. In Hamburg alone for example there were 300 local groups, some of these groups were purely local, others belonged to national political or religious bodies. National actions prompted coordination: the Krefeld Appeal against the NATO missiles was an initial focus, and the Bonn demonstrations of 1981 and 1982 were called by loose coalitions following a number of 'Action Conferences'. A more formal body for demonstrations emerged in 1983, the Coordinating Committee, which soon comprised thirty peace organizations and set up a small office in Bonn.[39] In Italy the Communist Party provided organizational support, but the peace movement as a whole was fragmented, and as in Germany only achieved formal coordination in 1983. About 700 delegates from 150 groups met in January and created a committee to decide the main programme of protests for 1983 and to issue a journal. Both the committee and journal survived after 1983, despite the drop in peace activity.[40]

The IKV, which after 1977 had about 400 local groups, was the most important organization within the Dutch peace movement; but it was only one of nine peace groupings within the umbrella body, the No Cruise Missiles Committee, which called the mass demonstrations in October 1983 and May 1984. Peace activity in Belgium, like all forms of politics, developed separately in Flanders and French-speaking Wallonia. Opposition to the missiles in both regions was channelled through coalitions. The Flemish Action Committee Against Nuclear Weapons was set up in 1979 specifically to resist cruise deployment. The Walloon National Action Committee for Peace and Development, which had been set up some years earlier, linked about forty groups, but could not match the vigour of the Flemish campaign.[41]

No simple conclusions can be drawn about the effect of organization on a movement's ability to mobilize large numbers or to act creatively. The *ad hoc* improvisation for West German demonstrations brought more people onto the streets than CND's central planning in Britain, but this might be explained by a greater sense of urgency in front-line West Germany or by CND's more radical policy limiting its appeal. Conversely, while CND's centralized and traditional structure did not encourage new ideas, groups arising around CND developed new tactics. There was indeed less strain than might have been expected between CND leaders and radicals committed to informal networks and direct democracy. This was partly because CND leaders were not, as in 1958, self-selected personalities but elected activists; and partly because CND was much more willing to endorse civil disobedience than twenty years earlier. Both factors were reflected in the election of Greenham Common peace camp women to posts in CND.

Organizational factors did influence policy and tactics. While a wide range of political views and types of protest flourished, pressure to act jointly meant in many countries adopting minimal policies and orthodox methods of campaigning at a national level. Extending policy demands could mean, as in West Germany, many months of negotiation. Tolerance of movement diversity could also give way to bitter internal disputes.[42]

BELIEFS AND POLICIES

The movement of the 1980s was informed by a widespread sense that Europe in particular, and the world in general, faced the imminent danger of nuclear war. This belief led the young Protestants who demonstrated against nuclear weapons in Hamburg in June 1981 to challenge the biblical injunction 'Fear not' by adopting the slogan 'Have Fear'. CND marched in October 1980 under the slogan 'Protest and Survive', which was the title Edward Thompson had used for his best-selling pamphlet attacking civil defence, adapted from the government civil defence pamphlet 'Protect and Survive'. The END Appeal began. 'We are entering the most dangerous decade of human history.'[43] One reason for this belief was renewed awareness of the danger of accidental war. Martin Ryle, Cambridge professor of Radio-Astronomy, stressed computer error in his 1981 pamphlet 'Towards the Nuclear Holocaust': 'We have recently seen US alerts around the world, with aircraft taking off due to (a) the running of a "war games" program without switching out the connection to the "Alert" system and (b), twice in three days, a faulty silicon chip.'[44] Ryle went on to note that the aircraft which took off could be recalled, but cruise missiles could not. The new missiles, accurate enough to destroy missiles on the other side, were seen as especially menacing because they could be used as 'first-strike' weapons. There were disagreements among protesters whether all forms of nuclear deterrence were fundamentally flawed as a strategy, or whether minimal deterrence between the USA and USSR was reasonable in the interim until full nuclear disarmament became conceivable.

The peace movements were in general agreed in condemning a number of NATO policies: for example NATO's explicit strategy of being ready to use nuclear weapons first; the thousands of 'tactical' atomic weapons in Central Europe, and the proposed new strategy of 'Airland Battle' which blurred distinctions between conventional and nuclear and chemical war and implied willingness to take the offensive.

Campaigners, especially in the Mediterranean countries, also expressed disquiet about American pressure to extend NATO's role to the Middle East and other parts of the world. The 1986 US bombing raid on Libya from British bases enhanced this concern. After 1983 European peace activists also opposed the new Strategic Defence Initiative ('Star Wars') programme and European involvement in SDI research. The extent of hostility to NATO as an alliance depended on the political views held by movement members. Apart from the Spanish No To NATO campaign, CND was the only major nuclear disarmament campaign calling for immediate and unconditional withdrawal from the Alliance, and by no means all CND members supported this policy, though it was repeatedly reaffirmed by the national conference.

The majority of protesters were critical of aspects of Soviet policy and stressed their opposition to the SS20 missiles. Eurocommunists were willing to criticize the invasion of Afghanistan and the Soviet nuclear force. However, the wing of the West German movement which was linked to the Communist Party and the German Peace Union refused to oppose any Soviet missiles publicly until 1984, when it agreed to criticize Soviet deployment of new SS21 and 22 missiles. The END call for an end to both the military blocs reflected the attitudes and aspirations of many campaigners, but jarred not only on those left-wing socialists who saw the USA as the more aggressive power, but on moderate socialists who accepted the orthodox view that NATO was crucial to ensure European stability. This latter view was held by the wing of the West German movement attached to the SPD. When the END perspective was linked to the possibility of a united and neutral Germany, as it was by some West Berlin intellectuals, it became even more controversial, since it posed a challenge to the legitimacy of the German Democratic Republic and raised the spectre of German nationalism. Religious as well as the centrist and left political circles in the West German coalition tended to reject proposals for German unity.[45]

The most direct challenge to official Soviet and East European policies was, however, posed by END and organizations such as IKV and the German Greens actively encouraging individuals and autonomous groups in the Soviet bloc to condemn Soviet policies. Official peace committees, especially in the USSR and Czechoslovakia, were outraged when peace movement representatives pursued contacts with 'dissidents'. At the same time, in many unofficial groups, such as Charter 77 in Czechoslovakia, were deeply unhappy when Western peace groups seemed to give the official peace committees legitimacy.

Many Western peace organizations, while rejoicing in the emergence of unofficial peace groups, or the willingness of some opposition circles to consider peace issues, were torn between fostering these contacts and trying to exert pressure on official committees through dialogue. CND compromised by accepting peace committee invitations, but insisting on meeting with unofficial groups as well, despite the difficulties involved. END activists gave priority to unofficial contact, but had some links with official peace committees.

Both END policy and the attitudes of the official peace committees varied over time. Soviet Peace Committee President, Yuri Zhukov, launched a violent attack on END in December 1982, partly in connection with its planned Convention in Berlin. But when END modified its policy and invited official committees to its 1984 Convention, alongside unofficial groups, the official peace committees sent delegations to Perugia, although their presence created tensions.[46] END organizers of the 1987 Coventry Conference were bitterly divided when invitations were sent out by the Russell Foundation to East European Communist Parties as well as to peace committees. (See Chapter 7 for a more detailed analysis of independent peace groups in Eastern Europe and their relations with Western movements.)

The European movements differed in the extent to which they embraced a wider anti-militarist case beyond the missiles and nuclear weapons. CND was formally opposed to all weapons of mass destruction and endorsed the ultimate goal of general disarmament, but was primarily concerned with nuclear weapons. In Italy, however, the campaigners opposed stationing of Italian troops abroad, and conventional arms policies. The West German movement hammered out a new Peace Declaration in 1986, which not only demanded removal of the missiles and opposed SDI research, but called for rejection of all 'offensive' weapons by the German armed forces, cuts in the military budget, an end to the arms trade and greater rights for conscientious objectors.[47] Most campaigns expressed dismay at the waste of resources on the arms race, and the role of the arms trade, at a time of increasing poverty in the Third World. CND for example centred some of its demonstrations on the theme 'bread not bombs', and a group at the peace camp at Molesworth cruise base grew wheat on part of the scheduled base area for delivery to Eritrea to alleviate famine.[48]

One of the most important policy questions was how far campaigns pressed for unilateral action to halt nuclear weapons. One issue here was meshing the demands of moral rejection of genocidal weapons with political realism; another was an assessment of the role of arms-control negotiations. Most protesters expressed moral abhorrence at the prospect of possible nuclear war, either on the grounds of a humanist rejection of genocidal weapons or in the case of religious groups because they believed use of nuclear weapons could never be justified in terms of just war principles. A strictly moral renunciation of possession of nuclear weapons implies abandoning them unconditionally, but many groups tempered this conclusion with considerations of political practicality. All the European campaigns demanded that NATO should abandon its deployment plans unconditionally, while urging Soviet reciprocation. Many in addition urged further unilateral steps. West German Christian groups for example endorsed the concept of 'graduated unilateralism' (taking small steps at a time), and IKV called on The Netherlands to lead the way. British CND went further than any of its counterparts in advocating a comprehensive policy of unilateral nuclear disarmament (including, as already mentioned, withdrawal from NATO).

TACTICS AND OFFICIAL RESPONSES

Campaigners used standard pressure group tactics – petitions, lobbying, literature sales, canvassing and public meetings – as well as holding mass marches and rallies to prove they represented a new movement. They also adopted the symbols of the previous nuclear disarmament movement, for example commemorating Hiroshima. Many disarmers took up the tradition of non-violent direct action at bases or military centres; the numbers were much larger than in the 1960s and styles of protest more varied. In addition the movement threw up a number of quite new tactics.

Civil disobedience based on strict Gandhian principles was represented in Britain by the 'Snowball Campaign', which began in October 1984 and two years later had inspired thousands to court arrest after symbolic acts of civil disobedience at over thirty bases. In addition mass blockades took place at major nuclear bases, Christian CND civil disobedience demonstrations led to numerous arrests, and CND itself organized a number of more token sit-downs.[49]

Large numbers took part in a variety of direct action demonstrations in West Germany, where 3,400 joined blockades at twenty military sites in December 1982. In the context of large rallies and marches in October 1983 protesters blocked the port at Bremerhaven used by the US military, the proposed Pershing II base at Neu-Ulm, and the right-wing Springer Press offices. When the West German movement next mobilized a mass legal protest three years later, bringing 180,000 on 11 October 1986 to the Hasselbach cruise base, more than 800 had been arrested during a four-week blockade at the Pershing II Mutlangen base.[50]

Peace camps at about a dozen bases in Britain became a symbol of peace movement resistance, and also became centres for non-violent direct action. The best-known and most innovative camp was at Greenham Common. After a group of women had marched from Wales and chained themselves to the fence of the Greenham base, in imitation of the suffragettes, they decided to maintain a permanent presence there. The camp evolved into a women-only grouping and attracted feminists who wanted a 'women's space'. Women stayed at the base throughout the 1980s, through several freezing winters and despite frequent personal harassment and almost continuous attempts to move them away and sequester their belongings. Greenham women who adopted a militant interpretation of non-violent action, defied military security by climbing over the fence, cutting the wire or pulling the fence down, dancing inside the base and on top of missile silos. They also attracted thousands of women to show support. In the most effective demonstration, which drew 30,000 in December 1982, women formed a human chain to 'embrace' the base and decorated the fence with personal mementoes.[51] Greenham inspired a more short-lived feminist camp at Comiso; a women's camp at an underground bunker near Viborg in Denmark; and a women's summer camp at the Hasselbach cruise base which began in 1983 and was held each year until 1986.[52]

Government responses to protests at the bases varied, and so did those of the local people. When, for example, peace campaigners bought a peace house near the Florennes cruise base in Belgium, they found the police imposed stringent regulations, which made protest activity at the base difficult to pursue. Most local people welcomed the base for economic reasons, so sympathy for campaigners was limited.

Conditions were, however, much more difficult at Comiso. Local cultural and political pressure made it hard for Sicilians, especially women, to join peace camps. Peasants were afraid, because of Mafia influence, to offer campers land immediately by the proposed cruise missile base. Local resistance was strengthened by supporters from the Italian mainland and from elsewhere in Europe, but the protesters met with considerable police violence. Police and military police attacked a peaceful blockade on 8 August, 1983, for example, injuring a hundred people, twenty seriously. The police also refused to grant residence permits to enable Italian campaigners to stay in Sicily, and expelled numbers of international supporters; a group of women trying to maintain the Spider's Web women's camp at Comiso were banned from re-entering Sicily. Seven of these women were arrested for illegal entry when they returned to Italy, but won a court case in Bologna in 1984, when the court declared the original expulsion orders were unjustified. The Green Vine camp at Comiso for both women and men (but predominantly male) worked with local farmers on the land and managed to maintain a presence longer than the women-only camp.[53]

The British Government adopted an *ad hoc* approach to peace camps and non-violent direct action at bases. Campers at Molesworth were moved off land scheduled for the base in a military-style operation at dawn, but the most systematic attempts to move campers were made at Greenham by a road-widening scheme incorporating common land and use of military bye-laws. The courts generally imposed fines or fairly brief prison sentences. When a vicar's wife was sentenced to a year's imprisonment in 1985 there was widespread publicity and protest. The most serious legal move to deter action at bases occurred in 1984, when nine campers at the Alconbury base (linked to Molesworth) were charged with conspiracy to commit criminal damage. Only five were found guilty at their trial in July 1985 and they were given suspended sentences or community orders.[54] The decentralized nature of the peace camps, and the variety of magistrates and crown courts involved, made it difficult for the state to impose deterrent sentences on central organizers of the kind that damaged the Committee of 100 in 1962.

Local attitudes to peace camps varied. The Greenham women evoked a good deal of hostility and were often threatened by aggressive youths. Their relationship with soldiers guarding the base also seems to have been mainly confrontational, though a few soldiers revealed privately to peace campaigners that they sympathized with the women. The campers at Faslane, the Clydeside base for Polaris submarines, prompted much less local antagonism and one of its founders was elected to the local district council of Dumbarton in 1984. Many sailors and workers from the base visited the camp for a variety of motives – one sailor went to stay at the camp while absent without leave – and the relations between camp and base seemed remarkably friendly.[55]

Once cruise missiles had arrived, a group of activists in Britain began a new form of direct action by setting up 'Cruisewatch'. Their aim was to track the missile convoys, which periodically left the base at night to practise dispersing into the countryside, as they were meant to do if nuclear war was imminent. The Greenham women alerted Cruisewatch when convoys left at night, so that supporters could drive after the convoys, note their route and try to obstruct them. Tracking and publicizing the convoys provided a focus for continued resistance and a reminder of the presence and purpose of the missiles.[56] Campers at the West German Pershing II base at Mutlangen also took up the tactic of trying to follow convoys and block them.[57] Although British protesters had begun to track convoys carrying nuclear warheads as early as 1982, such tactics could only be used where weapons were being moved, and so were not as widely adopted as peace camps.[58]

The nuclear disarmers of the 1980s used the courts far more extensively than their predecessors had done. Campaigners in several countries challenged the new missile bases under international or constitutional law. The German Greens asked the West German Constitutional Court to rule that the missiles were illegal, on the grounds that the deployment decision should have been statutory; the court found in favour of the Government in December 1984. The Foundation to Forbid Cruise Missiles issued a writ claiming that The Netherlands state was contravening the civil code by cooperating with cruise deployment and secured 20,000 signatures supporting the request for an injunction to halt government action, and several Belgian groups took legal action to try to prove US-controlled missiles were unconstitutional.[59]

Protesters taking direct action at nuclear bases often invoked international law to justify their infringement of national law or local regulations. Although most courts turned down this defence, a Frankfurt court unexpectedly ruled in June 1985 that Pershing II missiles were aggressive weapons contrary to the Constitution, and controverted the goal of unification by threatening East Germany, and so acquitted six defendants who had blocked a Pershing base.[60]

The Greenham women initiated a court case before a US Federal Court in New York, in November 1983, demanding an injunction to halt cruise deployment in Britain. They appealed to the United Nations Charter, which states a threat of force is illegal, to the Nuremberg principles, and to the argument that genocide is a crime under international law. The action brought together campaigners in Britain and the USA and won widespread publicity. The court ruled in August 1984 that the judiciary lacked the expertise to determine this kind of issue and that an injunction to stop deployment would damage the USA's relations with its allies; but the judge did uphold the right of the plaintiffs to bring the case.[61]

The tactic of tax refusal combined civil disobedience with political pressure to change the law. The Movement for Refusing Defence Taxes, which arose in The Netherlands immediately after the NATO dual-track decision, called on citizens to withhold one cent for each of the 572 new NATO missiles. The movement's goal was to win the constitutional right not to pay for weapons and to divert the money to a Peace Tax Fund.[62] Some campaigners in Britain began to refuse a proportion of their taxes likely to be spent on nuclear weapons, taking up a form of protest tried out on a very small scale in the early 1960s. Taxpayers for Peace in France announced a campaign in January 1983, calling on sympathizers to refuse to pay 3 per cent of their taxes as a protest against modernization of the French nuclear force.[63] The growing campaigns of tax resistance in many European countries, including Britain, tended, however, to adopt a more comprehensive anti-militarist stance. (See Chapter 8.)

Local government support for nuclear disarmament gave a new dimension to the 1980s nuclear disarmament movement. Sympathetic local councils could create international links with other councils. David Blunkett, then leader of Sheffield City Council, urged that town-twinning could be lifted 'from the *bonhomie* of official banquets' into constructive dialogue. Sheffield itself was twinned both with Bochum in the Ruhr and Donetsk in the Ukraine.[64] The central tactic, however, was for councils to declare their areas 'nuclear-free zones'. Manchester City Council took the first step in November 1980, and five years later 180 councils in Britain had followed suit. The whole of Wales became a nuclear-free zone. The declaration had symbolic significance but did also imply council action, for example disseminating information about nuclear weapons. 'Nuclear-free' councils were also likely to oppose transport of nuclear weapons or materials through their locality. The central issue in Britain, however, became civil defence. Nuclear-free councils combined with CND in a campaign which forced the Government to abandon a nation-wide civil defence exercise, 'Hard Rock', planned for autumn 1982. Subsequently the Government tightened up civil defence obligations of local authorities, many of which continued to maintain their nuclear-free status.[65]

The idea of nuclear-free zones spread rapidly to other countries. For example Trömso in Norway declared itself a nuclear-free harbour in December 1985 as a challenge to a proposed NATO exercise in

1986. Trömso became the seventeenth local government body to declare itself a nuclear-free harbour; in some cases this had meant imposing a local ban on ships carrying nuclear weapons and in others appealing to the Norwegian Government to enforce such a ban.[66] Nuclear-free zones began to spread in West Germany in 1982 with the idea of beginning to implement on a small scale the grand aim of a nuclear-free Europe. When higher authorities vetoed such declarations local councils appealed to the courts.[67] The first international conference of nuclear-free local authorities was held in Manchester in 1984, and the second in Cordoba, a year later.

MOVEMENT PARTICIPANTS

Long-established peace organizations played a part in the new nuclear disarmament movement. War Resisters' International sections were active in the West German movement, and in Belgium where the WRI branch had long campaigned against NATO. The first sign of growing peace awareness in Italy was a larger turnout for the annual anti-militarist march from Perugia to Assissi organized by the Italian WRI section.[68] The Women's International League for Peace and Freedom decided in 1980 on a campaign to Stop the Arms Race, which was launched in 1982 and mustered 10,000 women for a march and rally in Brussels in March 1983.[69] Pax Christi had been set up as an international Catholic peace organization immediately after the Second World War, and its branches were prominent in the movements in West Germany, The Netherlands and Belgium. Quakers took the lead in campaigning in 1980 in East Anglia, then believed to be the destination for cruise missiles. Pacifists were in many countries to the fore in non-cooperation and civil disobedience, for example in the peace tax campaigns and in protests at bases.

The feminist and environmentalist movements of the 1970s had, as we have noted, created local and national groups which in many cases were ideologically predisposed to join the campaigns against the missiles. Radical feminists were most attracted to the women-only camps but in some countries, for example West Germany, there were women's peace organizations with a clear feminist standpoint. Environmental groups as well as Green or ecology parties made connections between nuclear weapons and wider nuclear power issues and joined in the campaigns, playing a particularly important role in West Germany. In some peace coalitions, for example in both

Flanders and Wallonia, groups with a primary focus on Third World development joined in.

Religious backing for the European movement for nuclear disarmament was quite strong, most obviously through IKV in The Netherlands where the Chairman of the National Council of Churches and the Catholic Bishop Ernst joined the National Committee for Recommendation for the 1985 'Citizens' Petition' against cruise deployment, although the churches did not officially support it.[70] The Protestant Action for Reconciliation, which was behind the 1958 campaign in West Germany, took part in the revival of the nuclear disarmament movement, as did Action for Community Service and Peace, a coalition of Protestant groups.[71] CND had a Christian CND section, which could draw 900 to a conference at Coventry Cathedral in 1981. In addition, Catholic Peace Action was set up in 1981 to witness against nuclear weapons and to enter into dialogue with officials at the Ministry of Defence, and Clergy Against Nuclear Arms began in 1983.[72] The Catholic Workers' Association supported the anti-cruise demonstrations in Italy.[73]

Members of many professions supported the new European movement by signing petitions, joining in demonstrations and speaking on public platforms, but above all by offering their special expertise. Scientists and doctors were prominent in analysing the likely effects of a nuclear war, lawyers examined the legality of nuclear weapons, academics promoted seminars and research, writers and publishers brought out numerous books, and musicians and actors arranged special performances. Professional groups committed to nuclear disarmament sprang up in a number of countries, but a particularly wide range existed in Britain, including psychologists, architects, engineers and electronics experts.[74]

More surprisingly, the European campaigns gained support from former and serving members of the armed forces. Contingents of Ex-Services CND on British demonstrations signalled that opposition to nuclear weapons did not imply unwillingness to defend one's country. Open protests against nuclear weapons by serving soldiers were, however, much more significant. In The Netherlands the Union of Conscripted Soldiers belonged to the Cruise Missiles No Committee, and soldiers in uniform joined in the November 1981 Amsterdam demonstration.[75] In addition the Soldiers Against Nuclear Weapons Committee, founded by about thirty conscripts in January 1981, planned to disseminate information about nuclear weapons and to refuse all duties involving nuclear weapons. Conscripts were of course more likely to mirror public attitudes than professional soldiers, but the protests by Dutch soldiers reflected the remarkable degree of freedom allowed in the armed services as well as the strength of anti-cruise feeling in the country. Some soldiers in the West German army also began to organize against the missiles in 1983, collecting signatures for the Krefeld Appeal and marching under a banner 'Soldiers Against Nuclear Missiles'. Groups in battalions at Luneburg and Oldenburg declared their batteries 'nuclear-free zones' and the Luneburg group announced to the press that they would not join in any preparations for nuclear war.[76] High-level military opposition to the NATO deployment plans had been voiced by General Gert Bastian as early as 1979. Shortly afterwards he retired in order to campaign more vigorously and joined a select international group convened by retired Brigadier Michael Harbottle, 'Generals for Peace'.[77] This group of former generals and admirals made contact with military representatives in the Warsaw Pact to discuss strategy and arms control.

If movement activists and supporters are broken down into age groups, there is a good deal of evidence that young people predominated. A US Information Agency survey of the November 1983 demonstrations against cruise found that half of the protesters in Italy and Belgium were under thirty-five, as were around two-thirds of protesters in The Netherlands and Britain and over four-fifths in West Germany.[78] It is not surprising that the young are more willing to march or take non-violent direct action, but there was also some indication from Eurobarometer polls that the twenty-five–thirty-four age group was in general much more willing to support the peace movement than the thirty-five–forty-four age group. A 1982 CND survey of its own national members found 20 per cent were students and almost half were twenty-five–forty. Individual members who paid a subscription to CND national office, were not necessarily representative of local group members and demonstrators, and likely on average to be somewhat older. A large increase in paid-up national members by 1985 did not, according to a follow-up survey by Paul Byrne, suggest any significant change in the pattern of membership.[79] Less than half were involved in local groups in 1985. The second wave of nuclear disarmament movements clearly captured the idealism of the young as the first wave had done, but their appeal to those under forty might reflect the fact that they had not experienced the more extreme attitudes of the Cold War, or that they had been influenced by the social movements and changing attitudes of the 1960s and 1970s.

Women were prominent in the movement. In addition to the established women's peace organizations and specifically feminist groups new bodies arose, such as Women Oppose the Nuclear Threat in Britain, Women Against Nuclear Weapons in The Netherlands, and the German Women for Peace.[80] But it is not clear that more women than men supported the campaigns for nuclear disarmament. CND's own membership survey showed men and women more or less equally represented.

The second movement against nuclear weapons, like the first, drew most of its committed support from the middle-classes. Certainly this was true in Britain. CND's own survey found that their national members were predominantly middle class and highly educated, and that about half were members of professions, and Byrne found that 63 per cent had middle-class occupations. A sociological enquiry by John Mattausch, comparing CND activists in a Scottish city and a new town in south-east England, concluded that CND tended to represent employees of the welfare state who were resisting the demands of the 'warfare state'.[81] Although one-third of CND's membership poll belonged to trade unions, many of these were in white-collar unions, as was the case with many Dutch activists who were teachers or social workers.[82]

SUPPORT IN SOCIETY

The affiliation of activists in the campaigns did not necessarily indicate wider institutional support. For example 23 per cent in CND's membership survey said they were practising Christians, but the churches hesitated to adopt a strong unilateralist position, although the British Council of Churches did propose in 1983 that Britain should gradually phase out its independent nuclear force. The Church of Scotland voted in 1983 for a negotiated freeze, and the Methodists supported a freeze on new nuclear weapons, which meant opposing cruise and Trident deployment. The most dramatic development was the publication of a report by a Church of England working party in 1982 which called for Britain to give up its nuclear weapons unilaterally, though when debated by Synod in 1983 a three-to-one majority voted against the report. The Synod did, however, oppose the first use of nuclear weapons, which indicated a moral unease about the justification for fighting a nuclear war.[83]

Strong opposition to the new missiles among 'progressive' groups in the German Protestant Churches was represented at the two yearly Kirchentag. In June 1985, for example, around 150,000 people met in

Düsseldorf to discuss the arms race, the Third World and other social issues, and endorsed the Düsseldorf Theses stressing Christian opposition to nuclear weapons.[84] But the West German Protestant churches did not officially support the peace movement. The closest links between the nuclear disarmament campaigns and the churches existed in The Netherlands through IKV. The Dutch Reformed Church, encompassing 23 per cent of the Dutch people, had strongly opposed nuclear arms since 1962. The Synod of the separate 'Reformed Churches' explicitly distanced itself from IKV at the beginning of the anti-missile campaign, but by 1984 had come out against cruise.[85]

The Catholic Church throughout Western Europe generally condemned the prospect of nuclear war as morally unjustifiable, but supported nuclear deterrence and opposed unilateralism. The political attitudes of national Catholic hierarchies had, however, been influenced by wider political and social changes, reflected in the Marxist–Christian dialogue started in the 1960s, liberation theology and moves towards Church unity. Although the changes in the Catholic Church in Europe were less dramatic than in the USA, greater tolerance for peace movements was suggested by the willingness of the Church to allow Monsignor Bruce Kent to act as CND Secretary in the controversial period of the early 1980s, although he felt under increasing pressure in the Church and eventually left the priesthood.

Despite the large number of campaigners in professional jobs, professional associations were unlikely to endorse peace movements. Professional bodies might, however, give indirect assistance to campaigners if drawn into debate on nuclear policies. The British Medical Association for example, issued a report strongly critical of government assumptions about civil defence and the possible role of the medical services:[86] Elitist professional bodies are, however, by tradition reluctant to take controversial political stances and many of their members would be politically hostile to any campaigning initiative. Where professional associations have absorbed some of the political ethos of trade unions, as in the case of some teachers' unions, explicit support for peace movements becomes more likely.

Union backing for campaigns against the missiles grew in several of the countries when deployment was scheduled, despite the relatively small proportion of working-class activists in the movement. The Dutch Trade Union Federation moved from official neutrality towards the 1981 national demonstration against the missiles to active endorsement by 1983. In West Germany the metalworkers sent a large contingent to the 1981 demonstration, but the Trade Union Federation would only call for multilateral agreement to restrict nuclear weapons and held back from unconditional opposition to the missiles. In late 1983, however, the Federation came out against stationing new missiles, and many unions backed the October demonstration. The CND Trade Union section won a good deal of support from unions at both a local and national level: twenty-one national unions affiliated to CND. The support of the TGWU, with its block vote of over one million, at the Labour Party Conference was especially important.[87] Individual union leaders spoke at the 1981 Rome rally, but the Italian General Confederation of Labour (covering Communists and socialists) remained cautious about committing themselves to the peace movement because they were trying to maintain links with the Christian and Social Democratic unions.[88] The Dutch and German Trade Union Federations were prepared to support token industrial action in the form of stopping work for fifteen and five minutes respectively in October 1983. The Dutch railway unions were, moreover, willing to suspend a strike to carry demonstrators to The Hague protest that month.[89] Unions in Florennes did ask members to try to find alternatives to work on the missile base,[90] but no major unions called for a total boycott of the bases.

Official union support at local or national level does not of course indicate that the passive majority of union members share these views. On the other hand poll evidence does not seem to indicate major differences between classes in their views on peace movement policies. A *Sunday Times* MORI poll in January 1983 did not find that the 23 per cent who supported unilateral nuclear disarmament were predominantly members of the professions.[91] Poll evidence about public attitudes is not a satisfactory guide, because of the complexity of the issues involved in the nuclear weapons debate and the degree to which answers can be structured by the way the question is asked. Proportions opposing the NATO missiles tended to vary by about 20 per cent: stressing the Soviet SS20s for instance could reduce hostility to NATO deployments, while underlining that the missiles were 'new' and 'American' increased resistance. But some broad trends in public opinion do emerge.

West Europeans (like North Americans) became markedly more worried about the danger of nuclear war in the early 1980s, which created a favourable context for the peace movement, though fear of nuclear war does not automatically translate into support for specific policies. Indeed, one analysis of West European opinion indicated that fear of war began to decline in many countries by the end of 1981, and that public loss of confidence in US leadership was more significant by 1982.[92]

Comparison of polls in 1980 or 1981 and polls in 1983 suggests opposition to the NATO missiles increased in this period. A May 1981 poll in West Germany found 39 per cent against new missiles and about one-third still undecided. By early 1983 opposition to the missiles was around 60 per cent, although by the end of the year it had fallen to around 50 per cent. A Belgian poll in 1980 found 42 per cent against new missiles on their territory, but as the debate intensified opposition grew to between 62 per cent and 78 per cent, depending on the question.[93] There was also a tendency to be more willing to accept the principle of new deployments than to accept missiles in one's own country. In all countries support for NATO remained high – for instance 67 per cent of those West Germans against missile deployment believed in NATO.[94] Not surprisingly polls also suggested that resistance to new missiles was much greater than support for measures of unilateral nuclear disarmament: a January 1983 Marplan poll found 61 per cent in Britain against cruise but only 21 per cent for unilateral nuclear disarmament. Polls in October and November 1982 after the Labour Party Conference voted for unilateralism found 35 per cent and 41 per cent in favour, but the figure was more often between 20 and 30 per cent, much the same proportion as in the first phase of CND.[95]

Public opinion clearly has some influence on government policies. In Belgium and The Netherlands – where about two-thirds or more of the electorate were hostile to missile deployment – the governing coalitions looked for compromises to make the missiles more acceptable. Party policies on defence do not, however, directly reflect public attitudes. There is indeed evidence that party supporters quite often diverge from the views of their parties. A 1982 Eurobarometer poll found that only 32.4 per cent of German SPD supporters and 44.7 per cent of Labour supporters strongly approved of the peace movement, although the SPD swung to the peace movement position in 1983 and the Labour Party voted for unilateralism in 1982. Conversely, voters for centrist parties might be more sympathetic to the peace movement than their parties. The British SDP broke away from Labour partly on the issue of defence, but 30.4 per cent of its supporters were 'strongly in favour' of the movement against the missiles; so were 31.9 per cent of supporters of the West German Free Democratic Party.[96]

THE POLITICAL PARTIES

Only minority parties have strongly and consistently endorsed the aims of nuclear disarmament campaigns. These include the Pacifist Socialist Parties set up in a number of countries in the early 1960s for this purpose, and the later wave of Ecology or Green Parties, of which by far the most important has been the German Greens who swept past the 5 per cent barrier in the 1983 West German national elections. The Italian Radical Party, reconstituted in the early 1960s to promote peace policies, and also reflecting feminist and Green concerns, combined both categories. Communist Parties active in promoting action against US missiles were, not surprisingly, less inclined to endorse peace movement criticisms of the Soviet Union, although the Italian PCI was a major exception. Marxist parties to the left of the Communists, such as the Italian Democratic Party of Proletarian Unity, have strongly opposed NATO (and been in varying degree hostile to the Soviet Government) and so have joined in major peace movements. The Scottish and Welsh Nationalists do not fit any of these ideological moulds, but have for historic reasons been hostile to defence policies decided in London and to the nuclear bases on their territories.

The major parties most likely to endorse at least some nuclear disarmament policies have been the socialists. Within Socialist Parties rank-and-file activists, youth sections and individual MPs were more likely to back nuclear disarmament campaigns, and the leadership more likely to lean towards orthodox NATO positions. Bettino Craxi imposed unconditional acceptance of the NATO missiles on his Italian Socialist Party by dismissing six deputies who opposed him. (Thus, when Craxi became the first Italian Socialist prime minister since the war in August 1983, Italy's deployment of cruise missiles was assured, though many government deputies abstained during a November debate on the missiles in Parliament.)[97] Although both Michael Foot and Neil Kinnock were personally sympathetic to unilateralist policies, the doubts of many other Labour leaders undermined the party's attempt to present a positive unilateralist case to the electorate in 1983 and 1987. Socialist parties have also been much more likely to accept nuclear disarmament policies when in opposition than when in power. Helmut Schmidt held off gathering opposition to the missiles in the Social Democratic Party even after he lost power in the autumn of 1982 when his Free Democrat coalition partner defected, until after the 1983 election in which the SPD was defeated.[98] The Flemish and Walloon Socialist Parties, which had been represented in a government which gave provisional support to acceptance of the missiles in 1980, went into opposition after the 1981 elections and then came out against deployment.[99] The Dutch labour party was most consistently opposed to the missiles, and was backed in this position by about 90 per cent of their voters.[100]

Right-wing parties such as the British Conservatives, the Belgian 'Liberals' or the Italian 'Republicans' were strongly in favour of deployment, as was the Bavarian Christian Social Union. Right-wing Dutch Liberals also unequivocally supported cruise, but the left Liberals who had broken away in 1966 opposed the missiles. The Christian Democrats in Italy and West Germany upheld NATO policy in line with longstanding attitudes towards defence and foreign policy. The great asset of both the Dutch and Belgian movements was that the centre right Christian Democratic Parties in The Netherlands and in Flanders split on the issue of the missiles, partly reflecting the strength of opposition within the churches.

The fact that both The Netherlands and Belgium are governed by multi-party coalitions, whereas West Germany and Britain have been more polarized between major parties of the Right and Left may have helped the Dutch and Belgian movements. It was also important that, for strategic and political reasons, defence and full allegiance to NATO and to Washington were more crucial and emotive issues in West Germany and Britain. The British debate was further complicated by Britain's own nuclear force. Public opinion appeared to favour the British Bomb much more strongly than US bases or cruise missiles, but the military and political establishment was even more unequivocally committed to NATO and the US Alliance than to the British nuclear force. CND was therefore trying to win arguments on several fronts. A UK campaign for a Nuclear Freeze tried to mobilize the much wider support available for stopping cruise and Trident unconditionally – a policy supported by the Liberal Assembly in 1981. The UK Freeze campaign in 1983 and 1984 had the backing of the United Nations Association and the British Council of Churches. But because of the prominence of CND, much public debate continued to focus on unilateral nuclear disarmament.[101]

Both the West German and British peace movements suffered a setback in the 1983 elections, partly due to political and social factors which had nothing to do with policy on the missiles. But the British general election did focus to a quite unusual degree on nuclear weapons and defence, and CND dubbed it the 'nuclear election'. It could therefore be argued that CND had failed to transform the terms of the defence debate and influence public attitudes in depth, so that the Conservatives, instead of feeling vulnerable on nuclear weapons, launched a pre-election 'Peace-with-Freedom' campaign directed against both CND and the Labour Party, and saw defence as their strongest suit. CND was, however, confronting a Conservative Government able to mobilize the resources of the Ministry of Defence, MI5, well-funded right-wing groups and a predominantly Conservative press to engage in a campaign against CND which, in the words of one of those involved, used 'information, disinformation and character assassination'.[102] The West German movement, despite its impressive size, also failed to secure a firm enough base in public opinion and in the SPD itself, as well as proving unable to make inroads on the Free Democrats or Christian Democrats.

The Dutch and Belgian movements did have much greater success in winning public support and a cross-party alliance against the missiles, and the deployment issue influenced the 1984 EEC elections in these countries. The Dutch and Belgian governments were forced by external pressures from Washington, Britain and West Germany, and from NATO to agree to deployment against domestic preferences. Therefore many campaigners could conclude (as some already believed) that internal democratic processes were ultimately irrelevant to defence decisions involving NATO. Defence policy was apparently made by military intelligence and foreign policy bureaucracies responding to the dominant power within the NATO structure, the USA. These views could find further confirmation in the about turn of the Papandreou Government on US bases. The fate of the campaign in Spain against NATO membership might also provide at least partial proof of this thesis.

SPAIN

The Spanish nuclear disarmament campaign focused on three main issues. Following the precedent of proposals for nuclear-free zones in the Balkans and in the Nordic areas, Spanish and Portuguese activists called for removal of all nuclear bases in the Iberian peninsula. A conference of intellectuals, peace groups and town mayors at Lisbon in November 1984 launched the campaign for an Iberian nuclear-free zone, which was linked to moves for municipal 'nuclear-free zones' initiated by the Spanish Human Rights Association in 1983. By 1986 about 400 town councils in both Spain and Portugal had declared themselves nuclear-free areas.[103]

The second focus of protest has been the presence of US military bases in Spain. These were initially established after General Franco signed a treaty with the USA in 1953, and a new agreement was negotiated in 1982. The most important bases were the Rota naval base and the Torrejon base for fighter aircraft. The first big Spanish peace demonstration, which took place in January 1981, was a march by 20,000 from Madrid to Torrejon.[104] Although the USA withdrew its nuclear-missile submarines from Rota in 1979, and had apparently promised not to store nuclear weapons in Spain, peace researchers revealed early in 1985 that Joint Chiefs of Staff Deployment Contingency Plans envisaged basing nuclear depth bombs in both Spain and Portugal. The Spanish Government professed itself ignorant of these plans.[105] Spanish public opinion was generally hostile to the bases, believing Washington had propped up the Franco dictatorship and that the bases gave the Americans influence over Spanish affairs. The danger of US nuclear weapons had been dramatized in 1966 when a B52 bomber collided with a tanker aircraft in mid-air and crashed with four H bombs aboard. It took the USA 10 weeks to find the bombs and much longer to remove tons of the worst irradiated soil. When President Reagan visited Spain in 1985, trade unionists, Socialists and Communists demonstrated at the US bases to show continued opposition to them.[106]

After June 1982, however, when a Conservative Government took Spain into NATO, the central aim of the Spanish peace movement was to bring Spain out of the Alliance as soon as possible. During the 1982 autumn election the Spanish Socialist Workers' Party (PSOE) campaigned against NATO membership and promised to hold a referendum on the issue. The PSOE won the election and the new prime minister, Felipe Gonzalez, halted moves towards military integration in NATO and reaffirmed commitment to a referendum. It soon became apparent, however, that once in government the Socialist Party was reluctant to withdraw from NATO and the referendum was delayed until March 1986. By then Spain had after prolonged negotiations achieved entry into the EEC. Despite the setback to the movement for withdrawal from NATO created by the PSOE change of policy, the peace movement was encouraged by its own strength. In addition to the coalition of pacifist, anti-militarist, feminist, environmental and religious groupings to be found elsewhere in Europe, there was extensive opposition to NATO membership in existing left-wing organizations in factories, work-places, towns and neighbourhoods. The rank and file of the PSOE had also remained hostile to NATO. Public pressure ensured that the long-promised referendum was eventually held. Moreover, public opinion polls consistently showed that a majority of the voters were against NATO membership: for example a poll in April 1985 found 54 per cent against membership and only 19 per cent in favour.[107]

The Socialist Government did not argue that NATO membership would increase Spain's military security, but stressed instead that it was linked to EEC membership and a symbol of Spain's new status among the democratic nations of Western Europe. Gonzalez also made concessions to the peace movement by guaranteeing that Spain would not join the NATO integrated command structure, that it would not have nuclear weapons on its soil and that the number of American troops would be cut. The referendum result was a severe shock to the National Coordination of Peace Organization and a defeat for the whole European nuclear disarmament movement – British CND had in particular backed the anti-NATO campaign by sending prominent personalities to speak at rallies. In the event about 40 per cent of the electorate abstained in the referendum, over half of those voting favoured staying in NATO and only seven million out of twenty-eight million voters opted for leaving.[108] Government tactics no doubt influenced the result: Gonzalez implied that the anti-NATO campaign was dominated by Communists and refused to allow any debates on the issue on television. The radio and most of the press backed NATO membership, but government domination of television was probably most significant, especially given the still quite high illiteracy rate. Many observers thought the crucially determining factor was that the Government persuaded many voters that leaving NATO would have repercussions in the EEC and lead to economic loss for Spain.[109]

FRANCE

If government and institutional forces could defeat the peace movement in Spain, they could ensure in France that no major movement arose to capitalize upon potential sympathy among the French public. Interestingly, opinion polls in France in the 1980s indicated that only about half the population supported the *force de frappe* (52 per cent in a November 1982 poll), but since 1977 all the main political parties have favoured an independent French nuclear force.[110] Moreover, a poll in 1981 on attitudes to West European demonstrations against the missiles found that 50 per cent of French citizens questioned did approve of the protests (almost as many as in Britain), yet the French non-aligned peace movement was a great deal weaker than CND.[111]

Some of the reasons for the absence of a significant independent nuclear disarmament campaign were the same as twenty years earlier, for example the dominant role of the Communist Party and its Movement for Peace in peace action, and the lack of a recent peace tradition among French Socialists. Many factors were, however, more specific to the condition of French politics in the 1980s. For example, the fact that the Socialist and Communist Parties, after a long period of at least formal opposition to the French nuclear force, had switched to endorsing it in 1977, meant that there was no authoritative support for nuclear disarmament within political parties. Jolyon Howarth has also pointed to the 'Cold War' attitude in France in the early 1980s, encouraged by the belated recognition of many former Communists or Maoists of the 1960s of the realities of Stalinism. Moreover, the French Communist Party had moved away from Eurocommunism by 1980 and reverted to unquestioning support of the Soviet Union, including the invasion of Afghanistan.[112]

France had only political ties to NATO and so was exempt from the requirement to accept new American missile bases on its soil. This meant that President Mitterrand could vociferously call for deployment by other countries, while his own citizens were not alarmed by possible loss of sovereignty or worried about becoming prime targets in a nuclear war. Nor did the French public appear to be worried about the possible dangers of their own nuclear force, which was viewed mainly as a symbol of state prestige. There has been no public debate in France in Parliament or the media about the military or technological aspects of the *force de frappe*, in marked contrast to Britain. The difference in attitudes between France and most other West European countries is illustrated by the fact that many members of the vigorous French movement against civilian nuclear power did not see any necessary connection with the military nuclear programme.[113]

The coalition of autonomous groups that came together in late 1981 as the Committee for Nuclear Disarmament (CODENE) therefore remained weak. CODENE was created by Claude Bourdet's 1960s nuclear disarmament body, Movement for Democracy, Peace and Liberty, which drew in pacifist, feminist and ecological groups, and was backed by the left socialist party, PSU. In its policies CODENE was close to END, supported 'phased elimination' of all European nuclear weapons and developed contacts with Eastern European independent groups. It also called for a halt to French nuclear tests and to modernization of the *force de frappe*. After organizational difficulties, CODENE, tried again to regroup its forces in August 1983 and met at Larzac, symbol of a successful anti-militarist campaign (see Chapter 1).[114] As a result CODENE did take part in the wave of European protests in October 1983, and managed to secure very limited and provisional support from the Christian Trade Union Federation (CFDT) for this demonstration.[115] The fragmented nature of the French peace movement has been cited as one reason for its relative lack of impact: a University of Grenoble study found fifty-nine groups representing differing ideologies and aims who were willing to cooperate in the survey.[116] Certainly there was a strong contrast between CODENE and CND, but, as we noted earlier, the decentralized and variegated nature of the West German campaign was not an obvious weakness. It is, however, easier to mobilize diverse groups round a central issue, such as the Krefeld Appeal against the missiles, and the French campaign lacked such a clear and simple focus.

ASSESSING THE MOVEMENT FOR EUROPEAN NUCLEAR DISARMAMENT

The nuclear disarmament campaigns of the 1980s attracted millions of active supporters throughout Western Europe. Not only was the movement larger than its predecessor twenty years earlier, it was also more sophisticated in its campaigning tactics and able to draw on a wide range of professional expertise. Activists often were very knowledgeable about nuclear weapons and policies and able to engage in strategic debate. They were assisted by investigative journalists and academics in making a great deal of telling information available to the general public. The earlier campaigns had challenged the then fairly rudimentary official concepts of deterrence and exposed accidents with nuclear weapons, but in the 1980s groups linked to the movement produced detailed analyses of strategic developments and proposals for alternative defence policies which both the media and official strategic circles took seriously, however strongly they disagreed with them.[117] The peace research institutes and departments which had grown up in the 1960s and 1970s played a major role in the theoretical side of the movement.

The European peace movement in the 1980s was, by any criterion, a significant political force. The tangible results it could claim were, however, very limited. In Britain CND had its greatest success in discrediting government civil defence plans. Mrs Thatcher's Government had given specific impetus to CND by stressing the importance of the British nuclear force, deciding to buy new Trident missiles from the USA, and by making an issue of civil defence preparations. This emphasis on civil defence was a tactical error. Campaigners had no difficulty in showing the ludicrous inadequacy of plans to shelter the population, and government estimates of casualties in a nuclear attack became a focus for competing scientific and medical analysis, and drew medical staff into the debate. The numerous local councils who declared themselves 'nuclear-fee zones' could also challenge the government over civil defence plans.

CND made little headway, however, on the much more central issue of the British nuclear force. There was significant public opposition to Trident, because the missiles would be new, because they represented a significant increase in the nuclear warheads which would be available to Britian and because of the expense of buying the missiles from the USA. Scottish CND set up a separate campaign to oppose Trident (which like Polaris would be deployed from a Scottish base). The Liberal Assembly voted against Trident in 1981. The Liberals had opposed a British nuclear force since 1957, but under SDP pressure in the mid-1980s the Liberal leadership accepted the case for maintaining such a force, though the Liberal–SDP Alliance looked for alternatives to the Trident missile. The Labour Party went into the 1983 and 1987 elections with a programme of opposing both the British Bomb and all US nuclear bases – and made this policy more coherent in the second election. But with only a minority of the public in favour of unilateralism, and with opposing parties and the media attacking Labour defence policy, the apparent result – especially in 1983 – was to marginalize further a Labour Party already losing support to the Alliance. After 1987 the Labour leadership jettisoned all elements of CND policy, even though in a rapidly changing international context the objective case for re-evaluating Britain's defence policy was stronger than ever before. Unilateralism had been damagingly equated with the left-wing of the Labour Party and was widely regarded as incompatible with winning an election.

The major focus of CND and other European campaigns was of course the new NATO missile deployment. Because the missiles were new, a broad coalition could unite against them and public opinion was more easily roused, so they provided a natural target for the new nuclear disarmament movement. In addition demonstrators could easily group at bases for land-based missiles, and the NATO deployment timetable provided a framework for protest. Although there were tactical advantages in concentrating primarily on the missiles, and supporters of nuclear disarmament had no moral or political choice but to oppose them, there were also grave disadvantages in too exclusive an emphasis on stopping the missiles. Firstly, while using the missiles to illustrate the very real dangers of nuclear deterrence and the latest nuclear weapon technology, some campaigners tended to exaggerate the immediate danger of nuclear war if deployment went ahead.[118] Secondly, campaigners opposing NATO deployments were, through the logic of the situation, promoting the Soviet goals of preventing cruise and Pershing II, which Moscow saw as a direct threat. Moreover, even if protesters stressed opposition to the Soviet SS20s, they could not directly influence their deployment. While claims by some right-wing groups that the USSR was orchestrating the protests were clearly false, it was true that the Soviet Union was happy to offer every encouragement, which made the campaigns more vulnerable to allegations of Soviet influence.[119]

The campaigns against the missiles had a direct impact on negotiations between the USA and USSR in a number of ways. The first was to exert pressure on West European governments, who in turn persuaded key figures in the Reagan Administration to start INF talks late in 1981. The second was that the Reagan Administration took up the END slogan – No Cruise and Pershing, No SS20s – as the basis of its negotiating stance at Geneva. At the time this seemed an astute move to wrongfoot the peace movement, who then had to argue that there is a difference between a slogan and a serious negotiating position; and Washington could rest assured that Moscow was not willing to destroy hundreds of missiles already in place against 'paper missiles'. Those who genuinely wanted an arms control agreement envisaged some arrangement which would allow limited NATO deployments against cuts in SS20s along the lines of the abortive 'walk in the woods' proposal by the heads of the US and Soviet delegations in Geneva in late 1982.[120] However, when both sides resumed serious INF negotiations after 1985 NATO was somewhat reluctantly hoist with its original negotiating proposal.

During the crucial year, 1983, the peace movement failed to stop the beginning of the missile deployment, the USA and its NATO allies refused to make any concession to the USSR by delaying deployment, and the USSR in turn showed its intransigence by walking out of the nuclear arms control talks and putting extra missiles into East Germany and Czechoslovakia. The peace movement had failed to limit the spread of nuclear weapons in Europe or to mitigate Cold War hostilities between Washington and Moscow. At worst it might have made both sides more intransigent, by making the missiles a test of NATO solidarity and encouraging the USSR to believe it need not make negotiating concessions.

When Gorbachev and Reagan met in Washington in December 1987 to sign an INF Treaty which provided for the removal of all intermediate and shorter-range missiles from Europe, and for strict verification of the destruction of the missiles, both right-wing governments and the peace movement claimed a victory. The governments argued that once the NATO missiles were in place the USSR had a motive to negotiate seriously and that Western pressure had forced the Soviet Government to overcommit its resources to arms, so that there were strong economic incentives for Moscow to seek cuts in nuclear arsenals. The peace movement argued that their pressure ensured NATO governments were ultimately willing to dismantle all the NATO missiles as part of an INF Treaty. It was certainly true that Mrs Thatcher, Chancellor Kohl and top NATO generals showed initial reluctance to dismantle the missiles, which they now stated were designed primarily to strengthen US nuclear commitment to Europe and a strategy of flexible deterrence.[121]

Primary responsibility for the 1987 Treaty seemed to lie with Gorbachev, who set the pace for rapid moves forward during 1987, made a series of concessions to overcome Western objections, and showed an unprecedented Soviet willingness to dismantle many more missiles than the West (1,752 Soviet missiles to 859 US missiles in the final treaty) and to accept detailed on-site verification. The peace movement could, however, argue that Gorbachev and some of his advisers appeared from 1987 to have been influenced by some of the ideas put forward by peace research and arms control circles in the West. These were minimum nuclear deterrence, non-offensive conventional defence and the value of significant measures of unilateral disarmament in promoting multilateral agreement. Gorbachev's references to 'nuclear sufficiency', plus concessions on INF and acceptance of the goal of 50 per cent cuts in strategic nuclear arsenals, all indicated a change in official Soviet nuclear strategy. Soviet proposals to the new Conventional Forces in Europe talks in 1989 stressed reductions in 'offensive' potential on both sides and minimizing the fear of a surprise attack. Moreover, in December 1988 Gorbachev announced that the USSR would withdraw 50,000 troops and 5,000 tanks from Eastern Europe, and reduce the total Soviet armed forces unilaterally by 500,000 men. Since influential research institutes and party officials had shown serious interest in Western

149

peace research proposals through the 1980s, after Gorbachev came to power it became clear that links between Western campaigners and researchers and levels of the Soviet establishment could be constructive.[122]

Rapid political change in the late 1980s also demonstrated the value of contacts between Western peace movements and Eastern Europe at the very different level of dialogue with opposition groups. The END policy of trying to win support from autonomous circles in Eastern Europe resulted in a dialogue, which raised long-term questions about the possibility of a future Europe without military blocs and promoted citizen-to-citizen links across the East–West divide, which even opponents of the peace movement conceded were significant.[123] Because END policy transcended opposition to INF and SS20s, END Conventions remained potentially significant after 1987; and some participants in the dialogue with Western peace movements came to power, as in Czechoslovakia at the end of 1989.

The balance sheet of peace movement success and failure in terms of political impact in the 1980s is therefore mixed and open to varying interpretation. Both supporters and critics often agree, however, on one secondary result of the peace protests: that they led to the democratization of debate on defence policy.[124] Nuclear strategy and deployments, the minutiae of arms control proposals and debates about NATO military policies have normally been arcane and highly technical subjects confined to defence experts and academics specializing in strategy and arms control. Very few knew the details of the 1979 SALT II Treaty. After 1980 there was an explosion of articles, pamphlets, books and television programmes covering Western and Soviet arsenals and strategies and monitoring progress (or lack of it) in arms control talks. The peace campaigns and research institutes produced their own literature and journals. However, in addition commercial publishing recognized a booming market and the mainstream media responded to public interest and political controversy. This public debate may only have involved a minority – some European polls suggested that by 1984 only 10–15 per cent of the population was interested in the details of foreign policy and defence – except in West Germany, where the figure was 28 per cent.[125] But it must have significantly increased the circle of informed people and generated a sense that people had the right to know the details of defence policy and deployments.

Whether public debate and pressure on defence policy is intrinsically desirable, and whether there is a conflict between the requirements of state security and the principle of democratic accountability, are wider issues raised by all peace campaigns. These questions are addressed in the final chapter of this book.

NOTES AND REFERENCES

1. For example President Carter had tried to limit the spread of plutonium to curb proliferation. See Walter C. Patterson, *The Plutonium Business: and the Spread of the Bomb* (London, Paladin Books, 1984).

2. CND drew attention to the military use of plutonium from civil UK nuclear reactors and gave evidence against the proposed siting of the first UK Pressurized Water Reactor at Sizewell at the 1983–85 public inquiry. Jonathan Porritt and David Winner, *The Coming of the Greens* (London, Fontana, 1988), p. 41.

3. Dorothy Nelkin and Michael Pollak, *The Atom Besieged: Anti-nuclear Movements in France and Germany* (Cambridge, Mass., MIT Press, 1978); and Dave Elliott, *The Politics of Nuclear Power* (London, Pluto Press, 1978).

4. Elliott, *The Politics of Nuclear Power*, pp. 121–2.

5. Feminism was in part a reaction to the male domination of the 1960s New Left and its emphasis on machismo, though it had more substantial roots in the economic and social subordination of women. See Juliet Mitchell, *Women's Estate* (Harmondsworth, Middlesex, Penguin, 1971).

6. Bruce Russett and Donald R. Deluce, 'Theater Nuclear Forces: Public Opinion in Western Europe', *Political Science Quarterly*, **98**, 1983, pp. 179–86.

7. For differing perspectives on the 'Second Cold War' see Fred Halliday, *The Making of the Second Cold War* (London, Verso, 1986, 2nd ed); and Raymond L. Garthoff, *Detente and Confrontation: American Soviet Relations from Nixon to Reagan* (Washington DC, the Brookings Institution, 1985).

8. For the background to the INF negotiations see Strobe Talbott, *Deadly Gambits: the Reagan Administration and the Stalemate in Nuclear Arms Control* (London, Pan Books, 1985).

9. Ibid, pp. 27–8 32–3.

10. Egbert Boeker, 'On the Way towards Consensus?', *END Bulletin*, **4**, February 1981, pp. 5–7.

11. END Briefing Notes: 'The Netherlands'.

12. Jon Grepstad, 'Norway's Ongoing Struggle', *END Bulletin*, **3**, 1980, pp. 14–15.

13. Illustrated by Talbott. On Administration attitudes to deployment see for example p. 187: '"We don't care if the goddam things work or not", said Burt in a meeting with his staff. "After all, that doesn't matter unless there's a war. What we care about is getting them in." The comment was perfect illustration . . . of the essentially political – as opposed to military – purpose of nuclear weapons in general and Pershing II in particular.'

14. See Marco De Andreis, 'The Nuclear Debate in Italy', *Survival*, May–June, 1986 and Bruno Gabrielli, 'Comiso and Beyond', *END Journal*, **16/17**, Summer 1986, p. 32.
15. *END Bulletin*, **3**, 1980, p. 16.
16. Iikka Taipale, 'Action in Finland', *END Bulletin*, **9**, May–June, 1982, p. 23.
17. Jan Andersson and Kent Lindkvist, 'The Peace Movement in Sweden', in Werner Kaltefleiter and Robert L. Pfaltzgraff (eds), *The Peace Movements in Europe and the United States* (London, Croom Helm, 1985) pp. 13–22.
18. Olafur Grimsson, 'Passionate Campaign in the Land of Ice-caps', *END Bulletin*, **10**, July–August 1982, pp. 12–13.
19. Interview with Andreas Papandreou by Mary Kaldor, *END Journal*, No. 2, February–March 1983, pp. 12–13. See also Rita Sanderson, 'Greek Government Seeks Non-Aligned World Stance,' *Sanity*, November 1983, pp. 20–1.
20. 'Pasok Caught by Turkish Threat', *END Journal*, **10**, June–July 1984, p. 27. In 1988 Papandreou prevaricated on signing a further bases agreement. His Government lost the 1990 elections.
21. 'Turkey', END Bulletin, **10**, July–August 1982, pp. 5–7.
22. Chris Horrie, 'Turkey's Most Famous Man of Peace at Last Gets Bail', *Sanity*, February 1983, pp. 16–17; Jean Furtado, 'The Land Where Peace is Illegal', *Sanity*, December 1983, pp. 22–3. Kevin Watkins, 'More Turkish Peace Trials', *Peace News*, 2 November, 1984, p. 6.
23. *END Bulletin*, **2**, 1980, p. 6; **3**, 1980, p. 21.
24. Rainer Santi, 'Draft for Brochure on History of the International Peace Bureau', October 1989.
25. Dimitri I, Roussopoulos, *The Coming of World War Three*, Vol. 1 (Montreal, Black Rose Books, 1986), pp. 147–203 covers END and its Conventions.
26. See *NATO Review*, **3/4**, 1983 and **1**, February 1982.
27. Jon Grepstad, 'Norway's Fight Against New European Nuclear Weapons', *END Bulletin*, **2**, 1980, pp. 19–20.
28. *END Bulletin*, **2**, 1980, p. 6.
29. John Minnion and Philip Bolsover, *The CND Story* (London, Allison and Busby, 1983), p. 36.
30. Ulrich Albrecht, 'The Great Hamburg Peace Demonstration', *END Bulletin*, **6**, Autumn 1982, p. 10; and 'European Notes', *END Bulletin*, **8**; Joyce Marie Mushaben, 'Cycles of Peace Protest in West Germany', *West European Politics*, **8**, 1, January 1985, p. 32.
31. *END Bulletin*, **5**, Summer 1981, pp. 3–4; **6**, Autumn 1981, pp. 8–9.
32. *END Bulletin*, **8**, Spring 1982, pp. 14–16.
33. 'Message from Europe', *END Bulletin*, **10**, July–August 1982, p. 3.
34. Alice Cook and Gwyn Kirk, *Greenham Women Everywhere* (London, Pluto Press, 1983) p. 32.
35. Jane Dibblin, 'An Outpouring of Protest – Peaceful and Determined', *END Journal*, **7**, December 1983–January 1984, pp. 10–12.
36. See 'Peace Movement's Cruise Triumph', *Sanity*, July 1984, p. 4 and 'Belgians Deploy Cruise on Time', *END Journal*, **15**, April–May 1985, p. 5 and END Briefing Notes on 'The Netherlands' and 'Belgium'.

37. Thomas R. Rochon, *Mobilizing for Peace: the Anti-nuclear Movements in Western Europe* (Princeton, New Jersey, Princeton University Press, 1985), pp. 84, 86–9;
38. CND leaflet, 'Questions and Answers about CND', Autumn 1985 and *CND Story*, p. 30.
39. Peter Findlay, 'Inside the Protean Peace Movement', *END Journal*, **20**, February–March 1986, pp. 13–15.
40. 'Five Years On', *END Journal* Supplement, Summer 1985. Diana Johnstone, *The Politics of Euromissiles: Europe's Role in America's World* (London, Verso, 1984) p. 144.
41. See END Briefings on 'The Netherlands' and 'Belgium'.
42. CND nationally did not entirely escape rifts over ideology or tactics. For example the CND Executive dismissed Youth CND officers in 1983 on the grounds that they were elected at a conference dominated by Trotskyists (*Peace News*, 16 September 1983, p. 5).
    When CND demonstrated against Reagan's visit in the summer of 1984, a breakaway group demanded more radical action and organized a sit-down outside the US Embassy. Feminist separatism was not always readily accepted, despite widespread admiration for the Greenham Common women. In the late 1980s a bitter dispute with roots in the earlier feminist movement developed at Greenham itself when the Kings Cross 'Wages for Housework' group took over at the 'Yellow' gate to the base. Beatrix Campbell 'Crisis at Greenham?' *Sanity*, November, 1987, pp. 19–21; letters *Sanity*, December 1987.
43. A text of the Appeal can be found in *END Bulletin*, **1**, 1980, pp. 3–4.
44. Martin Ryle, *Towards the Nuclear Holocaust* (London, The Menard Press, 1981) p. 11.
45. For a survey of West German groupings and policies see Findlay, *END Journal*, February–March 1986.
46. See 'The Zhukov File', *END Bulletin*, **12**, 1983, pp. 13–22. On the Perugia Convention see: 'Five Days of Discussion', *END Journal*, **11**, August–September, 1984, pp. 9–10; and Chiara Ingrao, 'Perugia Convention', *Sanity*, September 1984, p. 4. See also Dimitrios I. Roussopoulos, *The Coming of World War III*, Vol. 1, pp. 147–203.
47. See END Briefings on 'West Germany'.
48. Tim Wallis, 'Ploughshares Campaign', *Peace News*, Molesworth Broadsheet, in *Peace News*, **2257**, 15 November 1983.
49. Chris Booth, 'The Snowball Keeps Rolling On . . .' *Peace News*, 12 December 1986, p. 7 explains the Snowball campaign. On Christian CND 'Peace Pentecost' at Upper Heyford and later four-day blockade organized by peace camp in 1983, see Dave Wainwright and Barbara Eggleston 'Oxford Base focus for Direction Action' *Sanity*, July 1983, p. 17. These were early examples of non-violent direct action.
50. *Peace News*, 28 October 1983, p. 6; 17 October 1986, p. 3; 7 January 1983, p. 5.
51. Alice Cook and Gwyn Kirk, *Greenham Women Everywhere*, especially pp. 30–3.
52. On Comiso, see Patricia Melander, 'Machismo and the Military in Sicily', *Peace News*, 7 March 1986, pp. 8–9. On Viborg, see *Peace News*,

5 October 1984, p. 7. On Hasselbach, see *Peace News*, 17 October 1986, p. 3.

53. See Ben Thompson, *END Special Report; Comiso* (London, END and Merlin Press, 1982) See also *Peace News*, 16 September 1983, p. 6; 16 November 1984, p. 6; and Pat Sinclair, 'The Growing Militarisation of Sicily', *Peace News*, 14 December 1984, pp. 14–15; *Sanity*, November 1983, p. 17; and *WRI Newsletter*, No. 193, April 1983, pp. 1–2; No. 198, February 1984, p. 5; and No. 200, July–August 1984, pp. 3–4.

54. On vicar's wife, Ann Francis, see *Sanity*, June 1985, p. 6. On Alconbury trial see *Sanity*, February 1985, p. 5; and *Peace News*, 12 May 1985, pp. 12–13; 12 July 1985, p. 3.

55. *Faslane: Diary of a Peace Camp* (Edinburgh, Polygon Books, 1984).

56. Sian Williams, 'Cruisewatch', *Sanity*, July 1985, pp. 36–7; 'Bringing Cruise Home', *Peace News*, 22 February 1985, pp. 8–9.

57. *Peace News*, 10 August 1984, p. 6.

58. *Peace News*, 27 February 1987. p. 10.

59. Gunter Offczors and Matthias Ruete, 'Law and Peace in West Germany', in John Dewar *et al.* (eds), *Nuclear Weapons, the Peace Movement and the Law* (London, Macmillan, 1986) pp. 219–30; Theo De Roos, 'Nuclear Missiles in The Netherlands', in Dewar, pp. 237–8; END Briefing Notes on 'Belgium'.

60. *Peace News*, 28 June 1985, p. 6. See also Offczors and Ruete, pp. 227–8.

61. Jane Hickman, 'Greenham Women Against Cruise Missiles and Others v. Ronald Reagan and Others', in Dewar, pp. 200–18.

62. *Disarmament Campaigns*, **2**, May 1980, p. 7; **19**, February 1983, p. 5.

63. *WRI Newsletter*, **207**, September–October 1985, p. 14.

64. David Blunkett, 'Nuclear-Free Zones – Silly or Sane?', *Sanity*, November 1984, pp. 16–17.

65. 'Nuclear-Free Zones: the First Five Years', *Sanity*, November 1985, pp. 13–18.

66. *Disarmament Campaigns*, February–March 1986, p. 2.

67. Offczors and Ruete, pp. 221–15.

68. Johnstone, *The Politics of Euromissiles*, p. 144.

69. Women's International League for Peace and Freedom, 'International Women's Day Brussels, March 1983', (Geneva, 1983).

70. Dion van den Berg, 'Cruise in The Netherlands', *Sanity*, September 1985, pp. 20–1.

71. Thoman R. Rochon, *Mobilizing for Peace: the Antinuclear Movements in Western Europe* (Princeton, New Jersey, Princeton University Press, 1985) pp. 12–20.

72. David Ormrod, 'The Churches and the Nuclear Arms Race, 1945–85', in Richard Taylor and Nigel Young (eds), *Campaigns for Peace* (Manchester, Manchester University Press, 1987) p. 214.

73. 'Five Nations Supplement', *END Journal*, **6**, October–November 1983.

74. Minnion and Bolsover, *CND Story*, p. 39.

75. 'Two Million on the Street', *END Bulletin*, **8**, Spring 1982, p. 16; *Disarmament Campaigns*, **5**, April 1981, p. 11.

76. *Peace News*, 10 June 1983, p. 6.

77. Johnstone, pp. 47–8; Rochon, pp. 137–8; *Observer*, 1 April 1984, p. 11.

When the West German Admiral Elmar Schmäling was dismissed in January 1990 for criticizing NATO nuclear strategy, *Sanity*, March 1990, interviewed him and ran a parallel article on Generals for Peace, *'Breaking Ranks'*, pp. 15–16.

78. Rochon, p. 37.
79. Paul Byrne, *The Campaign for Nuclear Disarmament* (London, Croom Helm, 1988) pp. 54–6.
80. Lynne Jones (ed.), *Keeping the Peace* (London, Women's Press, 1983) has chapters on both the Dutch and West German Organizations, and on WONT
81. John Mattausch, *A Commitment to Campaign: a Sociological Study of CND* (Manchester, Manchester University Press, 1989).
82. Rochon, p. 149. Byrnes in fact found that union membership was slightly higher among those in middle-class jobs than in working-class jobs.
83. Ormrod, pp. 211–12.
84. *END Newsletter*, **1**, 1985, p. 2.
85. Boeker, *END Bulletin*, February 1981, p. 7; Rochon, p. 130.
86. The Report of the British Medical Association's Board of Science and Education, *The Medical Effects of Nuclear War* (Chichester, John Wiley, 1983).
87. Rochon, pp. 140–3.
88. Johnstone, p. 144.
89. Rochon, p. 142.
90. *Peace News*, 22 March 1985, p. 6.
91. Bruce George and Jonathan Marcus, 'Unilateralism's Second Wave: The 1983 General Election and After', *Political Quarterly*, **55**, 1, 1984, p. 63.
92. Bruce Russett and Donald R. Deluca, 'Theater Nuclear Forces: Public Opinion in Western Europe', *Political Science Quarterly*, **98**, 1983, pp. 179–96.
93. Malvern Lumsden, 'Nuclear Weapons and the New Peace Movement', *The Arms Race and Arms Control 1983: the Shorter SIPRI Yearbook* (London, Taylor and Francis), pp. 100–1 for 1980 and 1981 figures; for 1983 figures see Eymert den Ouden, 'Public Opinion and Nuclear Weapons', *The Arms Race and Arms Control 1984: the Shorter SIPRI Yearbook* (London, Taylor and Francis) p. 16, for West Germany, and END Briefing Notes on Belgium.
94. A poll of university-educated Europeans suggested those over fifty were most pro-NATO, but a majority in all age-groups backed NATO. Russett and Deluce, pp. 185–7.
95. On Marplan poll see Tony Chafer, 'Politics and the Perception of Risk: A Study of Anti-Nuclear Movements in Britain and France', *West European Politics*, **8**, 1, 1985, p. 22, n. 28; and on 1982 polls see Lumsden, p. 101.
96. See Rochon, p. 159.
97. Johnstone, pp. 141.–2.
98. Johnstone, p. 50–1.
99. Goedele de Keersmaker, 'The Future in the Balance', *END Journal* **14**, December 1984–January 1985, pp. 20–1.

100. Rochon, p. 159.
101. On UK Freeze proposals see Christopher Meredith, 'First Step, the Freeze', in Ron Huzzard and Christopher Meredith (eds), *World Disarmament: an Idea Whose Time Has Come* (Nottingham, Spokesman, 1985), pp. 177–82.
102. 'Secret Society: Cabinet', TV programme on Channel 4, 9 April, 1991. Government sensitivity to these revelations was demonstrated by a Special Branch raid on BBC Scotland in 1986, before the programme was broadcast, and by its successful pressure on the BBC Governors to suppress the programme, Channel 4 remade the programme from the original BBC script.
103. Mariano Aguirre, 'An Iberian Nuclear Free Zone', END Papers 12, Spring 1986 (Bertrand Russell Peace Foundation), pp. 23–4.
104. END Briefing 'Spain and NATO'.
105. See Gregory F. Treverton, *Spain: Domestic Politics and Security Policy*, Adelphi Paper 204, London, IISS, 1986; Aguirre p. 24.
106. Treverton, p. 31.
107. Ibid, p. 12.
108. Ruth Stanley, 'How Felipe Won the Referendum', END Papers 12, pp. 66, 71.
109. Jonathan Steele, 'Spain Says "Yes, But" to NATO', *END Journal*, **21**, April–May 1986, p. 3; Stanley.
110. Jolyon Howarth, 'The Stumbling Block of Europe', *END Journal*, **3**, April–May 1983, p. 15.
111. Rochon, p. 104, on poll results.
112. Howarth, pp. 14–15.
113. Chafer, p. 12.
114. David Arnott, 'Movement in France', *Peace News*, 30 September 1983, p. 12.
115. Rochon, p. 144.
116. Chafer, p. 17.
117. See Bruce George and Jonathan Marcus, 'Unilateralism's Second Wave: the 1983 General Election and After', *Political Quarterly*, **55**, 1, January–March 1984, p. 70 for a comparison of first and second phases of CND.
118. Dan Smith, 'Who Needs the Peace Movement?' *Sanity*, November 1989, p. 12.
119. Esko Antola, *Campaigns Against European Peace Movements* (International Peace Bureau and Peace Union of Finland, 1984) examines smear campaigns alleging Moscow control or funding, but notes that in some cases government complaints that Soviet Embassy diplomats tried to influence national peace groups – for example in Denmark and perhaps Switzerland – have been proved to be true (p. 59).
120. Talbott, pp. 116–51.
121. April Carter, *Success and Failure in Arms Control Negotiations* (Oxford, Oxford University Press for SIPRI, 1989), Chapter 8 analyses the second stage of INF negotiations 1985–87.
122. Stephen Shenfield, 'In Quest of Sufficient Defence', *Détente*, **11** pp. 26–9; Gerard Holden, 'Alternative Defence and the Warsaw Treaty

Organization' in Michael Randle and Paul Rogers (eds), *Alternatives in European Security* (Aldershot, Gower, 1990), pp. 71–90.
123. Timothy Garton Ash, 'Raising the Iron Curtain', *New Society*, 18 April 1985.
124. Bruce Kent, 'I Knew We Were on to Something', *Sanity*, November–December, 1990, p. 12; John Barry, 'Just Who is Deterred by the Deterrent?', *The Times*, 18 August 1981.
125. Stephen F. Szabo, 'European Opinion After the Missiles', *Survival* November–December 1985, pp. 265–72.

CHAPTER SIX
Nuclear Disarmament Campaigns in North America and the Pacific in the 1980s

INTRODUCTION

Peace campaigns in the 1980s shared a strong sense of solidarity in a common struggle against the threat of nuclear weapons and often drew on popular desire for national autonomy and on resistance to being dominated by the rivalry of the USA and the Soviet Union. Campaigning priorities were, however, different in various parts of the world. Whereas in Western Europe new nuclear missiles and the political and military division of Europe were the central issues, in the Pacific nuclear weapons tests and environmental damage from radiation prompted protests and aroused public opinion. Opposition to US nuclear bases and to superpower rivalry in the Pacific was also important, especially for countries with bases, but inevitably more contentious.

The USA had significant military interests and political influence in both Western Europe and in the Pacific, and so American peace activists naturally made links with campaigners in both regions and offered campaigning support. Given the world impact of US military strategy and deployments, American peace researchers and defence experts also had a crucial role in providing information about US military programmes and analysing US policies.

Since groups within the USA played a major part in creating the 'Second Cold War', internal politics reflected renewed hostility to the Soviet Union, desire for greater US military strength and suspicion of liberals who were 'soft' on Communism. When President Carter attended the June 1979 Summit to sign the SALT II Treaty to set a ceiling to totals of nuclear missiles and warheads, hawkish Senator Henry Jackson publicly compared him to Chamberlain at Munich.

Carter later decided against asking the Senate to ratify SALT II because of the Soviet invasion of Afghanistan, but experts doubted whether he could in any case have secured ratification.[1] In this swing to the Right Ronald Reagan secured the Republican Party nomination to contest the 1980 Presidential election, which he then went on to win. It was scarcely surprising, therefore, that peace activity in the USA did not immediately match the swelling opposition to cruise and Pershing in Western Europe in 1980–81. Reagan's rhetoric and policies were, however, soon counterproductive. In June 1982 between 800,000 and one million demonstrators mustered in New York to demonstrate for an end to the arms race;[2] and the November 1982 mid-term Congressional elections showed that the growing American peace movement had significant support among the public and in the Democratic Party.

THE PEACE MOVEMENT IN THE USA

There was no single central peace organization in the USA comparable to CND in Britain, and campaigners had a variety of policy goals. The initiative which gained widest support was the call for a bilaterally negotiated freeze on the nuclear arsenals of the two superpowers. The Freeze strategy was to maximize popular and Congressional support for a limited, relatively non-controversial and respectable campaign. At the other end of the spectrum, religious and pacifist groups undertook imaginative and committed forms of direct action, which in some cases drew jail sentences of eight to eighteen years. A strong women's peace movement, which embraced both conventional lobbying and feminist peace camps, also existed. In the early 1980s the main focus was on nuclear weapons; by the mid-1980s there was increasing emphasis on opposing US intervention in other countries, and in particular in Central America. As in Europe and the Pacific there was also a tendency to combine opposition to nuclear weapons with protests against nuclear power.

All sections of the American peace movement offered assistance to the European campaign against cruise and Pershing II. Old and new organizations cooperated in a coalition for this purpose, including SANE, the nuclear disarmament grouping founded in 1957, and the pacifist Fellowship of Reconciliation. Their main aim was to lobby Congress and inform the public.[3] US peace researchers and activists toured Europe talking to European peace movements and attended

159

END conferences, and organized speaking tours for European peace representatives in the USA. Greenham women received strong support in taking their case against the missiles to the American courts. When Europeans demonstrated *en masse* in October 1983, Americans protested in sympathy in over a hundred towns and cities, and over 1,300 took part in non-violent direct action, in many cases against companies producing components for the missiles.[4]

Nevertheless, the primary emphasis of American researchers and activists was on the totality of the USA's nuclear arsenal and its world-wide strategy. The *Bulletin of the Atomic Scientists* continued to be an influential voice, calculating on its hypothetical clock in January 1981 that the world stood at 'four minutes to midnight' of a nuclear holocaust. *New Yorker* journalist Jonathan Schell wrote the most eloquent book on nuclear war, *The Fate of the Earth*, which became a best-seller, and American scientists investigated the theory, first fully analysed in *Science* in 1983, that a nuclear war would create a 'nuclear winter'.[5] Former members of the American military and arms control establishment, like Admiral Gene LaRocque of the Centre for Defence Information, criticized aspects of US and NATO strategy. Once the Reagan Administration had launched its SDI programme a wide range of scientific, defence and arms control experts subjected it to sustained criticism. Some of the critics of Reagan's policies were close to the peace movement, others were much more politically orthodox. But the fact that prominent figures such as former Defence Secretary Robert McNamara were publicly raising questions about existing policies, and arguing for a policy of 'No First Use' of nuclear weapons, lent a good deal of weight to peace movement opposition.[6]

The Freeze campaign, which had by far the widest political impact, had its origins in the difficult days of 1980. Randall Forsberg, researcher at the Institute for Defense and Disarmament Studies, drafted a four-page proposal 'Call to Halt the Arms Race' proposing a bilateral agreed freeze on testing, production and deployment of nuclear weapons, missiles and bombers. Her proposal circulated among peace groups during 1980, and during the November 1980 election peace activist Randy Kehler tested popular response in three senatorial districts in West Massachusetts, where 60 per cent voted for a freeze in a local referendum. When the National Freeze campaign was officially launched in March 1981, Randy Kehler became its national coordinator. The strategy of the campaign was to build up strong local support across the USA before trying to influence the Congress and eventually the Administration. Early action included using the forum provided by the New England town meeting to get citizens in New Hampshire and Vermont to debate and vote on Freeze resolutions. The Freeze also looked for endorsement from city and state bodies – the National Conference of Black Mayors and state legislatures in Massachusetts, Oregon and New York had voted in favour by mid-1981.[7]

Growing support for the Freeze by 1982 reflected both a response to the mass peace demonstrations in Western Europe in the autumn of 1981, widely reported in the US media, and a reaction to President Reagan's policies. His public statements about the possibility of fighting a nuclear war in Europe caused alarm, and his major investment in military projects created controversy. People saw the Administration slashing expenditure on social services in the 1981 and 1982 budgets while increasing the defence allocation. Since the President had also slashed taxes, by 1982 Congress too was becoming alarmed at the prospect of a spiralling budget deficit.[8]

Congress did indeed debate Freeze proposals in 1982. Senator Edward Kennedy's attempt to get a Senate debate was blocked by Republican control of the Senate committees, but in the House of Representatives a Freeze motion failed by only two votes in August 1982. The Reagan Administration had to lobby hard to persuade some reluctant members to oppose the Freeze. There was a long-standing liberal lobby in Congress favourable to arms control, but many members of Congress were also responding to the growing wave of support for the Freeze across the country. By late 1982 Congress had pressured a reluctant Administration to reopen negotiations with the Soviet Union on long-range strategic nuclear missiles under the new acronym START (Strategic Arms Reduction Talks). The November 1982 mid-term Congressional elections then returned an increased Democratic majority to the House of Representatives including, Freeze advocates claimed, thirty-nine more supporters of their position.[9]

Freeze campaigners across the USA mobilized public backing during the run-up to the 1982 elections. Nine out of ten states and thirty-four out of thirty-seven cities and counties voted in favour of Freeze proposals by majorities of about 60 per cent. Although the original support for Freeze had been primarily in New England – where by the end of 1982 over 440 town meetings had backed it – voters backed Freeze proposals in mid-western and western as well as eastern states, and in both rural areas and big cities. In California, where Reagan had previously been governor, a highly professional campaign drew on backing from a Los Angeles millionaire and prominent personalities to secure the 346,000 signatures needed to get a Freeze proposal on the ballot and then to campaign for it. Over 30 per cent of the electorate were able to vote for Freeze propositions and Randy Kehler claimed that this approximation to a national referendum was 'a victory for democracy itself'.[10]

When Freeze representatives met in February 1983 they already had plans to hold a mass lobby in Washington in March to press for the House of Representatives to pass the Freeze resolution scheduled to come before it. In May 1983 the House did indeed pass a Freeze resolution by 278 to 149 votes. The Conference agreed to organize demonstrations across the USA in October 1983 in solidarity with West European resistance to cruise and Pershing II, either at local town halls or at nuclear weapons bases or facilities. In addition the Conference responded to a call from Randall Forsberg to look ahead to the 1984 elections and set up a task force to plan measures to ensure that no candidate could get elected unless pledged to support the Freeze.[11]

Freeze groups intervened systematically in the long-drawn-out electoral process to influence the outcome. Their tactics in 1984 included programmes of voter registration – since increasing numbers of the poor or ethnic minorities and of women qualified to vote would swell probable support for more expenditure on welfare and less on weapons. Freeze supporters also used electioneering by candidates as an opportunity to distribute leaflets to waiting crowds and to ask the candidates questions about defence. The campaign organized demonstrations at the Party Conventions in the summer and tried to influence the party platforms adopted there. Freeze had no success with the Republicans, where the liberal wing had lost out to the Right and Reaganism, but in the Democratic Party many county conventions passed Freeze policies and all the main Democratic contenders for the presidential nomination looked to the peace groups for support. So in the Convention all the main speakers endorsed the idea of a nuclear freeze. The most important campaigning tactic of all was for the Freeze to support individual candidates. Here the peace movement borrowed from the far-Right, sent out carefully selected mailings to garner thousands of individual contributions to campaign funds, and set up Political Action Committees designed to help pro-Freeze candidates win against opponents of Freeze where their intervention might tip the balance. The Political Action Committees – Freeze Voter 84, and national PACS set up by the Council for a Livable World, SANE and Women's Action for Nuclear Disarmament – concentrated resources in key constituencies to canvass voters and to get their supporters to the voting booths.[12]

After Reagan won the 1984 election the Freeze movement reassessed its strategy. The campaign already had a sophisticated lobbying operation in Washington and decided to make renewed attempts to get Congress to refuse funds for new nuclear weapons and to call for an agreed moratorium with the Soviet Union on testing of both warheads and missiles. The fifth Freeze conference also agreed to try to strengthen its local constituences.[13] Radical critics of the Freeze had noted that its supporters were predominantly white, prosperous and middle class, although by mid-1983 it had the backing of ten labour unions, and black leaders like Jesse Jackson endorsed it. The conference committed itself to reach out to more trade union and minority organizations. In addition the Freeze included in its policy opposition to US intervention in Central America and agreed to join in demonstrations in Washington in April 1985 which combined demands to halt the arms race and to end intervention. During 1985 Freeze collected a million signatures to a petition for a comprehensive nuclear test ban. Nevertheless, the movement was losing its momentum.

The Freeze campaign, like its West European counterparts, had won support among many professional groupings who both helped to alert a long apathetic public and to influence their professional colleagues. The Union of Concerned Scientists, for example, contributed to teach-ins at universities, and Physicians for Social Responsibility, Educators for Social Responsibility and the Lawyers' Alliance for Nuclear Arms Control offered their expertise.[14]

The moral authority and respectability which public endorsement by the churches conferred counted for more in the USA than in some of the more secular societies of Western Europe. The Freeze had by 1981 won support from the Unitarians and the United Presbyterian Church, and dioceses within the Episcopalians and the National Council of Churches then gave their backing.[15] Bruce Kent noted that on his 1982 speaking tour in the USA, sponsored by Clergy and Laity Concerned, almost 'every large evening meeting was held in a church'; and he spoke in Pittsburgh on the same platform as an American cardinal.[16] The role of both the Protestant and Catholic Churches indicated the change in church attitudes since the 1950s, influenced by the Vietnam War. The American Catholic Church in particular had altered a good deal since Cardinal Spellman used to epitomize unyielding Cold War attitudes. Now some Catholic bishops were at the forefront of opposition to nuclear weapons: for example the Bishop of Amarillo, Texas, who called on workers not to assemble nuclear warheads at the local factory and the Archbishop of Seattle who urged tax resistance.[17] The official statement produced by the US bishops in their Pastoral Letter on War and Peace in the Nuclear Age, published in 1983, expressed grave reservations about many aspects of nuclear strategy, opposed NATO's 'first use' policy and called for immediate negotiated agreements to halt testing, production and deployment of new nuclear weapons.[18]

Whereas the Freeze sought political influence by winning maximum support on a minimum programme, the emphasis of protesters at nuclear bases and production plants was not on numbers, but on arousing public conscience and finding appropriate forms of direct resistance. Pacifists had initiated civil disobedience in the 1970s, well before the development of a mass movement, and continued their actions throughout the 1980s. The Trident submarine base at Bangor, Washington State, was the focus of one campaign; 112 demonstrators were jailed for six months for trespassing on the base in October 1979.[19] The Ground Zero Centre set up outside the base extended its protests to the 'white trains' carrying nuclear warheads from Texas to the Bangor base. The 'Tracks Campaign' aimed to alert communities along the route by holding vigils and by trying to halt the trains by sitting down on the tracks after giving the train drivers due warning.[20] A coalition of non-violent action groups brought a thousand to a MX missile base in January 1983 to oppose missile tests; protesters blocked the entrance and sat on silos inside the base.[21] A new national organization, American Peace Test, was set up early in 1986 to attract Freeze supporters to commit civil disobedience; this brought 250 to the Nevada test site in May 1986 to resist underground nuclear tests for the SDI programme.[22]

The most dramatic nonviolent direct action campaign was the 'Plowshares Action', which drew inspiration from the biblical injunctions to beat swords into ploughshares. In September 1980 eight Christian pacifists entered a General Electrics factory in Pennsylvania, which made nose cones for Minutemen missiles. The men and women hammered on the cones and spilt their own blood over them. Among the protesters were two Catholic priests, the Berrigan brothers, who had burned draft cards with napalm during the Vietnam War, and who believed that peace required total sacrifice. Eight years later over eighty people had undertaken similar demonstrations; many had been sentenced to terms of seven, eight or ten years in prison.[23] The Plowshares concept was adopted later by activists in Germany, Australia, The Netherlands, Sweden and Britain.

The women's movement for peace also embraced non-violent direct action. On 4 July 1983 2,000 women surrounded the Seneca Army base, believed to be a storage point for cruise and Pershing II missiles. They attached symbols to the fence and began to climb it, whereupon the police arrested them. Women then started a permanent camp at the base, consciously modelled on Greenham Common, so encouraging creation of women's camps elsewhere.[24] Women in the War Resisters' League helped to promote the Seneca camp and were also behind the Women's Pentagon Action, founded in 1980, which stressed the links between feminism and peace activity.

There were other women's peace organizations which were much more orthodox in their style of campaigning. Women Strike for Peace, set up in the early 1960s, undertook public education and pressure on Congressional candidates, and gave priority to preventing new missile deployments. Women's Action for Nuclear Disarmament, created by Dr Helen Caldicott, an eloquent speaker and author on the dangers of nuclear weapons and of radiation, focused on electoral activities.[25] The oldest organization, the American section of the Women's International League for Peace and Freedom (WILPF), put cruise and Pershing II at the forefront of their campaign in the early 1980s. After US intervention in Grenada in 1983 WILPF took up the controversial issue of American military involvement in Central America: it co-sponsored a conference on Nicaragua and peace in Central America early in 1984, and organized a speaking tour on Central America.[26]

WILPF was prepared to oppose American military intervention when WAND chose to limit itself to nuclear weapons and the Freeze was trying to maximize its popular support and avoid divisive questions about the USA's world role and its attitude to leftist regimes. However, many of the more radical peace groups began from 1984 to lay increasing emphasis on opposing Washington's role in Central America. While this emphasis was in tune with END's call for an end to superpower domination and bloc politics, and was approved by many European peace groups, it switched the emphasis away from nuclear weapons to a different kind of peace campaigning. Mobilization for Survival, which was set up in 1975 and had been primarily responsible for the June 1982 protests, had by 1985 developed into a network of about 160 groups campaigning both on nuclear weapons and nuclear power, and on non-intervention.[27]

ASSESSING THE US MOVEMENT

Comparison of the peace movement in the 1980s with the protests against nuclear testing and nuclear weapons in the late 1950s shows a spectacular increase in the number of political activists and in those willing to commit civil disobedience. The campaigns of the 1960s and changed attitudes in many sectors of American society had created an entirely new climate for peace protest, despite the reassertion of right-wing politics and Christian fundamentalism which helped Reagan to win the 1980 election. A specific comparison between the quite minor campaign mounted by SANE between 1957 and 1960 and the achievements of Freeze between 1981 and 1985 indicates how much closer peace campaigners had come to influencing US policies.

Nevertheless, we need to look critically at what the Freeze actually did achieve, beyond its impressive ability to mount locally based campaigns in 1982 and to bring pressure to bear in the 1984 election. Freeze chalked up significant public support for its aim to halt the build-up of nuclear weapons. The depth and seriousness of much public support was, however, questionable. Despite the educational efforts of the Freeze, several polls in 1984 suggested that many who supported the idea thought that President Reagan did so too.[28] Apart from fundamental problems about the level of political knowledge among large sections of the electorate, the Freeze also had difficulties in maintaining the clarity of its own initial policy. In order to maximize support, the authors of resolutions in Congress, those framing propositions for the voters and candidates for political office were often inclined to tone down the call for an immediate moratorium on weapons development. Politicians supporting Freeze would, moreover, sometimes endorse military projects if local votes seemed to be at stake.[29]

If the Freeze is measured by its direct effect on the Reagan Administration, then it had no immediate impact on arms and arms control policy during Reagan's first term. The Administration continued its drive for military superiority and refused to negotiate seriously on arms control. On the other hand by 1984 the strength of public opinion supporting the Freeze had an influence on Reagan's election rhetoric, and may have encouraged his remarkable conversion to an advocate of détente and arms cuts by 1986.

The Freeze campaign did have a significant impact on Congress and therefore indirectly helped to curb some elements of the Administration's ambitious arms programme. While the House and the Senate were clearly alarmed about the economic implications of Reagan's policies, and also motivated by a growing desire to assert Congressional powers over the defence budget, Freeze had a leverage on public opinion and the electorate that certainly could not be ignored. Moreover, Freeze provided a policy platform that many members of Congress were happy to promote because it provided a basis for resisting a military build-up, while sounding reassuringly moderate.

Freeze reflected many of the strengths and weaknesses of the political process in the USA. It illustrated the scope for citizens' initiatives to use the numerous channels of influence on legislators and government and the array of campaigning techniques developed by numerous pressure groups. It also demonstrated, however, the superficiality of much public opinion and the narrow scope for advocating alternatives imposed by political orthodoxy in Washington. In addition political activists were even more vulnerable than their West European counterparts to swings in fashion for liberal causes. By 1985 many campaigners turned their attention from nuclear weapons to the issue of apartheid in South Africa.

THE PROTESTS IN CANADA

Canada's foreign policy was shaped by its proximity to the USA and by its links to Europe, and tended to combine loyalty to the Atlantic Alliance with displays of limited independence on nuclear weapons and disarmament issues. The Liberal prime minister, Pierre Trudeau, in office almost continuously since the late 1960s, pursued this approach by proposing policies to limit nuclear weapons at the United Nations in 1978, but endorsing the NATO 1979 dual-track decision on deploying ground-launched cruise missiles. The evolution of peace protest in Canada also reflected the influence of both the American and European campaigns.

There was no single issue or organization to focus protest at the beginning of the 1980s, and most peace groups were purely local in membership and influence. Two organizations which did emerge out of the 1970s with a wider base were Project Ploughshares, which was centred on Ontario and had church backing, and Operation Dismantle, with an office in Ottawa. Both engaged in campaigns on the case for disarmament and both endorsed proposals for nuclear-weapon-free zones locally and advocated a nuclear-weapon-free Canada. The Canadian peace movement gained momentum in 1981 in response to European missile protests and the growing Freeze campaign in the USA, and at that stage directed much of its energy towards the June 1982 UN Special Session on Disarmament. Thousands in East Canada travelled to New York on 12 June 1982. By the end of the year, however, most Canadian activists had switched their energies to trying to prevent the testing of US air-launched cruise missiles over Canada.[30]

Governmental discussions between Ottawa and Washington had begun in 1978 on the possibility of testing US weapons in Canada and in 1980 Carter specifically asked for arrangements for testing air-launched cruise missiles. According to a press leak in Washington in March 1982 Trudeau had reached a secret agreement with Reagan to allow cruise tests, but a formal 'umbrella agreement' on US weapons testing in Canada was not signed until February 1983. The agreement allowed for testing cruise over Northern Alberta, and in July 1983 the Canadian Government announced that it would permit up to six test flights of air-launched cruise missiles a year over its territory.[31]

Demonstrations against cruise testing began when 15,000 protested in Ottawa in the autumn of 1982 and there were further marches and rallies in major cities when the umbrella agreement was signed and after the Government's July 1983 statement. About 35,000 delivered letters of protest to Trudeau, who reacted to growing opposition with an Open Letter in May 1983 in which he argued that Canada's NATO obligations required agreement to cruise testing and accused his critics of anti-Americanism. Operation Dismantle began a court case against the federal Government under Article 7 of the new constitution, claiming that cruise testing would infringe rights to life and security. The strength of opposition was indicated when up to 65,000 converged on Vancouver, British Columbia, in April 1983 and up to 75,000 protested in forty different towns and cities in October that year.[32]

Opposition to cruise testing was widespread in Canada during 1983, when opinion polls indicated over 50 per cent of the public were against the tests. The main opposition party, the Conservatives, endorsed testing, but the ruling Liberal Party was divided on the issue, and according to rumour doubts extended to the Cabinet. The more left-wing New Democratic Party unsuccessfully tabled a motion to stop the cruise tests in the federal Parliament.[33] The electorally insignificant Green Party had a comprehensive policy against nuclear weapons. Outside of the political parties the campaign for nuclear-weapon-free zones had influential backing from the Canadian Council of Churches, the Canadian Labour Congress and the Federation of Canadian Municipalities, and personal support from the mayors of Ottawa and Toronto. Several cities and the Province of Quebec as a whole voted to become nuclear-weapon-free zones in referenda.[34] In British Columbia, where 130 organizations including church and trade union groups combined in the End the Arms Race Committee, the Vancouver City Council distributed material on the effects of a nuclear attack.[35]

Once cruise testing had begun it ceased to be so central to protests. During 1984 the hundreds of local peace groups debated the desirability of a national body, and, despite opposition from those favouring a more decentralized structure, the Canadian Peace Alliance came into being.[36] A new Parliamentary Commission on defence and foreign policy, set up under the Conservative Government in 1985, encouraged public debate and gave peace activists a useful platform to present their views. The Canadian Peace Alliance also launched a campaign against any Canadian involvement in research for the US SDI programme in 1985.[37] The Canadian Government did distance itself from official participation in SDI research in 1986, but this allowed corporate research to continue.

Non-violent direct action campaigns sprang up alongside more conventional tactics, as they had elsewhere. There was a sustained protest against Canadian involvement in production of cruise missiles at the US-owned subsidiary Litton Systems in Toronto, where local papers announced a contract to make cruise missile guidance systems at the end of 1978. The Canadian Government gave a subsidy to the company, and news broke in late 1982 that the Government had also earlier granted a five-year interest-free loan. The Alliance for Non-violent Action and the Cruise Missile Conversion Project in Toronto ran a campaign at the factory from 1979 to 1983, which included civil disobedience demonstrations at the gates. These protests were not, however, so widely publicized as a bomb planted at Litton by a group prepared to use violence in October 1982, when several workers were hurt in the blast.[38] The Nanoose Conversion Campaign organized a peace walk to the US naval testing site at Nanoose Bay, Victoria Island, in August 1984 and set up a permanent peace camp there in April 1985.[39] Peace protest converged with environmental issues and the cultural rights of minorities when the Innu Indians decided to resist military low-flying by West German, British and Dutch aircraft training over their homeland in Labrador. Groups of Innu began to occupy bombing ranges and to obstruct aircraft on the runways at the Goose Bay NATO base until arrested. The Innu campaign included political and legal action – sending a delegation to Europe in 1989 to lobby, and to explore the possibility of injunctions against low-flying in West European courts. Two Canadian Government ministers agreed to meet the Innu to hear their complaints but did not promise to stop the flights; indeed the Government was urging expansion of the NATO base.[40]

The peace movement in Canada in the 1980s reflected the renewed fears of nuclear war felt in many parts of the world and the possibility of mobilizing widespread support to oppose new weapons policies. It also showed how local communities usually far removed from peace concerns – such as cattle and wheat farmers in Alberta – may react against the threat of military activity in their area.[41] Popular dislike of cruise testing drew in addition on a desire for Canadian independence from the USA. There were therefore some parallels with the West European campaigns against ground-launched cruise missiles and later against involvement in SDI research.

THE CAMPAIGN FOR A NUCLEAR-FREE PACIFIC

The campaign in the Pacific area had some similarities with the nuclear disarmament movements in Europe and North America, but was in a number of ways significantly different. The Pacific, like Europe, was a crucial area of strategic confrontation between the USA and USSR, and one of growing importance in the 1980s. So one facet of the movement was opposition to the string of US bases and military installations in Australia, Japan, the Philippines, Micronesia and in Hawaii. Protesters were also against missile testing in the Pacific by both the USA and USSR, and worried by the presence of US and Soviet fleets carrying nuclear weapons. This opposition was linked to a strong sentiment in favour of non-alignment especially in many of the Pacific Islands and in New Zealand.

The campaign against nuclear weapons received considerable impetus from continued French nuclear testing in the Pacific and growing awareness in the 1980s of the long-term impact of US and British nuclear explosions up to 1963. The nuclear tests aroused strong environmental concerns, and also symbolized great power arrogance, colonialism and implicit racialism in the arbitrary attitude displayed towards the rights and needs of the local people displaced and endangered by the tests. So the Green and peace movements fused in their opposition to nuclear testing. They made common cause too in resisting uranium mining in Australia, which provided potential material for nuclear bombs and also inflicted immediate damage on the local environment and health. Growing pressures for independence in Micronesia and Polynesia, and assertion of Aborigine rights in Australia, publicized their suffering due to their territories being used as nuclear testing grounds. The peace movement of the 1980s therefore drew on multiple sources of opposition to the Pacific being turned into a 'nuclear lake', and had its roots in campaigns of the 1970s.

The French nuclear tests provided a catalyst for developing anti-nuclear consciousness, and opposition to them provoked extreme reaction from the French authorites. After Algeria became independent, the French government had to abandon its Sahara testing ground and decided to continue nuclear testing in its Polynesian colony, taking over the uninhabited islands of Mururoa and Fangataufa. Here France exploded forty-four nuclear bombs in the atmosphere (asserting its right to flout the 1963 Test Ban Treaty, which it had not signed) between 1966 and 1974, and conducted numerous underground tests thereafter.[42] The environmental campaigning body, Greenpeace, took over from the nuclear disarmers of the 1950s and 1960s the tactic of trying to sail into the nuclear testing area, and achieved widespread publicity in the early 1970s when their yacht, the *Vega*, was rammed and boarded by the French navy. The Ecology candidate in the French presidential elections of 1981 sailed on the *Vega* towards Mururoa at the end of the year, but was persuaded to desist in return for a promise by the French Government that radioactive pollution in the area would be independently assessed. The same year the Polynesian Territorial Assembly voted for the first time for the testing programme to be suspended.[43] In the context of mounting anti-nuclear concern, the Greenpeace *Rainbow Warrior* was due to lead a flotilla of small ships into the Mururoa testing area in the summer of 1985. While it was moored in Auckland harbour, three French secret service agents blew up the boat, killing the Portuguese photographer who was on board at the time. The incident greatly angered the New Zealand Government, caused a world wide furore and provoked a political scandal in France itself which forced the resignation of the French Defence Minister.[44] Tahitian opponents of the French nuclear tests had planned to join the *Rainbow Warrior* protest in their canoes. Their leader was arrested for marching against the test by French colonial authorities – Tahiti being one of two Polynesian Islands still controlled by France in 1985.[45] Mitterrand's government showed no willingness to respond to protests from the peoples or governments of the Pacific.

While opposition mounted to continuing French nuclear tests, popular consciousness of the dangerous legacy of US and British nuclear explosions also grew. The USA had captured Micronesia from the Japanese during the war and in 1947 acquired 'Strategic Trusteeship' of the seven groupings of 2,100 islands. The US Administration then designated Bikini, within the Marshall Islands, as a nuclear testing site and transported the people living there to Rongerik; when in 1959 the USA chose Kwajalein (also in the Marshalls) for a missile testing site it again moved the several thousand inhabitants to a nearby island. By 1963 the USA had exploded sixty-six nuclear bombs in the Marshalls area. Although US atmospheric testing then ceased, the radiation lived on, and delegations from the Marshall and Marianas Islands and from Guam and Belau lobbied Congress in 1979. The people of Rongelap, showered with fall-out from the 1954 Bikini 15 megaton H bomb test, were found in 1976 to be suffering from a high proportion of thyroid tumours. The islanders also suffered from leukaemia, and babies were born deformed.[46] The Marshallese Government, established in 1983 in a Compact of Free Association with the USA, agreed the Rongelap islanders should move to a less contaminated island, but the 260 people living on Rongelap had to appeal to Greenpeace to get help with transport to the new island.

British nuclear tests had been carried out on Christmas Island and in Australia in the 1950s with the unquestioning cooperation of the Menzies Government. In the 1980s the Australian Government set up a Commission to investigate claims that Australians, in particular Aborigines, were harmed by the British tests in Maralinga, Southern Australia, and on the Montebello Islands. The Commission carried out a series of hearings in London in early 1985, and condemned the refusal of the British Government to make evidence available.[47] The Commission roused interest in the British media partly because British Veterans involved in carrying out the tests had been campaigning for compensation for exposure to radioactivity.

Growing desire for independence among Pacific Islanders encouraged resistance to a permanent US military presence. A number of the Kwajalein islanders evicted to make way for US missile testing began to return to the island.[48] The central struggle in Micronesia, however, centred round the Compacts of Free Association offered by the USA, which promised financial aid in return for the presence of US bases. Most of the new governments accepted these terms, but a significant section of the Belauan Islanders, who had opted for a new nuclear-free Constitution in 1979, voted repeatedly in successive referenda held by the pro-American authorities to keep their nuclear-free status and to reject the US Compact. When the President of Belau claimed that a referendum in August 1987 had endorsed the Compact by 73 per cent of the votes (and had also overturned the requirement for a 75 per cent vote to change the nuclear-free clause in the Constitution) women elders in Belau filed a lawsuit to contest the validity of the referendum. The court ruled in their favour in April 1988, but there were renewed pressures for a further referendum to be held in 1990. When this was held in February 1990, the Government again failed to achieve 75 per cent of the vote.[49]

The main symbol of the desire for a Pacific free of nuclear weapons was the 1985 Treaty of Rarotonga, agreed in 1985 by the members of the South Pacific Forum. The Treaty called for no nuclear testing, no nuclear waste dumping (planned in particular by Japan) and no stationing of nuclear weapons in the area. The Melanesian states, and the peace movements in Australia and New Zealand, had hoped to exclude the great powers from pursuing any military role in the Pacific, but the Polynesian states, especially Tonga, were not opposed to a continuing US presence. The Labour Governments of Australia and New Zealand insisted on limiting the Treaty's scope in return for their signatures. As a result Vanuatu, which had urged a wider treaty, refused to sign the Rarotonga Treaty. The Treaty has little practical effect, since the USA and Britain have not acceded to it (although they claim they do not contravene it) and France has simply ignored it.[50] But it does represent a formal governmental and legal endorsement of some of the aims articulated ten years earlier at the first of a series of international conferences for a nuclear-free Pacific held in Fiji.

Signing the Rarotonga Treaty was the major gesture made by the Australian Labour Government, elected in 1983, towards opposing nuclear weapons. Though the Government was also willing to refuse staging facilities in 1985 to US forces monitoring MX missile tests, it took no action against US or British ships carrying nuclear weapons using Australian ports. The peace movement grew as in other parts of the world. On Palm Sunday 1983 an estimated 200,000 turned out across Australia to demonstrate for disarmament; by April 1985 numbers had risen to about 400,000. The organizational basis and the strength of the movement varied in different states of Australia. People for Nuclear Disarmament was set up in Melbourne in 1981 and mustered support from the Roman Catholic and Anglican churches and from the Victoria state Government. A similar coalition based in Sydney, New South Wales, also had high-level church, union and political party backing. The peace movement was weaker in other states, though the Queensland campaign drew on an existing group resisting uranium mining, and there were long established peace bodies such as the Quakers and Women's International League for Peace and Freedom in Tasmania. By 1985 the movement had spread beyond the major cities; the first peace demonstration ever was held in Alice Springs, which is near to the Pine Gap US satellite communications base, one of the main US installations in Australia under the ANZUS Pact. The only Federal Party giving priority to nuclear and disarmament issues, however, was the Democratic Party, which had broken away from the Liberals and which had representation in the Senate.[51]

A much stronger nuclear disarmament movement existed in New Zealand. Hostility to French nuclear tests dated from the early 1970s, when the New Zealand Labour Government of that time had, together with Australia, taken France to the International Court, which issued an interim injunction against further tests. A popular campaign against US warships with nuclear weapons visiting New Zealand ports began in 1976, when activists in small boats tried to block a US vessel entering Wellington harbour and were backed by harbour workers. Majority popular opinion did not oppose such US naval visits until 1983; public opinion changed as hundreds of local community groups began peace campaigning and local councils declared themselves 'nuclear-free'. When a Labour government, under David Lange, was elected in 1984, committed to oppose ships carrying nuclear-weapons docking in New Zealand, popular pressure ensured that, for once, a socialist party in office maintained its election pledges on a disarmament issue. The Lange Government stressed loyalty to the ANZUS Pact and did not try to remove the US communications and monitoring bases on its territory. The US Administration brought strong political pressure on the Lange Government to abandon its ban on nuclear-weapons-carrying vessels, largely because it was afraid resistance to US nuclear strategy in the Pacific might spread to more strategically vital countries.[52] But public support for a nuclear-free policy grew. By 1987 polls indicated a majority favoured leaving ANZUS, and Labour won the 1988 election partly on the strength of its stand against the USA on nuclear-weapons ships.[53] US and British pressure on New Zealand had served to strengthen New Zealand national pride and sense of independence, while the people of New Zealand did not feel exposed to any major military threat which would justify subservience to the USA. The image and rhetoric of the Reagan Administration also alienated many New Zealanders.

Comparison of the New Zealand peace movement with its counterpart in Australia raises interesting questions about the conditions which promote success or failure. Andrew Mack, in an analysis of both campaigns, notes that in Australia opinion poll evidence suggests

174

that the movement managed to mobilize its natural constituency – about 20 per cent of the population – but that during the peak of peace protest between 1984 and 1985 popular support for the ANZUS alliance rose from 71 per cent to 77 per cent. So peace activism could be seen as partially counterproductive. In fact public attitudes to ANZUS, US bases and defence spending had been more favourable to the peace campaigners' policies during the earlier period of détente than in the early 1980s. The Second Cold War fears which created renewed peace activism also made it harder for the activists to win over public support in Australia.[54]

Mack ascribes the greater success of campaigners in New Zealand partly to the differences in public attitudes to nuclear weapons in the two countries dating back to the 1960s. He also suggests, however, that the New Zealand movement was more cohesive and had a more single-minded focus on banning visits by nuclear-armed vessels to its harbours. Prominent peace campaigners were, moreover, also leading Labour Party politicians and helped to hold the Labour Government to its commitment to stop visits by nuclear ships.

The campaign for a nuclear-free Pacific represented a major effort to achieve transnational coordination between the numerous small Pacific island communities and independent groups in the major Pacific rim states of Japan, Australia, New Zealand and the USA. The Conference for a Nuclear Free Pacific (launched in Fiji in 1975) met again in Hawaii in 1980. Later conferences were held in Okinawa in 1981, in the former French Polynesian colony of Vanuatu in 1983 and in Manila, the Philippines, in 1987. A resources centre for this movement had been set up in Honolulu in 1980.[55] Activists in the USA offered practical support – for example women lawyers began to assist the women elders in Belau who were challenging the 1987 referendum. Campaigners in Europe also established links with activists in the Pacific movement. Greenham Women organized a speaking tour of Britain for a Maori woman and a woman from the Marianas in 1985, and Women Working for a Nuclear-Free and Independent Pacific was established as a campaigning group in Britain.[56] The peace and environmental movement did begin to establish a transnational consciousness of events and issues the other side of the world. Roman Bedor, a Beluan lawyer campaigning to retain his island's nuclear-free status, had signatures to his petition from over eighty countries after eighteen months; and Tahitian activist Charlie Ching expressed surprise and pleasure at the support he received in France, West Germany and Britain.[57]

The campaigns for a nuclear-free Pacific have achieved little judged by their ambitious goals. But campaigners can claim a strong base in public opinion and wide-ranging support for at least some of their aims. The Pacific Conference of Churches for example passed a resolution in 1981 against all nuclear tests, passage of nuclear vessels and against nuclear dumping. One reason for the breadth of support has been that nuclear weapons were linked to wider environmental issues – opposition to proposed dumping of nuclear waste by Japan was a central part of the campaign. Nuclear testing, which combines refining nuclear weapons with widespread radioactive pollution, provokes strong resistance – as was shown in the 1950s. Finally, anti-nuclear campaigners have drawn on national pride and demands for democratic independence to resist the nuclear role of the USA and France. For example the Nuclear-Free Philippines Coalition, founded in 1981 primarily to oppose the building of a nuclear power plant, extended its opposition to US bases and US intervention in the Philippines in 1983 and joined in the movement to overthrow the Marcos regime.[58] French testing in its Pacific colonies aroused anger rather similar to the African response to French tests in the Sahara in the early 1960s. The Secretary-General of Vanuatu (which became independent of France in 1980) told a Nuclear-Free Pacific Conference that: 'it has always been my stern belief that nuclearism cannot be separated from colonialism, especially in the Pacific'.[59] The strong anti-nuclear stance of the Vanuatu Government was, however, vulnerable because of the extreme instability of its internal politics.

The Japanese peace movement played a less central role in the campaigns in the Pacific than might have been suggested by its place in the first phase of the nuclear disarmament movement, although the Socialist Party peace organization, Gensuikin, proposed the Conference for a Nuclear-Free Pacific in 1980. A historian of the movement suggested in the early 1980s that domestic circumstances were unfavourable to peace activism, since a more militant nationalism was emerging, which called for military prestige as well as economic power, since there was increased concern about the Soviet military threat and since the mood of young people was apolitical.[60] The divisions between the Socialist and Communist wings of the movement, even though Gensuikin and Gensuikyo began to cooperate again in 1977, also limited its potential.

Nevertheless, the renaissance of nuclear disarmament campaigns in Europe, the focus provided by the UN Second Special Session on Disarmament in 1982, and the USA's 1983 decision to deploy sea-launched cruise missiles on their Pacific fleet in 1984, all helped to revitalize peace action in Japan. Another split within the Communist Gensuikyo in 1984 created confusion, but led to a Non-Aligned Peace Office being created in Tokyo to coordinate grass-roots peace groups outside the political parties. A movement of petitions, songs, badges, mass demonstrations and token strikes against the missiles did involve many sections of Japanese society, including school children, in 1984. A nuclear-free-zones movement also took off, and by the end of 1984 included many towns and cities and the Prefecture of Kanagwa, which incorporated twenty military bases. Independent citizens groups had taken the initiative in the 1970s in protesting against US bases and in the early 1980s against visits by US vessels, after a former US Ambassador to Japan revealed in 1981 that the US navy docked in Japanese ports with nuclear weapons aboard. Although the Japanese Socialist Party seemed to be weakening in its opposition to the US military role in Japan during 1984, Gensuikin had adopted a policy against nuclear power and worked with the Nuclear-Free Pacific network to oppose Japanese nuclear dumping.[61] When Japanese participation in the US SDI research programme looked likely in 1985, the Japanese Scientists Association declared its opposition. Strong local campaigns also developed against the US military presence, especially where environmental dangers could also be invoked. For example about 85 per cent of the people in Miyake Island signed a petition against the building of a US airfield designed primarily for night flying.[62]

The variety of national and local initiatives against various aspects of the US superpower presence and the nuclear arms build-up of the Reagan Administration had no prospect of changing the policies of the ruling Liberal Democratic Party, which had been constantly in power since the period of post-war US occupation. The policies adopted by the Socialist Party were also of secondary importance so long as the party failed to pose a major electoral challenge to the Liberal Democrats, despite the crises and scandals which erupted in successive governments during the 1980s.

THE SCOPE OF THE TRANSNATIONAL NUCLEAR DISARMAMENT MOVEMENT

No campaign comparable to the agitation against nuclear weapons and nuclear pollution in the Pacific emerged in other regions of Asia or Africa, but there were signs of opposition in both India and the Indian Ocean. Since there has been a Gandhian movement in India, committed to non-violent social change, ever since Gandhi's death in 1948, and since the Indian Government exploded a nuclear device in 1974 (making India a potential nuclear-weapons state) the emergence of an Indian CND group in 1983 seemed overdue. The new group tried to draw on interest in US and Soviet nuclear weapons to explore the dangers of India's nuclear programme. Several other small groups concerned with nuclear proliferation emerged in major cities, attracting students and middle-class professional people.[63]

A more dynamic grass-roots campaign arose when the Indian Government attempted to take over land in Baliapal, Orissa, for a missile-testing range in 1985. The local people moved from petitions and protest meetings to militant resistance, in which the 126 villages in the area kept watch and then came together to drive off government officials trying to enter the proposed missile range. They also built barricades on the roads into the area and for three years ran their own local administration. Their resistance was so effective that early in 1987 the Government imposed an economic blockade on the area in an effort to quell the movement. Eventually in the 1989 elections the plan to convert the fertile agricultural area into a missile base was taken up by the opposition. When the opposition, pledged to stop the missile range, won the election the local people dismantled the barricades.[64]

When the farmers in Baliapal began to protest they were initially acting in defence of their traditional lands. They went on, however, to analyse the plans for the range, which included testing long-range missiles developed jointly with the USSR, and they extended their policy to call for no missile bases in India and for a zone of peace in the Indian Ocean. The aim of a peaceful Indian Ocean was taken up by a group in Mauritius, which began in 1985 to contact groups who might form part of a network in a campaign to achieve the goal embodied in a 1971 UN Resolution to demilitarize the Indian Ocean.[65]

Representatives of small new peace groups could meet with the larger and longer-established campaigns in the annual END Convention. The second Convention in West Berlin in 1983 included delegates from North America, Japan and the Pacific. At the 1984 Perugia Convention representatives from India, the Middle East and Central and South America joined in.[66] However, major regional campaigns with a primary focus on nuclear weapons were confined to Western Europe, North America and the Pacific, and it was between these regions that there was the greatest scope for cooperation. Broader political and economic issues in North-South relations arose at transnational conventions and were pursued by some peace groups, for example those campaigning on the arms trade (see Chapter 8). Many peace activists in the USA were also engaged in opposing US intervention in Central America and sympathetic to groups resisting dictatorship and militarism in Latin America. Nuclear weapons and the East-West confrontation tended, nevertheless, to dominate peace activity in the developed West, a focus sometimes criticized by Third World commentators. Indeed, overcoming the East-West divide in Europe and relations with unofficial peace and opposition circles in Eastern Europe often dominated the annual END Conventions.

NOTES AND REFERENCES

1. Strobe Talbott, *Endgame: the Inside Story of SALT II* (New York, Harper and Row, 1979); Raymond L. Garthoff, *Détente and Confrontation: American Soviet Relations from Nixon to Reagan* (Washington, DC, The Brookings Institution, 1985).
2. Thomas R. Rochon, *Mobilizing for Peace: the Antinuclear Movement in Western Europe* (Princeton, New Jersey, Princeton University Press, 1988), p. 5; The International Institute for Strategic Studies, *Strategic Survey 1982–1983* (London, IISS, 1983), p. 37.
3. Genie Silver, Speech to 8 March Rally, printed in Women's International League for Peace and Freedom, *International Women's Day, Brussels March 1983* (Geneva, 1983), p. 24.
4. Jane Dibblin, 'An Outpouring of Protest – Peaceful and Determined', *END Journal*, 7, December 1983–January 1984, p. 11.
5. Jonathan Schell, *The Fate of the Earth* (London, Pan Books 1982). On the theory of the nuclear winter see: 'The Nuclear Winter Debate', *Strategic Survey 1984–1985* (London, IISS, 1985). pp. 23–7; and Carl Sagan, 'Nuclear War and Climatic Catastrophe: Some Policy Implications', *Foreign Affairs*, Vol. **62**, Winter 1983–84, pp. 257–92.
6. See article written jointly with George Kennan, McGeorge Bundy and Gerard Smith, 'Nuclear Weapons and the Atlantic Alliance', *Foreign Affairs*, **60**, 4, Spring 1982, pp. 753–68.
7. Matthew Evangelista, Randall Forsberg and Mark Niedergang, 'END and a Nuclear Weapon Freeze', *ADIU Report*, **3**, 4, July–August 1981, p. 4 and Dimitrios I. Roussopoulos, *The Coming of World War Three*, Vol. 1, (Montreal, Black Rose Books, 1986), p. 141.
8. *Strategic Survey 1982–1983*, pp. 37–8.
9. Ibid., p. 37, *The Economist*, 14 August 1982, p. 38.
10. Randy Kehler, 'Reagan Feels the Freeze', *END Journal*, **2**, February–March 1983, p. 8; and Roussopoulos, pp. 142–4.
11. 'Freeze: a Mandate to Stop the Nuclear Arms Race', *END Journal*, **3**, April–May 1983, p. 6.

12. Sam Hirsch, 'Peace Movement Turns to Electoral Campaigning', *END Journal*, **12**, October–November 1984, pp. 8–9.
13. Melinda Fine, 'Letter from America', *END Journal*, **14**, February–March 1985, p. 10.
14. Maureen Davis, 'Americans Cool the Arms Race', *Peace News*, 16 April 1982, pp. 10–11.
15. Evangelista, *et al.*, *ADIU Report*, July–August 1981, p. 4; Pam Solo, 'From Strength to Strength', *Sanity*, June–July 1982, pp. 12–13.
16. Bruce Kent, 'Euro Peace Tour of USA', *Peace News*, 16 April 1982, p. 6.
17. *Disarmament Campaigns*, **7**, 1981, p. 13; **8**, February 1982, p. 7; *Guardian*, 5 April 1983, p. 15; 9 June 1984, p. 9.
18. The US Bishops' Pastoral Letter on War and Peace in the Nuclear Age, *The Challenge of Peace: God's Promise and Our Response* (London, CTS/ SPCK, 1983).
19. Jude Smith, 'Sentences and Actions', *Peace News*, 18 April 1980, p. 5; James W. Douglass, 'Confronting the Nuclear Monster', *Peace News*, 2 May 1980, pp. 10–11.
20. V.I.P. Short, 'Slow Train Comin'', *Peace News*, 11 May 1984, pp. 10–11.
21. 'MX Base Blockade', *Peace News*, 4 February 1983, p. 6.
22. Mike Holderness, 'Nevada Tests Draw Mass Protest', *Peace News*, 6 June 1986, p. 6.
23. *Peace News*, 17 October 1980, p. 5; Martin Holladay, 'Acts of Faith: the Purpose of Plowshares', *Peace News*, 19 September 1986, p. 7; Daniel Berrigan talks to Paul Miller, 'Waging Peace', *Sanity*, September 1988, p. 8.
24. Sandra Boston, 'Seneca', *Peace News*, 14 October 1983, p. 9; Gill Westacott, 'The Different Threads That Make Up the Web of the American Peace Movement', *Peace News*, 1 November 1985, pp. 12–13.
25. Marjoliyn de Jager, 'Making Links, the American Way', *Sanity*, March 1984, pp. 22–3.
26. Catherine Foster, *Women for All Seasons: the Story of the Women's International League for Peace and Freedom* (Athens, Georgia, University of Georgia Press, 1989), p. 93.
27. John Miller interview 'Protest in America', *Peace News*, 8 March 1985, pp. 12–13.
28. Ibid.
29. Randy Kehler (in discussion with Mary Kaldor) 'Learning from Each Other', *END Journal*, **2**, February–March 1983, p. 22; E.P. Thompson, 'Gissa Missile' *New Statesman*, 19 August 1983, p. 17.
30. Margot Trevellyan, 'On the Cold War's Front Line', and Eric Shragge, 'Cruise: the Test of Canada', *END Journal*, **7**, December 1983–January 1984, pp. 23–5.
31. Roussopoulos, pp. 132–3.
32. Shragge and Jane Dibblin, 'An Outpouring of Protest'/*END Journal*, **7**, December 1983–January 1984, p. 10.
33. Trevellyan.
34. Trevellyan.
35. Shragge.
36. Roussopoulos, pp. 135–8.

37. 'Canadians Watch SDI', *Disarmament Campaigns* in *END Journal*, **22–23**, Summer 1985.
38. Shragge.
39. Laurie Macbride, 'Campaign in Canada', *Peace News*, 10 January 1986, p. 9.
40. 'Innu People Resist Low-Flying Nightmare, *Peace News*, 27 October 1989, pp. 6–7.
41. Dave Wallis 'Cruise Over Canada', *Peace News*, 9 December 1983, p. 7.
42. John May, *The Greenpeace Book of the Nuclear Age* (London, Gollancz, 1989), pp. 132–33, 182–4, 246–8.
43. Jolyon Howarth, 'Mururoa: Lethal Legacy of France', *END Journal*, **4**, June–July 1983, p.18.
44. William Millinship and Robin Smyth, 'L'Affaire Greenpeace', *Observer*, 29 September 1985, p. 11.
45. Charlie Ching talks to Stephanie Mills, 'We Don't Ask for the Sky, It Isn't Ours', *Sanity*, July 1988, pp. 21–2.
46. May, pp. 76–9, 104–7; Griff Johnson, 'Paradise Lost', *Bulletin of the Atomic Scientists*, **36**, 10, December 1980, pp. 24–9.
47. Robert Milliken, *No Conceivable Injury: the Story of Britain and Australia's Atomic Cover-Up* (Harmondsworth, Penguin, 1986).
48. Derrick Purdue, 'The Struggle for a Pacific Pacific', *Peace News*, 21 January 1983, pp. 10–11.
49. Leonie Caldecott, 'Fighting in the Pacific for a Nuclear-Free Independence', *END Journal*, **4**, June–July 1983, pp. 20–21; *Peace News*, 11 September 1987, p. 3; *WRI Newsletter*, April–May 1988, p. 2; *Peace News*, 8 December 1989, p. 5; *Sanity*, March 1990, p. 6.
50. Greg Fry, 'Toward a South Pacific Nuclear-Free Zone', *Bulletin of the Atomic Scientists*, **41**, 6, June–July 1985, pp. 16–21 covers the background to the Treaty. See also: *Pax et Libertas*, **54**, 1, March 1989, p. 6.
51. Cathy Ashton and Mick Elliott, 'The Forgotten Peace Movement', *Sanity*, June 1983, pp. 8–9; *Peace News*, 19 April 1985, p. 6. For a brief overview of the 1980s movement see Malcolm Saunders and Ralph Summy, 'One Hundred Years of an Australian Peace Movement, 1885–1984; *Peace and Change*, **10**, 3/4, Fall/Winter 1984, pp. 39–75.
52. See James A. Kelly, Deputy Assistant Secretary of Defence for East Asian and Pacific Affairs to Subcommittee of Committee on Foreign Affairs, US House of Representatives, 18 March 1985 in *ADIU Report*, **7**, 3, May–June 1985, pp. 4–6.
53. Helen Clark MP, 'What Has Been Happening in New Zealand?' *Sanity*, July 1986, pp. 30–3; Helen Clark, 'Mainstream Disarmament', *Sanity*, January 1988, pp. 12–13; Kevin Hackwell, 'A Peace Movement Victory', *Sanity*, January 1988, pp. 13–14. See also P.F. Rogers and P. Landais-Stamp, *Rocking the Boat: New Zealand, the United States and the Nuclear-Free Zone Controversy* (Oxford, Berg Publishers, 1989).
54. Andrew Mack, 'Denuclearization in Australia and New Zealand: Issues and Prospects', *Australian Outlook*, **43**, 3, December 1989, pp. 18–50.
55. Peter D. Jones, 'From Tokyo to Tahiti', *Peace News*, 13 June 1980, p. 7; Peter D. Jones, 'For a Nuclear-Free Pacific', *Peace News*, 13 August 1983, p. 6; *Peace News*, 26 May 1981, p. 5; Zohl De Ishatar and Sian Evans,

'The Sword, the Cross and Coca Cola', *Peace News*, 11 December 1987, pp. 7–8.

56. Chailang, 'The Pacific Need for Peace', *Sanity*, May 1985, pp. 29–31.
57. Caldecott, *END Journal*, June–July 1983, p. 21; Ching, *Sanity*, July 1988.
58. *WRI Newsletter*, **194**, June 1983, p. 10 on launch of Anti-Bases Coalition.
59. Jane Dibblin, 'Paddling in the Nuclear Pool', *New Statesman*, 1 March 1985, pp. 18–19.
60. N. Bamba, 'Peace Movement at a Standstill: Roots of the Crisis', *Bulletin of Peace Proposals*, **13**, 1, 1982, pp. 39–43.
61. Peter D. Jones, 'Japan's Pro and Anti War Movements', *Peace News*, 25 January 1985, pp. 8–9; Hideaki Nagai, 'The Nuclear-Free Zone Movement in Japan', and Fumi Yamashita, 'Peace at the Grassroots', *Sanity*, August 1985, pp. 21–5.
62. Disarmament Campaigns', in *END Journal*, **22–3**, Summer 1985, p. 3.
63. Peter Jones, 'Movement in Asia Pacific', *WRI Newsletter*, No. 194, June 1983, p. 9; Achin Vanaik, 'How to Stop a Nuclear Arms Race Before it Starts', *Sanity*, November 1987, pp. 26–8.
64. 'Indian Missile Base Resistance', *Sanity*, April 1988, p. 6; and Narayan Desai, 'Farmers Resist Missiles in India', *Housmans Peace Diary 1991* (London, Housmans, 1990).
65. Radha Sunnassy, 'Resisting Military Bases: Demilitarisation of the Indian Ocean', *Peace News*, 18 April 1986, pp. 7–8.
66. Chiara Ingrao, 'Perugia Convention', *Sanity*, September 1984, p. 4.

CHAPTER SEVEN

Peace Protest in Socialist States

INTRODUCTION

The Soviet Union and other Socialist States stressed peace in their official rhetoric and established peace committees to campaign against Western militarism; but their political system was designed to prevent any autonomous political action independent of Communist Party control, and to suppress individual dissent. One of the problems facing Western peace groups in the 1950s and 1960s was the fact that their counterparts could not exist in the Soviet bloc.

Long-established international peace organizations, such as the War Resisters' International (WRI), did have some former members and individual contacts in Eastern Europe, but kept these confidential – except when public protest might serve to protect an individual under attack. For example, a Bulgarian lawyer, also a poet and a Tolstoyan pacifist, was released unharmed from prison early in 1959, following appeals from British MPs, and other well-known personalities. In addition some individuals and organizations seized opportunities to make contacts in Eastern Europe, for example by attending an Esperanto Congress in Poland in 1959.[1] (There have been close links historically between peace activists and enthusiasts for a universal language, and the fact that Esperanto was invented by a Pole and had adherents in Poland made it especially useful to pacifists trying to communicate with East Europeans.)

Pacifists have also periodically organized demonstrations designed both to demonstrate their willingness to protest against militarism in the Soviet bloc and to try to establish a dialogue with individual citizens in Eastern Europe and the USSR. The San Francisco to Moscow March gave out leaflets urging unilateral disarmament in

East Germany, Poland and the Soviet Union, but was only able to do so after negotiating permission from the authorities and as guests of the official peace committees. Other protesters have entered as tourists and then given out leaflets until stopped by the police. This tactic was adopted by War Resisters' International teams protesting in four Warsaw Pact capitals against the 1968 invasion of Czechoslovakia. After the International March for Non-violence and Demilitarization was halted at the Polish border in 1979, some members travelled as tourists to Warsaw, as did members of the 1980 International March who, after protests in France and Northern Italy, went on to Ljubljana and to Bucharest. The Italian Radical Party also initiated international 'Bread not Bombs' protests in Warsaw Pact capitals in April 1982.[2]

The first Western peace campaign to achieve a significant response to appeals for independent protest in Eastern Europe was the European Nuclear Disarmament (END) network. The response in most countries was slow and where autonomous protest did occur in the early 1980s – as in East Germany – it reflected internal political conditions and the political impact of major demonstrations in the West. Nevertheless, opposition circles such as Charter 77 in Czechoslovakia began to enter into dialogue with Edward Thompson, an initiator of the 1980 END Appeal for a nuclear-weapons-free Europe from Poland to Portugal, and to send policy statements to END Conventions.

When the END Appeal was launched in early 1980, Roy Medvedev, a well-known Soviet dissident who, unlike most dissidents in the USSR, still adhered to Marxism, signed it. So did former Hungarian Prime Minister, Andras Hegedus, by then a critic of the regime. But the prospect of wider support from Eastern Europe or the USSR then looked slight. Although there had been varying degrees of liberalization across the Soviet bloc, human rights activists and opposition groups faced harassment or prison. Publicity and protest about military bases, which challenged the Soviet military presence in Eastern Europe and concepts of national security, was likely to be met with much greater repression. Another barrier to interest in peace activity was that, despite pervasive peace propaganda, there was a dearth of public information about nuclear weapons and nuclear strategy. Indeed, for many struggling with the difficulties of minimal political activity, such as circulating underground '*samizdat*' publications, the concerns of Western peace movements seemed at best abstruse and remote. At worst many inside the Soviet bloc, including quite a few dissidents, saw the peace movements as dupes of the Soviet propaganda drive, a view reinforced by some prominent dissidents allowed or forced to go to the West. Many East Europeans also saw NATO as a valuable military and political check on Soviet ambitions and were especially critical of Western peace bodies which called for unilateral measures of disarmament. When the Polish Committee for Social Resistance (KOS) entered into critical dialogue with END, KOS specifically opposed Western unilateralism. Apart from the major reasons for Eastern European reserve about Western peace groups, there were more subtle issues of tone and style. Vaclav Havel, who explored all these problems in a penetrating essay sent to the 1985 END Amsterdam Convention, noted how the utopianism of some Western peace activists jarred on the scepticism and cultivated distrust of utopianism among Eastern European intellectuals.[3]

These political and psychological barriers remained significant despite the developing dialogue between Eastern European opposition groups and Western peace organizations such as the Dutch Inter-church Peace Council (IKV), the West German Greens and the French non-aligned Committee for Nuclear Disarmament (CODENE) as well as END representatives. Autonomous peace protests did, however, take place in East Germany, Czechoslovakia, Hungary and Poland. Independent peace activity also arose in Slovenia, the most 'Western' republic of Yugoslavia, which had been independent of the Soviet Union since 1948 but was a Communist Party state. Most surprisingly of all, individuals initiated peace proposals and undertook peace demonstrations on a small scale within the USSR itself.

Young people in Eastern Europe and the USSR were especially responsive to the wave of peace protests across Western Europe in the early 1980s. The young also responded eagerly to music and youth culture imported from the West, which created a base for independent cultural activity and sometimes encouraged peace protest. The Jazz Section of the Czechoslovak Musicians' Union, severely harassed by the authorities in the mid-1980s, became an important strand in the social resistance to party control and also gave support to END.[4] The former Beatle, John Lennon, associated with gestures for peace, also became a symbol of rebellious youth culture and of independent commitment to peace activity.

The most important influences on autonomous peace agitation in Eastern Europe and the USSR in the 1980s were, however, internal. Stationing of new short-range Soviet missiles in East Germany and Czechoslovakia in late 1983 evoked some internal protests in both countries.[5] A more permanent source of opposition was conscription, where anti-militarist and civil liberties issues overlapped, and where religious beliefs might challenge state ideology. Because conscription was so important for East Europeans, the END organization in the UK extended its remit in 1985 to take aboard this previously pacifist demand that rights to conscientious objection should be recognized.[6] Concern about the militarization of culture and society also prompted open resistance in a number of East European countries, notably East Germany and Slovenia.

A survey of autonomous peace protest in Eastern Europe and the USSR in the 1980s spans a period of astonishing political change, starting with the end of the Brezhnev era and a renewed Cold War atmosphere between East and West, and ending with the dissolution of the Soviet bloc. So individuals who were 'dissidents' in the early 1980s found themselves in government in 1990. They included Pastor Rainer Eppelmann, once imprisoned as a conscientious objector, who became Minister for Defence and Disarmament in the transitional East German Government, and Jiri Dienstbier, Charter 77 spokesperson engaged in dialogue with END, who after the 1990 elections was confirmed as Civic Forum's Foreign Minister. In the Soviet Union itself the increasingly insistent demands for national independence in many republics made service in the Soviet armed forces a focus for mass opposition rather than individual dissent.

An examination of dissent in the Soviet bloc must also take account of the considerable divergences between the states of Eastern Europe, based upon historical and cultural experience, and the even greater gulf between Eastern Europe and the USSR itself. So autonomous peace action can only be understood by a brief look at each country separately.

THE GERMAN DEMOCRATIC REPUBLIC

Unofficial peace activity was more widespread and sustained in East Germany than in any other East European country. Despite East German responsiveness to events in West Germany (and access to West German television), the initial impetus to peace action was internal, and reflected growing concern about the militarization of East German society. Conscription was not introduced in the GDR until 1962, after the building of the Berlin Wall made it possible to stop conscripts simply leaving the country, and prompted about 3,000 young men between 1962 and 1964 to refuse military service. When the Government introduced a Decree on Defence Studies in 1978, which required military training for older secondary school pupils, it led to public protests and petitions. A new conscription law in 1982 envisaged calling up women in an emergency and the creation of Women for Peace indicated significant opposition.

The Evangelical Protestant Church in the GDR played a crucial role in providing the network of autonomous peace groups, which had grown up by 1982, with a degree of legitimacy and protection. The majority of people in the GDR had been Protestants in 1949 and the Church still formally represented about half the seventeen million East Germans in 1979. The Church had over time evolved a position which combined acceptance of the state, and of socialist goals, while asserting a degree of independence and a right to criticize. In this context the Church used its influence to persuade the government in 1964 to recognize a limited right of conscientious objection – going further than other Socialist States – and to allow objectors to do non-combatant service in construction units within the armed forces. After the 1978 Decree on military training in schools, the Church promoted a programme of peace education for young people, and began in 1980 to hold a 'peace week'. The theme of this event was 'swords into ploughshares' and its logo depicted the Soviet statue before the United Nations building in New York based on this biblical concept. A year later the growing youth peace movement in the GDR made 'swords into ploughshares' its emblem.[7]

Autonomous peace activity in the GDR increased significantly in the early 1980s, partly in response to the planned NATO missile deployments and growing Western peace movement. A joint meeting of authors from East and West Germany in East Berlin in December 1981 gave an opportunity for some East German writers like Stefan Heym to make independent statements on peace. Then Pastor Eppelmann and Robert Havemann, a distinguished scientist and Marxist critic of the regime, jointly launched the 'Berlin Appeal' in January 1982 in response to the 'Krefeld Appeal' against the new NATO missiles in West Germany (see Chapter 5). The Berlin Appeal, which soon collected 300 other signatures, called for withdrawal of all nuclear weapons and foreign troops from both halves of Germany, and a nuclear-free zone in Central Europe. The West German peace movement publicized the Berlin Appeal, responding to a request from Havemann, who died shortly afterwards, and END also mustered left-wing support.[8]

The most important development, however, was an unofficial march and candle-lit vigil at the Church of Our Lady in Dresden in

February 1982 by about a thousand young peace activists commemorating the destruction of the city by saturation bombing in 1945. Independent peace demonstrations followed in Potsdam in June and in Jena in December 1982. The Catholic bishops, who had maintained a low profile in East Germany, where their congregation was small, publicly endorsed demands by women and youth groups for a constructive social alternative to military service in January 1983, and in February both Protestants and Catholics joined another peace action in Dresden.[9] Most peace activity was locally based, but a national peace seminar in Berlin in March 1983 gave the movement a central focus and another national conference took place in Eisenach in 1984.

The GDR Government hesitated over its response to the growing autonomous campaign and in 1982 engaged in a battle of slogans: 'swords and ploughshares' and 'peace must be armed' – while peace activists proclaimed 'make peace without arms' and wore the swords into ploughshares symbol as a badge. Then protesters in Jena were arrested in December 1982, members of Women for Peace were arrested in late 1983, and there was a wave of arrests in major cities in 1984. The Protestant Church, which could offer its premises and its protection for discussion circles and peace festivals, tried to balance maintaining reasonable relations with the Government with helping militant peace groups acting outside the Church. Sometimes clergy tried to defuse confrontation. For example, the Church arranged its own peace forum in Dresden in February 1982, which in the event preceded the smaller independent march and vigil. The bishops alienated some of their own clergy and congregations when in May 1982 they supported a regime ban on wearing the 'swords into ploughshares' badge, but urged keeping the slogan. The Church hierarchy did, however, maintain its independent, if cautious, peace programme when in September 1983 the Potsdam Synod urged both the USSR and the USA to desist from installing new missiles in Europe and called on the German Democratic Republic to oppose basing of new missiles on its territory.[10]

Many in the independent peace movement of an estimated 2,000–3,000 activists were practising Christians. But there were other sources of inspiration. Rock music linked students, young workers and avant-garde artists in Jena, and an anarchist-style commune acted as a centre for protest in Weimar. Women for Peace drew on a variety of backgrounds: Havemann's widow was one of the initial 150 signatories of a letter to Honnecker stating a refusal to be conscripted. The initiative began in East Berlin and then spread to other major cities, where women's groups sent similar letters and continued to meet for debate. Over 500 women declared their opposition to being conscripted.[11]

After the Government crackdown on the autonomous peace network in 1984 the peace groups reappraised their policies and tactics. Two Women for Peace activists, artist Barbel Bohley and historian Ulricke Poppe, arrested in December 1983 for treasonably passing on information to foreign agents under Article 99 of the GDR Code because they had met a British END supporter, were released in late January 1984. Peace groups in the West, appalled at a possible eight-year prison sentence for the two women, protested strongly on their behalf, and while in prison both women went on a twenty-two day hunger strike.[12] Western campaigners could not, however, intervene effectively on behalf of all those arrested or deported to West Germany. Some peace activists began to lay more emphasis on environmental issues, inspired by the West German Greens. Others turned to the example of Charter 77 and began to combine peace issues with much greater stress on human rights. Pastor Eppelmann was among those signing a public appeal early in 1985 calling for East German implementation of the UN Declaration of Human Rights.[13]

Two years later independent peace activists joined with ecological, human rights and feminist groups to protest against what they saw as the excessive willingness of the Protestant Church hierarchy to compromise with the state. The Church had been allowed to hold its first official gathering of East German Protestants in East Berlin since 1961 and had cancelled the usual annual peace workshop. The independent groups, after threatening a sit-in during the official celebration, were allowed to hold their unofficial gathering; but between 1,200 and 2,000 people handed out leaflets at the initial service in East Berlin on 24 June 1987, protesting against Church acceptance of the status quo.[14] The 'swords into ploughshares' symbol reappeared on the streets of East Germany in September 1987, when independent peace activists joined in a Church 'pilgrimage' which was part of the official Olof Palme Peace March. (West German and Austrian peace groups had combined with the official East German and Czechoslovak Peace Committees to demonstrate in favour of the nuclear weapon-free zone proposed by the Palme Commission in its 1982 Report on Common Security. Independents in East Germany used the opportunity to display their own demands on banners.[15]) The Government ordered new arrests in January 1988, but at the end of the 1980s combined peace action in Eastern Europe gained momentum in the context of wider political change.

CZECHOSLOVAKIA

After the Soviet Union invaded Czechoslovakia in 1968 to crush the Prague Spring and a new party leadership was imposed in 1969, Czechoslovakia became for the next twenty years one of the more repressive East European regimes in its political and cultural policies. Former reform Communists, intellectuals and student leaders created an opposition network, but its leaders were soon arrested and imprisoned. When Charter 77 emerged to demand the Government's compliance with the human rights guarantees it had endorsed in the 1975 Helsinki Final Act of the Conference on Security and Cooperation (CSCE), opposition gained international prominence. The Charter and its activist wing, the Committee for the Defence of the Unjustly Accused, covered a wide ideological spectrum, from rightwing Catholics to Eurocommunists, radical Catholics to revolutionary socialists, and those – like Havel – who adopted a broadly liberal position.[16] So Chartists naturally differed in their responses to Western peace movements, and there were varying emphases among those who did enter into an open dialogue.

The first response from Czechoslovakia to the END Appeal was hostile, a letter to Edward Thompson written early in 1981 under the pseudonym Vaclav Racek. Racek attacked the vision of a nuclear-free Europe as naive and asserted that Western arms helped to preserve freedom. In a further letter responding to Thompson, Racek urged Western peace movements to support East European dissidents and to endorse Western military forces as 'instruments of human rights confronting totalitarian systems'.[17] Racek's picture of an irreconcilable Western 'freedom' and Eastern 'totalitarianism' was repudiated in another open letter to Thompson, sent by Jaroslav Sabata in 1983. Sabata's influential document argued that independent campaigns for civil rights in the East and against the missiles in the West needed to converge, and to create a joint strategy for the democratic transformation of Europe.[18] Sabata, a regional Party Secretary under Dubcek, who had been sentenced in 1971 to six years in prison for opposing the regime, showed there was opposition support for END. So did fellow Charter signatory, former Foreign Minister Jiri Hajek, who issued a statement distinguishing IKV and END from the World Peace Council campaign of the early 1950s and suggested that Charter 77 was 'very close in spirit' to the independent peace movement.[19]

Charter 77's first cautious statement on the Western peace movement, made in November 1981, stressed the indivisibility of peace and freedom and called for adherence to the Helsinki Final Act of 1975 as a basis for both. This theme was developed in the March 1985 Prague Appeal to the END Convention, which urged the need for individual freedom and national self-determination in a united democratic Europe, and looked to the CSCE process to provide a framework for both. The Appeal also tackled the question of the division of Germany, and noted the right of West and East Germans to unite within their existing frontiers in the context of European *rapprochement*.[20] The Appeal encouraged Western peace activists to take the CSCE more seriously. Prominent Chartists later sponsored the idea of a Helsinki Citizens' Assembly to create initiatives from below which could promote the role of the CSCE.

The Charter 77 debates with END and IKV and its policy statements, such as the Prague Appeal, were politically significant because of the Charter's moral authority as the voice of Czechoslovak opposition, and because Charter 77 carried weight with opposition groups in other East European countries. The Polish Committee for Social Resistance (KOS), for example, wrote a careful if critical response to the Prague Appeal.[21] Charter 77 also combined with East German peace activists to sign a joint declaration on the 1984 anniversary of the stationing of new missiles in their two countries.[22]

Spontaneous peace demonstrations in Czechoslovakia drew on young apprentices, secondary school pupils and students. The official World Peace Council Assembly in Prague in 1983 prompted young people to march through the streets shouting 'We want both peace and freedom'. The commemoration of the fifth anniversary of John Lennon's death in December 1985 gradually developed into a march through Prague with songs and shouting of slogans and ended in the signing of an *ad hoc* petition against all nuclear weapons in both East and West Europe. The police later interrogated about eighty of the thousand youngsters involved, including the instigator of the petition.[23]

An Independent Peace Association was founded in April 1988 to call for the demilitarization of society, and its Bulletin demanded a legal right of conscientious objection. The author of this article was arrested in October 1988 for 'incitement' and two other Peace Association activists were also arrested for trying to call a demonstration to commemorate the fiftieth anniversary of the founding of the Republic.[24] The Czechoslovak authorities demonstrated their continued resistance to the Gorbachev trend of liberalization when in June 1988 they deported Western peace activists who went to Prague at the invitation of peace and human rights campaigners to attend a seminar.[25] The police were not, however, able to prevent a valuable dialogue.

HUNGARY

The Hungarian Government in the 1970s and 1980s pursued rather more liberal policies than its Czechoslovak neighbour, and as a result the Hungarian Peace Council was more flexible in responding to autonomous initiatives, and not viewed with such extreme distrust as the Peace Council in Czechoslovakia. Nevertheless, after a promising start attempts to promote autonomous peace action in 1982–83 ran into considerable difficulties. Firstly, there was a greater gulf than in Czechoslovakia between a younger generation responsive to peace appeals and an older group of committed political opponents of the regime. Secondly, young peace activists themselves soon split over the question of how far they should moderate their demands to remain acceptable to the authorities. Thirdly, the prospect of the breakdown of the INF talks in 1983 and of further missile deployments in Eastern Europe led the Hungarian authorities (like the GDR Government) to take more repressive action against a potentially radical independent grouping.

The majority of Hungary's political dissidents stood permanently aside from the peace dialogue of the 1980s, but two of the best known and most radical dissidents – Laszlo Rajk and Miklos Haraszti – took the initiative in launching a samizdat series of *Peace Notebooks* and translating Edward Thompson's pamphlet 'Beyond the Cold War'. They also used an official Soviet-sponsored peace march passing through Budapest in 1982 to hand out leaflets against Soviet troops and missiles in Hungary. Haraszti, a poet who had earlier been put on trial for writing too honest a survey of factory conditions in Hungary, insisted in a September 1982 statement that democratic rights were essential for the existence of a peace movement.[26]

Hungarian secondary school pupils and students at Budapest University tried in September 1981 and May 1982 to hold marches against all nuclear weapons. In both cases the Communist Youth League effectively took over the event – though in May some pupils held their own banners and slogans. Students at the university also tried to set up their own centre and peace journal. The Peace Group of Dialogue emerged with the aim of developing independently of both the official Peace Council and of the political dissidents, and remaining an open and public grouping which would not pose too direct a challenge to the state. The policies of Dialogue included calls for a nuclear-free zone in Europe, opposition to SS20s and NATO missiles and support for wider disarmament. When Edward Thompson visited Budapest late in 1982 he met a range of political opposition figures and the official Hungarian Peace Council, but founding members of the Dialogue Group acted as his hosts. A proposed lecture by Thompson at the University was cancelled at short notice.[27]

The Dialogue Group continued to grow in 1983. The Hungarian Peace Council allowed the group use of its premises for public meetings early in the year, but then set up its own youth section in opposition. Dialogue was never allowed its own peace centre, and harassment of its members grew, especially after Dialogue split at its April conference into moderate and radical wings over the question of how far to challenge the authorities. In the next two months Dialogue members spoke at a pop concert and attended an official Peace Council demonstration with their own banners, and at the end emulated Western peace demonstrators by lying down to illustrate deaths after a nuclear war. Dialogue planned a peace camp for July and invited Western peace activists, including Greenham women. The authorities deported the Western delegates and interrogated some of the Hungarians involved, and Dialogue decided to disband itself in face of police pressure, since it could not fulfil its original aims. Some members of Dialogue continued to meet and plan peace action, including circulation of a petition asking for a civilian alternative to military service. Others, including one of the founder members of Dialogue, opted for closer cooperation with the Peace Council and set up a Peace Club where former Dialogue members could meet.[28] Over the next two years youth clubs with a focus on peace sprang up round the country and the Peace Council, determinedly shedding its old-style image, offered practical help to the clubs when asked. The Council itself decided to hold a Star Peace rock concert in 1986, which would include a tribute to John Lennon, and signed the END Appeal in 1987.[29]

The break-up of the Dialogue Group in 1983 did, however, create despair and bitterness among many members and prompted a wave of personal accusations which Western observers found hard to assess. Some members of the group joined the political opposition they had previously rejected. Active identification of leading members of END with Dialogue might have increased difficulties in 1983, when the Soviet Peace Committee was waging a virulent campaign against END. But the lack of space for autonomous groups in this period probably reflected Soviet domestic and foreign policy and a worsening of East–West relations.

One remarkable grouping in the spectrum of peace activists in Hungary was little affected by these political influences because of its radical and uncompromising position. A Catholic priest who had been imprisoned during the Stalinist regime of the 1950s had established within the Church a movement of local communities striving to live according to the ethic of the original gospels. This belief in non-violence naturally meant rejecting military service. The movement was strongly condemned by the Catholic hierarchy, but had the support of a number of priests and a growing appeal to young Catholics. By 1982 there were about a hundred local communities of some thirty to forty people, and members set up a Committee for Human Dignity, which issued a statement in January 1982 opposing nuclear arms in both East and West. The main focus of the communities was, however, urging the right to conscientious objection and alternative service. The Hungarian Government did grant exemption to pacifist Christian sects like the Nazarenes and Jehovah's Witnesses, but the growing number of young Catholics refusing to serve in the forces were sent to prison, often for two to three years.[30] By 1987 penalties for Hungarian COs were becoming more rather than less harsh, and the Catholic Church leadership continued to condemn anti-militarism and refusal of military service.[31] The official Hungarian view on COs had changed radically two years later as a multiparty system challenged Communist Party rule.

POLAND

The Catholic Church in Poland was officially no more inclined to endorse anti-militarism than the Hungarian Church, but there were many other obstacles to independent peace action. An autonomous campaign, Freedom and Peace, did emerge and picked up a groundswell of support, but not until 1985. Polish nationalism, defined partly in opposition to a history of Russian and Soviet suppression, and a tendency to admire the Polish army as a defender of national independence, can be cited as reasons why Polish political culture has not been receptive to peace proposals. Polish opposition groups have also felt strongly the contempt for official Soviet-sponsored peace campaigns, and suspicion that Western peace movements were pro-Soviet, which characterized in varying degrees many oppositionists in Hungary and Czechoslovakia. The most important reason why independent peace activity developed slowly in Poland was probably, however, the fact that Solidarity was launched in 1980 and driven underground in December 1981. While the Western movement against the missiles was gaining momentum, Poles were absorbed in attempting the democratic transformation of their own society; and even if they had energy to consider wider foreign policy and defence issues, eschewed them as unnecessarily provocative.[32] After December 1981 the Reagan Administration imposed an economic embargo on Poland, and right-wing foundations offered funds to the opposition. Despite support from Western trade unions and socialist parties for Solidarity, the New Right offered more vigorous backing and these factors influenced the Polish opposition. Moreover, Western peace groups in general failed to demonstrate strongly in favour of Solidarity, hesitant to identify closely with opposition in Eastern Europe which was unrelated to peace issues. END did have contact with representatives of Solidarity in the West, and some pacifists saw Solidarity as an impressive example of non-violent resistance to dictatorship, but it took time for any mutual understanding between the Polish opposition and sectors of the Western peace movement to evolve.

Solidarity was a broad movement encompassing different ideological views, and as its activists began to regroup after the suppression of the Union they also began to react in different ways to the growing peace movement in Western Europe. During 1983 a group of well-known individuals associated with Solidarity in 1980 sent an 'Open Appeal' to the Polish Parliament, urging a fresh look at the 1950s Rapacki Plan for a nuclear-free zone in Central Europe; and a group in Cracow demonstrated at Easter with the slogan 'No Pershing, No SS missiles'. In addition, the influential circle of Solidarity intellectuals in the Committee for Social Resistance (KOS), formed after the declaration of martial law, began to engage in dialogue with Western peace groups, but strongly criticized proposals for Western unilateral disarmament. A leading figure in KOS, prominent in opposing the regime since the 1960s, was Jacek Kuron, who wrote an Open Letter to world peace movements in mid-1984, identifying the Warsaw Pact as the main threat to peace, proposing a demilitarized zone in Central Europe, and urging support for 'the peaceful struggle of Polish society against military dictatorship'. His letter was sent from prison. More encouraging news for END was contained in an article in the Solidarity underground newspaper in February 1984, carrying a declaration from a new 'Peace and Solidarity' group in Wroclaw, which demanded removal of nuclear weapons from Poland, and more information about nuclear issues, as well as removal of Soviet troops. The Wroclaw group indicated a desire to promote a nation-wide autonomous peace grouping.[33]

By the end of 1984 an intensification of dialogue between KOS and French and Italian activists had promoted better understanding. Nevertheless, the predominant tone of many pronouncements from the Polish opposition remained critical of the Western peace movements for failing to stress the threat posed by the USSR to both freedom and peace. It is indicative of the Polish tendency to give a higher priority to freedom that the spark for forming a militant autonomous peace campaign was the refusal by a young man to serve in the army because this involved also taking an oath of loyalty to the Soviet Union. Marek Adamievicz was sentenced to over two years in prison in December 1984. When young people started to fast in support of his stand in May 1985, the Freedom and Peace campaign was born. The campaigners' programme, issued in November 1985, stressed human rights and the struggle for national liberation before it discussed nuclear weapons and militarism. They also stressed that they were following the teachings of Pope John Paul II and had nothing to do with the official Peace Council.[34]

Nevertheless, Freedom and Peace identified itself with its allies in the Western peace movement, specifically CODENE, IKV and END, and declared its concern with environmental and Third World issues. The grouping soon moved towards a more radical pacifist position, endorsing non-violence both as a means of struggle and as a way of life, and calling for CO rights and alternative service on anti-militarist and internationalist grounds. Otto Schimek, an Austrian soldier executed in 1944 for refusing (according to the story surrounding his name) to shoot Polish civilians, was adopted as a symbol by the campaign.[35]

Freedom and Peace was illegal under Polish law, but activists organized openly in over fifteen cities producing newsletters for a wider readership. It drew on a rather diverse constituency of young intellectuals and workers, and the groups varied in their ideological stance. A British visitor to a trial of a Freedom and Peace activist was struck by similarities with trials of Greenham women: 'a crowd of scruffily dressed young people with "no proper respect for authority" treating . . . the courthouse as their own'.[36] The group's tactics were often militant, including scattering leaflets from roof tops, sit-downs, fasts and return of military call-up papers. Members also adopted the idea, promoted by East German and Hungarian peace activists, of individual 'peace treaties' with citizens from the West, with the aim of bypassing governments through citizen-to-citizen contact, for example making a mutual agreement not to join the armed forces. As in other East European countries, Freedom and Peace activists were mostly young – they included the son of Jacek Kuron. There were several hundred committed supporters, estimated at between ten and a hundred in each city group, but the newsletters reached a much wider circle of sympathizers.[37] Freedom and Peace demonstrations could attract up to 2,000 and their petitions up to 10,000 signatures.[38]

The openness and militancy of Freedom and Peace activities contrasted with the clandestine underground role of Solidarity, and gave a new dynamism to the Polish opposition. Some leading Solidarity intellectuals were drawn into support for the movement and became more sympathetic to associated Western peace groups. After the Chernobyl nuclear reactor disaster in the Ukraine in 1986, Freedom and Peace campaigned on the ecological dangers of nuclear power and opposed the building of a nuclear plant near Gdansk. By 1987 Freedom and Peace had acquired such a high profile in supporting CO rights that it was under attack from the Soviet government paper *Izvestia* and the Polish Defence Ministry.[39]

One major achievement for Freedom and Peace was to hold an international conference in Warsaw in May 1987, bringing together representatives from Charter 77 and the Slovene Peace Group with members of West European and North American organizations. The Polish authorities refused visas to twenty-two Western delegates, detained members of Freedom and Peace and created difficulties over a meeting place. However, a Warsaw parish priest made his church available despite official church pressure not to do so, and about 200 participants debated peace, environmental and human rights issues. Some East European groups prevented from attending by their own authorities sent policy documents.[40] The Warsaw seminar was part of a growing movement of cooperation and dialogue between East European groups.

ANTI-MILITARISM IN SLOVENIA

The Slovene Peace Group, which drew on students and academics at Ljubljana University, emerged out of the flourishing youth culture in the most northern of Yugoslavia's republics in the mid-1980s, and made contact with other East European civil rights and peace bodies and with END and WRI in the West. Peace activity in Slovenia reflected the growing divergence between the politics of the republic and developments in the south of Yugoslavia, and became a catalyst for further conflict between Slovenia and the Federal Government and Armed Forces.

Yugoslavia had for a long period been half in and half out of the Soviet bloc. After Tito broke with Stalin in 1948, Yugoslavia always remained formally non-aligned with an independent defence policy. Despite *rapprochement* with Moscow in 1955, and again in 1961 (after a further rupture at the end of 1956) Yugoslavia continued to be nervous of a possible Soviet invasion. Yugoslavia also enjoyed economic aid from the West and increasing Western tourism. On the other hand Yugoslavia remained a Communist Party state, and despite experiments in political and economic liberalization in the 1950s and 1960s, there was only limited space for autonomous political action. Moreover, the Communist regime drew its legitimacy from the partisan war against the German and Italian occupying powers during 1941–44, and Yugoslav defence was based upon universal military training and a commitment to heroic military resistance. Yugoslav political culture was therefore in general extremely hostile to pacifism, or to recognition of CO rights, especially in Southern republics with a long tradition of armed resistance to Ottoman rule. Therefore, although CND in the late 1950s was willing to cooperate with the official Yugoslav League of Peace, because it was non-aligned in the Cold War, WRI was addressing pleas to the Yugoslav Government on behalf of members of the Christian pacifist sect, the Nazarenes, being sentenced to an average of six years in jail for refusing to bear arms.[41]

Slovenia had always prided itself on being more 'Western' than other Yugoslav republics, and during the 1980s the Slovene Communist Party tolerated a radical youth culture in music and the arts which was linked to growth of environmental protest and agitation for rights for COs. There was also growing criticism of the Yugoslav political and economic system. *Mladina*, the organ of the official Slovene youth organization, was prominent in articulating this criticism.

The Ljubljana Peace Group announced its existence and policies to the Western peace movement in July 1986. It had only about twenty activists, but in addition to regular fortnightly meetings the group engaged in varied public campaigns. Late in 1986 members ran street stalls to publicize opposition to war toys and raised the wider issue of peace education in schools and universities. The group marched through Ljubljana to commemorate the anniversary of Chernobyl in April 1987 and in May organized a round table discussion on the right to conscientious objection, inviting lawyers from Serbia and Croatia, who had acted for Jehovah's Witnesses, to join in. Despite its small size the group claimed that opinion polls showed about half Slovenia's two million citizens were very sympathetic to their campaigns.[42] The youth paper, *Mladina*, gave them good coverage. The peace campaign also published its own information bulletin, *Peace Movement in Yugoslavia*, based in the Student Cultural Centre. The bulletin was also issued in an English language edition (later called *Independent Voices*) and informed Western peace groups about its campaigns, including its politically controversial activities on behalf of COs. Communist parties in other Yugoslav Republics, and the Federal Party Paper *Borba*, attacked the demand for an alternative to military conscription in January 1987.[43]

The Yugoslav military were by 1988 anxious to curb those opposing conscription and independent defence experts criticizing the defence establishment. *Mladina* had in early 1988 claimed that army conscripts were used to build a villa for the Minister of Defence. More seriously, the paper attacked Yugoslav arms sales to the Third World, in particular to the repressive Ethiopian regime, and revealed that the Defence Minister had visited Ethiopia. This article prompted the arrest of the chief editor of *Mladina* in March 1988, apparently due to Federal Government pressure. After hundreds demonstrated outside the court at his trial, the case was adjourned.[44] Soon afterwards rumours circulated of a threatened military coup in Slovenia. In May *Mladina* published an Open Letter to the Slovene Government, asking if it were true that there had been a plan by the Yugoslav Military Council to arrest up to 500 Slovene officials and intellectuals, and to use troops to quell popular resistance. Slovene party leaders had apparently blocked the plan, but were not anxious to have the details revealed. The *Mladina* Open Letter was suppressed, but Western journalists learned that its allegations were substantially true.[45]

Army pressure on Slovenia continued. At the end of May Janez Jansa, defence expert, campaigner for an alternative to military service and author of the Open Letter, was arrested and held in a military prison. He was charged with possession of a secret military document, which (it later emerged) related to the plans for a military coup, and which had been leaked to him by a sergeant in the army. The sergeant and another *Mladina* journalist, who had seen the document, soon joined Jansa in jail. The military subsequently charged the chief editor of *Mladina*, but he was not imprisoned at that stage. So when the military trial of the four took place in secret in July 1988, he was able to address a press conference each evening and to broadcast details of the trial on Radio Student in Ljubljana.[46]

The military court found the four men guilty, and sentenced the sergeant to four years in prison, Jansa and the chief editor to eighteen months and the other journalist to five months. All were released pending an appeal. The trial prompted widespread opposition to the use of military law and military courts to punish civilians. A Committee for the Defence of Human Rights sprang up in Ljubljana: eighty-eight intellectuals in Slovenia had immediately backed Jansa, and by the time of the trial 67,000 had signed a petition on behalf of the four defendants. The Committee drew 20,000 to a solidarity concert in June 1988 and numbers outside the court grew to around 10,000 on the last day of the trial. When Jansa was arrested on 5 May 1989 to begin his eighteen-month sentence, a crowd of 30,000 demonstrated in Ljubljana three days later demanding that all four defendants should go free.[47] By 1989 the Committee for the Defence of Human Rights was evolving into the nucleus of a new democratic front, engaging in a dialogue with the Slovene Communist Party and challenging its monopoly on power.[48] Peace campaigning and criticism of the military became more inextricably linked with the struggle for civil rights and pluralist democracy than in other parts of Eastern Europe. After multi-party elections in Slovenia in April 1990 ousted the Communist Party, Janez Jansa emerged as the Republic's new Minister of Defence.

The Ljubljana Peace Group was the only effective peace campaign in Yugoslavia, though students in the Croatian capital, Zagreb, also tried from 1986 to campaign on peace and environmental issues.[49] Nationalist conflicts increasingly dominated politics in most of Yugoslavia during the 1980s.

THE SOVIET UNION

Since the military policies of the Soviet Union, and fear of Soviet intentions, were central to the Cold War, Western peace groups were especially anxious to make contact with Soviet citizens. Given the efficiency of Communist Party control over society and official attitudes to Soviet defence, autonomous peace activity seemed however even less likely than in Eastern Europe. Moreover, the Soviet military guarded military information so jealously that even arms control negotiators in the Soviet Foreign Ministry did not have access to data on Soviet nuclear forces in the early SALT negotiations.[50] So for a long period the most promising basis for dialogue seemed to be with the liberal fringe of the Soviet intellegentsia through professional contacts.

Scientists have always tended to regard themselves as part of an international community of knowledge. In addition scientists enjoyed a privileged position within the Soviet Union and after the death of Stalin became relatively free from ideological controls over their work. The Pugwash Conferences, which began in 1957, enabled Soviet scientists to meet Western colleagues and to discuss such issues as a nuclear test ban (see Chapter 2). Over time Pugwash lost its unique importance as an East–West channel, as other personal and professional contacts developed, but the Pugwash annual conferences and working groups continued into the 1980s and allowed for exchange of information and ideas on a range of arms control problems.

The détente of the 1970s allowed a much wider exchange of academic and cultural personnel and made Western thinking, including theories of nuclear deterrence and arms control, much more available to the Soviet Union. A new group of Soviet civilian researchers expert in strategic affairs gained influence in the 1970s[51] and during the 1980s had frequent contact with Western peace researchers. Dialogue on arms control, nuclear deterrence and non-offensive forms of defence did have some repercussions on Soviet policy, as noted in Chapter 5. In addition Western and Soviet scientists were able to collaborate on very specific issues. Soviet scientists joined in research on the possible effects of a nuclear winter, and in 1986 Soviet and American scientists joined forces to experiment on detection of underground tests on Soviet territory at Semipalatinsk and at the US Nevada testing site.[52]

Liberal members of the Soviet establishment might exercise useful influence within it, but could not claim to be taking an autonomous stand openly critical of Soviet military policies. Soviet dissidents on the other hand concentrated primarily on human rights and religious or nationalist issues. They were, moreover, bitterly divided on questions of war and peace and the value of détente. Three leading dissidents, Alexander Solzhenitsyn, Andrei Sakharov and Roy Medvedev had engaged in debate on these issues in the mid-1970s, when Solzhenitsyn had bitterly opposed any *rapprochement* between the USSR and the West as betrayal of the cause of human rights in the East, and denounced liberal and left-wing opinion in the West favouring détente. Medvedev stood at the opposite extreme, both in his ideological evaluation of the Soviet Union – he remained a socialist – and his views on detente, which he saw as essential to create space for change in the Soviet Union. Sakharov took a middle position.[53] As an eminent nuclear scientist who had helped to develop the Soviet H bomb, Sakharov was well aware of the dangers of nuclear war. He had, moreover, urged Khrushchev not to resume nuclear testing in 1958, and his book *Progress, Coexistence and Intellectual Freedom* in 1968 called for internal Soviet reform and international cooperation to end the arms race.[54] During the 1970s Sakharov campaigned openly for human rights in the USSR, and expressed concern that the Western interpretation of détente did not put enough pressure on the Soviet regime to change, and could allow a strongly armed USSR with a closed society to become a greater threat to the world. Sakharov did, however, welcome the 1975 Helsinki Conference agreement, which made connections between security and democratic freedoms.[55] He was awarded the Nobel Peace Prize in the same year. By the early 1980s Sakharov was in internal exile, after publicly criticizing the invasion of Afghanistan. He was primarily concerned with civil rights, and his utterances on the international situation stressed the dangerous role of the Soviet Government.[56] When Sakharov was released from exile in December 1986, as a symbol of Gorbachev's commitment to change Soviet society, he plunged into the movement for democratic reform. He did, however, in the new domestic and world context show commitment to arms control by joining in Pugwash discussions. He also gave his name to the 1988 appeal by citizens from socialist states to the CSCE meeting in Vienna calling for a right to conscientious objection.[57] He never offered specific support, however, to Western peace groups, or to independent peace activity in the USSR.

When a small autonomous peace group appeared in Moscow in 1982, proposing a very moderate programme of peace education and initiatives to promote international trust, it stood between the established liberal intellectuals and the dissidents. The Moscow Trust Group therefore took on a symbolic and political significance disproportionate to its numbers, and non-aligned peace organizations in the USA and Europe hastened to make contact and offer support when group members came under pressure. The Soviet Peace Committee, asserting its claim to be the only representative of peace-loving Soviet citizens, denigrated the Trust Group as small and insignificant, and claimed that most members of it were Jews who had applied unsuccessfully to emigrate from the Soviet Union. The KGB soon began systematic harassment, which included sending several group members to psychiatric hospitals and having others sentenced to labour camps. Western peace groups campaigning for their release had some success, but not in all cases.[58]

The Moscow Trust Group was launched by fifteen intellectuals from the apartment of a twenty-six-year-old artist, Sergei Batovrin, on 4 June 1982, to coincide with the opening of the UN Special Session on Disarmament. The best-known member of the group was geographer Yuri Medvedkov, who had worked in the Ecology Unit of the World Health Organization in Geneva. A week after its initial public declaration of its aim the group members began to experience difficulties with the KGB. When the group planned to demonstrate outside the Ministry of Foreign Affairs on 27th June with the slogans 'No More Hiroshimas' and 'Peace Through Trust not Fear' they were prevented from leaving their flats. In July two members were arrested for 'hooliganism': and when Batovrin prepared an exhibition of anti-war paintings in his flat to commemorate Hiroshima, the KGB seized the paintings and sent him to a psychiatric hospital. Batovrin was released in September, but carpenter Alexander Shatravka, who had helped form the Moscow Trust Group and had a record of refusing military service in the 1970s, was arrested in July, when working in Siberia, for collecting signatures to the group's appeal to the governments and peoples of the USA and USSR. Despite the efforts of his fellow group members and Western peace groups, he was sentenced to three years in a labour camp in April 1983.[59]

The group began by addressing itself to organizations in the USA and developing proposals for increased contact between American and Soviet citizens. Over time it established links with many West European groups and with autonomous peace groups and opposition circles in Eastern Europe. The group continued to organize petitions, hold seminars and to plan demonstrations, for example on Hiroshima Day, during the next few years. It also became a focus for young people, who were often part of a Western-style youth culture and who linked the two by commemorating the death of John Lennon. Gradually the group extended the scope of its protests and tackled more controversial issues, such as environmental disasters, the war in Afghanistan and the rights of COs.[60]

The Moscow Trust Group was still meeting regularly at the end of 1988, despite constant KGB surveillance, searches and arrests between 1982 and 1988. A number of group activists were sent to psychiatric hospitals and several leading members were forced, or allowed, to go to the West. Even after Gorbachev became General Secretary of the

Communist Party, group activists faced severe sentences. Jewish doctor Vladimir Brodsky, who was a heart specialist, was sentenced to three years in a labour camp in 1985 and Larisa Chukayeva (whose husband was in prison for Social Democratic views) was sentenced to two years hard labour in July 1986, although she was pardoned in December that year.[61]

The Moscow Trust Group was the best known in the West, but was not the only expression of autonomous peace activity. Other Trust Groups arose in Leningrad, Odessa and Novosibirsk by the end of 1982.[62] A group emerged in Lvov in the Ukraine in 1987, including Pentecostalists and objectors to the war in Afghanistan, and staged a demonstration in September 1987 with slogans calling for nuclear disarmament by the USA and USSR and for *perestroika* inside the Soviet Union.[63] There were also signs of autonomous activity as early as 1982 from the Baltic States, where opposition to Soviet militarism could draw on strong national resistance to Soviet rule. Thirty-eight dissidents from Lithuania, Latvia and Estonia signed a public appeal to the Soviet and Scandinavian Governments that proposals for a Nordic nuclear-weapons-free zone should be extended to cover the Baltic States and the Baltic Sea.[64] Police broke up a summer peace camp in Latvia in July 1987 – allegedly looking for drugs – and by 1989 news reached the West of young Estonians objecting to military service in what they regarded as the occupying Soviet army.[65] As nationalist dissent swelled in Lithuania, young men went into hiding to avoid conscription. When the public confrontation between the new Lithuanian Government demanding independence, and the Soviet Government refusing to grant it, became acute (early in 1990) many Lithuanian soldiers deserted.[66]

EAST–WEST COOPERATION AND ITS PROBLEMS

A number of the autonomous peace campaigns in the USSR and Eastern Europe, such as the Trust Group and the Hungarian Dialogue Group tried to find a space for action between conformity with the official peace committees and open challenge to the Government. In practice this proved very difficult as the official reactions to both groups showed, and in both cases the original participants split between those who tried to continue to operate within limits acceptable to the regime and those who moved towards open protest and direct confrontation. In the USSR the Friendship and Dialogue Group of scientists from the Dolgoprudny sector of Moscow broke with the Trust Group in January 1983 over tactics, and instead of samizdat, petitions and public demonstrations concentrated on research, discussions and education.[67] In both cases divisions over tactics led to bitterness and accusations that those choosing the more cautious approach were collaborating with the regime.

A number of individuals and groups within the Western peace movement were also anxious to try to exploit possible space between the party and its political fronts and the minority of 'dissidents' openly challenging the party. This desire was sometimes heightened by awareness that the Western media and the political Right tended to publicize dissidents in the context of Cold War stereotypes. One such initiative was the Theology of Peace seminar held in Budapest in September 1984, organized jointly by the editor of the END Churches Register and the Hungarian bishop, Karoly Toth.[68] The churches in Eastern Europe had extensive experience of trying to maintain a sphere of autonomy while making compromises with the ruling Communist Parties, although only in East Germany had the Evangelical Church used its influence to oppose militarism. The seminar drew in Western religious peace organizations, such as the International Fellowship of Reconciliation (IFOR), and included a spectrum of views, including the pacifists within the Hungarian Catholic Church.

Professional links could span the East–West divide, as we have seen, though the degree of autonomy on the Eastern side remained problematic. The most ambitious organizational attempt to build professional contacts was International Physicians for the Prevention of Nuclear War, founded in 1980 jointly by an American cardiologist, Bernard Lown, and Yevgeny Chazov, a deputy Minister of Health (and Brezhnev's doctor), who had, however, a reputation for personal independence. Initially the organization concentrated on non-political issues, publicizing the probable effects of nuclear war. But by 1985 it also endorsed proposals for a comprehensive test ban, a No First Use of nuclear weapons commitment and a mutual, verified US–Soviet Freeze on new weapons development. International Physicians won the Nobel Peace Prize in 1985, when it claimed the support of 140,000 doctors in thirty-four countries, including Third World countries.[69] The right-wing press (for example *The Times*) denounced the award of the prize to an allegedly pro-Soviet body, without seriously documenting this claim. It was, indeed, true that members in Socialist states were responsible to their official medical academies, and refrained from public opposition to their own governments' policies.

Western members pointed, however, to the scope for debate on controversial issues – for example they could raise the question of Sakharov's exile and the arrest of Moscow Trust Group activist Dr Brodsky.[70] International Physicians could, therefore, be seen as one of the channels for promoting contact, dialogue and greater individual trust which the Moscow Trust Group had advocated.

Indeed, in terms of promoting dialogue there was an argument for Western peace campaigns to have contact with the official peace committees. Non-aligned peace organizations had varying attitudes to such contact, as noted in Chapter 5, depending partly on their own beliefs. Quakers for example had a long tradition of fostering debate with official bodies in the USSR and Eastern bloc. Western peace groups also found it hard to adopt simple policies on meeting with peace committees because the political colouring of peace committees themselves varied – they could be headed by hard-line party hacks or by more liberal-minded individuals seeking rather more freedom of manoeuvre. In addition the attitudes of independent peace groups and opposition groups in the East towards Western peace movement cooperation with the official committees varied. Western organizations such as CND could on accepting peace committee invitations then insist on visiting autonomous groups and so enhance their status. Moreover, Western cooperation with official committees could allow space for independents to demonstrate their own position, as on the Olof Palme Peace March in 1987. East German and Hungarian independent groups were therefore inclined to favour such contacts. The Poles, however, tended to be strongly opposed to any Western peace group recognition of the official committees.[71] Charter 77 was in general opposed to Western peace groups giving legitimacy to official peace committees, but at the time of the World Peace Council Congress in Prague in 1983 invited non-aligned Western peace groups to attend, in the hope that they could voice an independent policy position and would meet with members of the Charter.[72]

These complexities extended to the annual END Conventions and whether or not to invite official peace committees. Inviting the 'officials' could possibly make it easier for independent activists to get visas; on the other hand some independents – if they managed to get to the convention – felt extremely inhibited by the fact that official representatives were present. The END Liaison Committees for the conventions tended themselves to be divided on invitations to official Eastern bodies (see Chapter 5). When official peace committees did attend the 1984 END Convention in Perugia, a number of Eastern

European independents combined with some Western groups to set up the European Network for East–West Dialogue which became a focus for organizing cooperation between East European groups in the late 1980s.

The distrust initially felt by most East European opposition groupings towards Western peace campaigns was mirrored by the doubts of many Western peace activists about allying themselves with Eastern 'dissidents'. Western activists were aware that quite a few Eastern dissidents, especially some prominent dissidents forced to emigrate to the West, were ardent supporters of Reaganism and so looked to be opponents, not allies, of the peace movement. Western peace campaigners also hesitated to extend their demands to calls for human rights in Eastern Europe because they saw this demand being used selectively by Western governments for Cold War purposes, and because they thought that many pro-Western dictatorships were engaged in even worse abuse of human rights through widescale torture and murder. So emphasis on human rights would involve campaigning on multiple issues. When independent peace groups emerged, organizations like CND resolved their dilemma by calling for the right to demonstrate for peace in the East and by campaigning on behalf of individual peace activists who were arrested. CND remained cautious about alliance with other East European opposition circles.[73]

Even in END, which from the outset was committed to dialogue with opposition groups on peace issues, there was initial hesitation about fully accepting linkage between policies on nuclear weapons and demands for human rights and democracy in Eastern Europe. However, END's political vision of a reunited Europe transcending the East–West divide made it much easier for prominent END personalities to accept the political programme suggested by Charter 77's 1985 Prague Appeal. At the end of 1984 the Polish Group KOS agreed a statement with the French CODENE and Italian Environmental League (Lega Ambiente) on the goal of 'building a free and peaceful Europe beyond the order of Yalta'.[74] So from 1985 there was greater convergence between a section of the Western peace movement and some important opposition circles in the East. This convergence on policy was matched by growing sympathy and understanding between groups acting in opposition to their own governments, and encouraged by the solidarity shown, for example, by END, IKV the Greens, CODENE, WRI and Pax Christi in campaigning on behalf of activists imprisoned in the USSR and Eastern Europe. This sense of the indivisibility of human rights and transnational solidarity also led Eastern independent groups to protest about abuses in the West, such as the imprisonment of peace campaigners in Turkey. The Campaign for Peace and Democracy in New York was able to publish the signatures of prominent East European oppositionists in advertisements calling for the USSR to leave Afghanistan and the USA to end intervention in Nicaragua. A Freedom and Peace activist invited to meet the visiting US Vice-President, George Bush, had his invitation withdrawn by the Americans apparently because he planned to ask questions about an American CO imprisoned for three and a half years.[75] The coming together of the East European opposition and sections of the non-aligned Western peace movement was symbolized by Jacek Kuron's attendance at the 1988 END Convention in Lund, where he and Edward Thompson embraced each other on the speakers' platform.

Contacts between East European groups intensified in the late 1980s, when they addressed joint appeals and statements to the CSCE meeting in Vienna in 1988, and organized conferences for both Eastern and Western participants in their own countries. The Freedom and Peace seminar in Poland in May 1987 was followed by an East–West Dialogue Network seminar on the implications of Gorbachev's reforms, held in Hungary in November 1987, which included discussion of peace issues. Charter 77's interrupted seminar in June 1988 was followed by a meeting in Slovenia in August 1988, which focused on CO rights. During 1989, however, the rapid pace of political change both in Eastern Europe and the USSR itself meant that peace activity tended to be submerged.

CONCLUSION

The transformation of the Soviet bloc created a totally new context for the transnational peace movement. When the END Convention met in July 1990 in Helsinki, delegates could rejoice at the virtual dissolution of the Warsaw Pact, but worried about the implications of the maintenance of NATO. Moreover, the rise of nationalism throughout Eastern Europe and the USSR raised urgent questions about the compatibility of nationalist aspirations and a new peaceful order in the former Soviet bloc. The END Convention transferred half way through its deliberations to Tallinn in Estonia, where a speaker from the Estonian Parliament stressed the positive connections between national self-determination and disarmament goals in

Estonian pressure for a nuclear-free Baltic, and between 'internationalism' and recognition of national rights.[76] In Azerbaijan and Yugoslavia, however, the potential of nationalist passions to lead to civil war was more evident.

The END Convention in 1990 was the first one which autonomous peace groups from Eastern Europe and the USSR could freely attend and so reflected the possibility of a more truly representative dialogue about the priorities for promoting peace. Many prominent members of the autonomous peace groups and opposition groups in Eastern Europe were, however, by mid-1990 in government or advisers to government. This was especially true of Charter 77, but also applied to Freedom and Peace and the Ljubljana Peace Group.

The new governmental status of many in the Charter created some anomalies when the Helsinki Citizens' Assembly met in Prague in October 1990, because the original intention had been to give a voice to diverse social groups independent of governments. The assembly had been suggested by Charter 77 at its 1988 international conference, which had been broken up by the police. So although the assembly responded warmly to Foreign Minister Jiri Dienstbier, who had promoted the idea, and to President Vaclav Havel's opening address, there were some doubts about long-term government involvement. The policy statement for the Assembly reflected earlier Charter views and called for a new European security system without military blocs and troops on foreign soil, and without weapons of mass destruction. However, Western peace groups attending found that most East Europeans were less interested in these disarmament issues than in problems of nationalism and independence, and of economic reconstruction.[77] The prevalence of nationalist conflicts within Eastern Europe and the USSR suggested that in the future peace group concerns with reconciliation and peace keeping might become more central.

NOTES AND REFERENCES

1. *The War Resister*, **83**, 2nd Quarter 1959, pp. 8–9
2. On the San Francisco–Moscow march see Bradford Lyttle, *You Come with Naked Hands: the Story of the San Francisco to Moscow March for Peace* (Raymond, N.H., Greenleaf, 1966); on WRI Czechoslovakia protest, Michael Randle *et al. Support Czechoslovakia* (London, Housmans, 1968); on International Marches for Demilitarization and Radical Party protest

see *Peace News*, 31 August 1979, pp. 4–5; 5 September 1980, p. 5; 30 April 1982, p. 5.

3. Vaclav Havel, 'An Anatomy of Reticence', in Vaclav Havel, *Living in Truth* ed. Jan Vladislav (London, Faber and Faber, 1986).

4. The Jazz Section, founded in 1971, was part of the official Musicians' Union, but became a focus for independent cultural activity, including exhibitions and publishing, and had links with Jazz groups in other East European countries. See *East European Reporter*, **2**, 2, 1986, pp. 17–20; and *END Journal*, **14**, February–March 1985, p. 4.

5. Oliver MacDonald, 'Sudden Growth of Nuclear Pacifism', *Labour Focus on Eastern Europe*, **7**, 1, Winter 1984. Petitions against stationing the missiles circulated in Prague and over 1,500 signed a protest letter in Brno. The official party paper Rude Pravo received numerous letters on the new missiles and published a reply on 5 November 1983. Excerpts in *Survival*, January–February 1984, pp. 37–8.

6. *END Newsletter*, **2**, January 1986, pp. 4–5.

7. John Sandford, *The Sword and the Ploughshare: Autonomous Peace Initiatives in East Germany* (London, END/Merlin, 1983) is the major source up to 1983; Pedro Ramet, 'Church and Peace in the GDR', *Problems of Communism*, Vol. 35, July–August 1984, pp. 44–57 gives overview of the role of the Protestant Church. 'A History of the Peace Movement', *Labour Focus on Eastern Europe*, **8**, 1. Summer 1985, pp. 32–3 is a brief survey by an East German.

8. Joe Singleton, 'Eastern Europe's CND', *Labour Focus on Eastern Europe*, **5**, 1–2, Spring 1982, pp. 41–2; *END Papers 3*, Summer–Autumn 1982, 'Dossier on East Germany'; Sandford, pp. 52–67.

9. Gus Fagan, 'The Peace Movement Enters its Second Year', *Labour Focus on Eastern Europe*, **6**, 1–2, Summer 1983, pp. 18–21.

10. Stephen Brown, 'GDR: The Church, State and Peace', *Sanity*, October 1983, pp. 24–7; and Ramet, pp. 52 and 55 especially.

11. On Weimar peace activities see *Labour Focus on Eastern Europe*, Summer 1984, pp. 33–4 for two East German contributions. On the Women's Group see *END Journal*, **2**, February–March 1983, pp. 10–11 (includes text of letter).

12. *END Journal*, No. 8, February–March 1984, p. 5; *From Below: Independent Peace and Environmental Movements in Eastern Europe and the USSR* (New York, Helsinki Watch Report, October 1987), pp. 31–2.

13. Gunter Minnerup, 'The Round-up of Peace Activists', *Labour Focus on Eastern Europe*, **7**, 2, Summer 1984, p. 33; and 'East German Peace Activists Take Up the Human Rights Issue', *Labour Focus on Eastern Europe*, **8**, 2, May 1986, pp. 17–18; *From Below*, pp. 34–5.

14. *Ibid.* pp. 45–7; *Labour Focus on Eastern Europe*, **9**, 2, July–October 1987, p. 48.

15. Stephen Brown, 'Gorbachev, New Thinking and the Church in the German Democratic Republic', *Sanity*, November 1987, p. 33. For Palme Report see *Common Security: a Programme for Disarmament* (London, Pan Books, 1982).

16. Vladimir V. Kusin, *From Dubcek to Charter 77* (Edinburgh, Q Press, 1978); and Gordon H. Skilling, *Charter 77 and Human Rights in Czechoslovakia* (London, Allen and Unwin, 1981) give the political background.

17. See Jan Kavan and Zdena Tomin (eds), *Voices From Prague* (London, END and Palach Press, 1983), p. 16. The first exchange between Racek and Thompson was published in the *New Statesman*, 24 April 1981.
18. Kavan and Tomin, pp. 52–72.
19. Kavan and Tomin, p. 40.
20. Kavan and Tomin, pp. 22–3 print the first Charter statement. For the Prague Appeal see *END Journal*, April–May 1985.
21. *East European Reporter*, **1**, 5, Autumn 1985, p. 38.
22. *END Journal*, **14**, February–March 1985, p. 30.
23. Jan Kavan, 'Spontaneous Peace Demo in Prague' and 'Participant's Report', *East European Reporter*, **1**, 4, Winter 1986, pp. 27–9.
24. END Statement, December 1988; and *Labour Focus on Eastern Europe*, **2**, 1989, p. 48.
25. *END Newsletter*, July 1988.
26. Bill Lomax, 'The Hungarian Peace Movement', *Labour Focus on Eastern Europe*, **5**, 5–6, Winter 1982–83, pp. 35–6. Laszlo Rajk's father had been executed in a notorious Stalinist show trial in Hungary in 1949 (he had been Interior Minister and then Foreign Minister in the post-war government). Rajk became a prominent dissident in the 1960s.
27. Ference Koszegi and E.P. Thompson, *The New Hungarian Peace Movement* (London, END/Merlin Press, 1983).
28. Bill Lomax, 'The Dialogue Breaks Down', *Labour Focus on Eastern Europe*, **7**, 1, Winter 1984, pp. 23–5; and Lynne Jones, 'Keeping Dialogue Open', *END Journal*, **6**, October–November 1983, pp. 11–12.
29. Bob Dent, 'Hungary: Peaceful Developments', *Sanity*, March 1986, pp. 24–6.
30. Bill Lomax, 'Pacifist Movement Within the Hungarian Catholic Church', *Labour Focus on Eastern Europe*, **5**, 3–4, Summer 1982, pp. 30–1 (based on article by Haraszti in Hungarian samizdat journal *Bezelo*); 'Catholic Conscientious Objectors', *East European Reporter*, **1**, 1, Summer 1985, pp. 31–4; and Koszegi (in Koszegi and Thompson), p. 12 (who cites 300 groups).
31. 'Putting Conscience Before the State', *Peace News*, 16 January 1987, p. 9.
32. Solidarity is authoritatively covered in Neal Ascherson, *The Polish August* (Harmondsworth, Penguin, 1982) and Timothy Garton Ash, *The Polish Revolution: Solidarity 1980–82* (London, Cape, 1983), who also discusses Western reactions.
33. For Jacek Kuron's letter and Wroclaw Group statement see *END Journal*, **11**, August–September 1984, p. 8; see also 'Polish Attitudes to Foreign Affairs', *END Journal*, **15**, April–May 1985, pp. 6–7 (translated from French Solidarnosc information bulletin).
34. *East European Reporter*, **2**, 1, Spring 1986, pp. 44–6 (prints Freedom and Peace Programme) and **2**, 3, 1987, pp. 39–41 (prints interview of Polish peace activist for Hungarian samizdat).
35. *From Below*, pp. 78–9.
36. Lynne Jones, 'Peace in Poland', *Sanity*, June 1988, p. 17.
37. Ibid.
38. *From Below*, p. 77.
39. Ibid., pp. 92–3, 85–6.

40. 'Freedom and Peace International Seminar', *East European Reporter*, **2** 3, 1987, pp. 56–9.
41. *The War Resister*, **82**, 1st Quarter 1959, pp. 3–4.
42. *END Newsletter*, **9**, January 1988, p. 2.
43. *From Below*, pp. 181–203 cover Ljublajana Peace Group and reactions to it.
44. Michele Lee, 'Awaiting the Future', *Labour Focus on Eastern Europe*, **10**, 1, April 1988, p. 42; and 'Opposing a Military Coup in Yugoslavia', *Prisoners for Peace* (London, WRI, 1988).
45. *Independent*, 20 May 1988, p. 10.
46. *New Statesman and Society*, 14 June 1988, p. 7; *Prisoners for Peace*, 1988.
47. *Keesings*, Vol. 35, May 1989, p. 36663.
48. Michele Lee, 'Will the Centre Hold?' *Labour Focus on Eastern Europe*, **1**, 1989, p. 38.
49. *From Below*, pp. 203–4.
50. John Newhouse, *Cold Dawn: The Story of SALT* (New York, Holt, Rhinehart and Winston, 1973), pp. 55–6.
51. J.F. Hough, 'The Soviet View of the Strategic Situation', in R. Kolkowitz and N. Joeck (eds), *Arms Control and International Security* (Boulder, Colorado, Westview Press, 1984).
52. The Natural Resources Defence Council in New York signed an agreement with the Soviet Academy of Sciences in May 1986 allowing American scientists to set up their seismic instruments near the Semipalatinsk testing site in the USSR and in November Soviet scientists visited the USA to examine possible sites in Nevada to set up their own instruments. This initiative by scientists was of course authorized by the US and Soviet Governments. *ADIU Report*, **8**, 4, July–August 1986, p. 21; **9**, 1, January–February 1987, p. 23.
53. Joshua Rubenstein, *Soviet Dissidents: their Struggle for Human Rights* (London, Wildwood House, 1981), pp. 196–9.
54. H.F. York, 'Sakharov and the Nuclear Test Ban', *Bulletin of the Atomic Scientists*, **37**, 9, November 1981, pp. 33–7.
55. Andrei Sakharov, *My Country and the World* (New York, Vintage Press, 1975).
56. For example Sakharov supported development of the US MX missile as a bargaining chip in negotiations with the USSR, see *From Below*, p. 106.
57. *East European Reporter*, **3**, 2, March 1988, pp. 68–9.
58. Jean Stead and Danielle Grunberg (eds), *Moscow Independent Peace Group* (London, Merlin Press/END, 1982) covers the origins of the group. END Briefing Sheet, 'Moscow Trust Group', summarizes the first few years.
59. *Trustbuilders Newsletter*, **7**, 1985 (UK Trustbuilders' Group).
60. *END Journal*, **14**, February–March 1983, p. 27; **12**, October–November 1984, p. 7; **14**, February–March 1985, p. 6; and *Peace News*, 9 December 1988, p. 6. See also *From Below*, pp. 107–35 for a more detailed history of the group up to 1987.
61. END Briefing Sheet, 'Moscow Trust Group' and *END Newsletter*, July–September 1986, p. 3 on arrests. *Keesings*, October 1987, p. 35471, covers Chukayeva's release.
62. Stead and Grunberg, p. 43.

63. *Peace News*, 11 December 1987, p. 6 (Source: London-based Ukraine Peace Committee).
64. *Peace News*, 19 March 1982.
65. *Peace News*, 9 October 1987, p. 6 on Latvian camp and *WRI Newsletter*, No. 226, September–October 1989, pp. 24–5.
66. *Guardian (Weekend)*, 7–8 April 1990, pp. 24–5.
67. *From Below*, pp. 135–8.
68. Bill McSweeney, 'A New Politics in the East–West Dialogue?', *END Journal*, **13**, December 1984–January 1985, p. 28.
69. *Observer*, 13 October 1985, p. 13.
70. Lynne Jones, 'Inside IPPNW', *END Journal*, **9**, December 1985–January 1986 pp. 10–11.
71. I am indebted to comments by Howard Clark of WRI here and at several other points in this chapter.
72. Kavan and Tomin, pp. 7–8.
73. See Bruce Kent on CND policy and his disagreements with Solidarity demonstrators when he had visited the Polish Embassy: Bruce Kent, 'I Knew We Were onto Something', *Sanity*, November–December 1990, p. 14.
74. 'Polish–French–Italian "Beyond Yalta" Statement', *END Journal*, **13**, December 1984–January 1985, pp. 31–3.
75. Jones, *Sanity*, June 1988, p. 18.
76. *Sanity*, September 1990, pp. 6–7; *CND News*, Autumn/Winter 1990, p. 12.
77. *Sanity*, April 1990, p. 8; Howard Clark, '"Helsinki from Below" Process Starts in Prague', *Peace News*, November 1990, p. 5.

CHAPTER EIGHT
Pacifism, War Resistance and Reconciliation

INTRODUCTION

Previous chapters explored the major campaigns against nuclear weapons and against the Vietnam War, which brought peace movements onto the front pages of newspapers and which challenged governments to change course. This chapter looks at examples of longer-term pacifist action designed to alter ideas and attitudes or influence policies on arms and military defence. Continuity in peace activity has been encouraged by national and international peace organizations dating from before the Second World War, but many new peace groupings have sprung up to pursue specific issues such as the arms trade.

Surveying the scope of peace campaigning and the degree of popular or official support for particular demands, such as recognition of conscientious objectors (COs), the contrast between the late 1940s and the late 1980s is striking. Some obvious reasons for the dearth of non-aligned peace campaigning in the 1940s – the impact of the Second World War and the evolution of the Cold War – were examined in Chapter 2. One positive reason for the impetus given to pacifist campaigns has been the cumulative effect of the nuclear disarmament campaigns and of the opposition to the Vietnam War. These movements swelled the constituency of people receptive to anti-militarist ideas and provided examples of resistance to military policies, encouraging for instance refusal to be conscripted into the armed services. These movements also generated energy and new ideas. During the 1980s it became difficult to distinguish between campaigns against nuclear weapons and those against all weapons. The Peace Tax campaign, for example, combined elements of both.

The other significant trend in Europe has been the strengthening of liberal values and the institutional scope for promoting liberal principles through the Council of Europe, the European Community and the European Court of Human Rights. The last forty-five years have seen widening recognition of conscientious objection to military service as an individual human right, as more states have thrown off repressive or dictatorial regimes, and as European bodies have expressed support for CO rights. Peace campaigners have also been able to appeal to liberal attitudes and beliefs to gain some parliamentary or government support on issues such as opposing the sale of war toys.

If pacifists have benefited from increasing liberalism, their campaigns have in turn contributed to acceptance of liberal attitudes on military matters. Pacifist criticism of the armed forces has exposed restrictions on freedom of speech and pacifist publication of military information has illustrated how claims of military secrecy curb freedom of the press and can bypass parliamentary democracy. Establishing the right to conscientious objection as a liberal principle has only been achieved gradually after hard-fought campaigns in many countries, and through the determination of individual resisters to military service. The right is not yet fully established in Europe and in only a handful of countries outside it.

Opposition to military policies and support for basic human rights have often coincided, especially where repressive military regimes are in power. Campaigns against the arms trade have combined general opposition to arms sales, which opponents claim divert economic resources and often intensify local conflicts, with specific human rights objections to regimes acquiring the arms. Pacifists locally and internationally have also supported resistance to military service prompted, as in South Africa and Israel, more by commitment to human rights and social justice than by anti-militarism.

Established peace organizations have usually played some part in opposing the armed forces, or trying to promote inter-communal reconciliation, in specific wars or conflicts. But significant movements of war resistance, or campaigns for peace, have depended on spontaneous action by women and men rebelling against the injustice or violence of their situation, as the brief studies of South Africa, Israel and Northern Ireland illustrate. The scope for organized transnational action by pacifists is examined in the penultimate section of this chapter. Many aspects of peace campaigning came together in opposition to the 1991 Gulf War and a brief survey of this movement concludes our discussion.

PACIFIST PROTEST

The most distinctive element in pacifist thought and action is individual commitment to refuse cooperation with the armed services and military preparations, and the campaigns to promote refusal of war taxes and conscientious objection to military service are considered at some length in this chapter. A good deal of pacifist campaigning is, however, directed towards challenging a culture which accepts war as normal and constantly promotes images of war and violence. Many who do not accept the pacifist conclusion that all military defence should be abandoned have rejected trends towards a militarization of culture, as the campaigns against war toys have suggested.

In the affluent societies of North America and Britain appealing to parents to think about the presents they give their children has obvious potential. Protesting against war toys also gives scope for lobbying shops and toy manufacturers and for offering positive alternatives. So, for example, the No War Toys groups, formed in California in 1965 to focus on Christmas that year, had by December launched a campaign of publicity on radio and television, issued lists of films and books on peace issues and set up a centre in Los Angeles to provide creative toys in exchange for war toys.[1] Twenty years later the Canadian Alliance for Non-violent Action called for a boycott of war toys, which were being sold in increasing numbers, partly because of a boom in the production of American war toys in the early 1980s. The boycott had the backing of church and Third World groups, and of women's, parents' and children's rights organizations, as well as peace groups.[2] The Peace Pledge Union in Britain produced a petition against advertising war toys and a leaflet, and the group Play for Life had by 1985 moved on from vigils at toy fairs to promoting creative and traditional toys.[3] Official support for limits on war toys has so far, however, been limited to Europe. West Germany has been concerned about military toys, and has banned replicas of Second World War German military equipment, while Sweden decided to impose a total ban on war toys in 1980, but made an exception for models of pre-1914 weapons. The European Parliament urged limits on war toy advertising in 1982[4].

Military toys have evoked opposition in a variety of political and cultural contexts. A number of peace activists in Socialist States concerned about the militarization of education and society – the Moscow Trust Group, the East German campaigners and the Ljubljana Peace Group – took up the issue of war toys. Opposition within the military-dominated societies of Latin America has also sometimes focused on children. A pacifist group in Uruguay reported in 1949 that it was protesting both against military training in school and against war toys. In General Pinochet's Chile, the Committee on Denuclearization and Demilitarization and the Chilean Greens tried to promote peace education in schools and protested against war toys in 1987 and 1988.[5] The Caribbean Project for Peace and Justice, based in Puerto Rico, which was campaigning in the late 1980s against military bases, also opposed the influence of the USA on local culture represented by war toys.[6] In South Africa, in the context of mounting resistance to the role of the armed forces, the End Conscription Campaign in Durban took time in 1986 to protest against the sale of war toys, in particular models of the troops vehicles widely used in the black townships.[7]

Public protest against military traditions can arouse controversy, as the Peace Pledge Union discovered when it began in 1980 to sell white poppies for peace to counter the official military ceremonial associated with Remembrance Sunday, which honours the dead servicemen and women from the two world wars. Members of the group also laid a wreath of white poppies at the Cenotaph to commemorate all those who had died in past wars and as a pledge to try to prevent future wars. They were reviving an idea initiated by the Cooperative Women's Guild in the 1930s. The white poppies became news when the *Star* led the tabloid press in November 1986 in attacking 'the lily livered and white feather brigade', and Mrs Thatcher voiced her 'deep distaste' for the pacifist poppies.[8]

Pacifist groups propagate their views, like many other groups, through posters, leaflets, pamphlets and periodicals, which for the most part do not attract wide notice. Occasionally, however, pacifist publications have provoked responses by the state which raise important issues about the freedom of expression and the power of the armed forces in that society. In one noted case in Italy the Secretary of the Movement for Non-violence was sentenced to four months in prison for producing a poster which 'slandered the armed forces'. He was convicted by a court in Perugia. But another court in Campobasso acquitted a pacifist distributing the same poster, the judge commenting that it was time to accept that Italy was a democracy. When the Supreme Court upheld the original conviction in June 1974, its ruling was challenged by widespread distribution of the poster, which had by now been signed by several well-known Italian personalities committed to the principle of freedom of expression. The offending text summarized the record of the Italian army from the 1920s to the 1940s.[9]

Where to draw the line between freedom of information and the requirements of military security is inevitably contentious, even in quite liberal societies. The editors of the Norwegian War Resisters' magazine, *Ikkevold* (Non-violence), went too far for the Norwegian state when in September 1983 they published details about the Andoya naval base in north Norway. *Ikkevold* drew on the press, military journals and US Congress papers (supplemented by phone enquiries to the military) to reveal that Andoya was not really a Norwegian facility, but a US Sound Surveillance System base for tracking Soviet submarines. This claim was highly sensitive since Norway had not officially accepted US bases on its territory. The Norwegian security police raided the offices and homes of the *Ikkevold* staff, and the seven editors were charged with endangering the state, a charge carrying a maximum sentence of twenty years imprisonment. It emerged at the trial that only three members of the Norwegian Parliamentary Defence Committee knew the real purpose of the base. The court ruled in May 1985 that the defendants had not been spying, but found them guilty and sentenced one editor to nine months in prison and six to suspended sentences. On appeal the prison sentences were quashed.[10]

The ultimate pacifist goal is not only to change popular attitudes to war, but to alter government policies on military defence. An ambitious campaign designed to achieve both these aims took place in Switzerland, where citizens voted on 25 November 1989 in a referendum on whether to abolish the armed forces. Switzerland has a long tradition of armed neutrality and its democratic ethos has tended to equate citizenship with willingness to fight for the republic – conscription has been in force since 1848. So evidence of a widespread mood of anti-militarism is especially interesting. The Swiss had been influenced by the 1980s movement against nuclear weapons in Western Europe, and in January 1988 over 700,000 had voted in an earlier referendum to give citizens the final say on military expenditure. The turn-out for the referendum on the abolition of the armed forces was in fact unusually high, with 68.7 per cent of the electorate voting, of whom 35.6 per cent (1,052,218) opted for abolishing the army. Analysis of the vote showed that a majority of those under thirty-five voted for abolition, and that urban areas were more favourable than rural. The cantons of Geneva and Jura showed majorities for the proposition. Afterwards the Defence Minister announced the formation of a working party to examine criticisms of the military and the size of the defence budget made during the referendum campaign.

The initiative for a referendum came from the Switzerland Without an Army Group, which was formed in 1982 with the aim of developing a non-violent society. The group had over 1,000 members by the late 1980s and an additional 1,200 subscribers to its newsletter. It launched a campaign for signatures to a constitutional initiative in March 1985, and by September 1986 had collected over 111,300 signatures calling for a referendum (100,000 are required). The signature campaign prompted widespread debate about the purpose of military defence and its relevance in an age of nuclear weapons. The Swiss Group was anxious to build up international support for its goals, and at the time of the referendum a new West German Group for a Federal Germany Without an Army blockaded their Ministry of Defence.[11]

OPPOSING THE ARMS TRADE

Pacifists oppose all arms sales, but they have often made common cause with groups principally concerned about selling particular types of weapon to particular regimes, or about the political and economic impact of Western arms exports. The campaigns which developed in the 1970s were primarily related to Third World issues. The British Campaign Against the Arms Trade was set up in 1974, in the aftermath of the 1973 Arab-Israeli War, in which both sides relied heavily on their Soviet and US arms supplies. The campaign engaged in research on British arms exports as well as mounting regular protests at exhibitions of defence equipment. For example, the campaign picketed a Defence Components Exhibition in Brighton in May 1981, where over 130 companies took part; next door, at the Grand Hotel, the Campaign held its own exhibition of technology appropriate to Third World development. During the 1982 Falklands War the campaign published details of the weapons Britain had supplied to Argentina.[12] Earlier, the Campaign had won influential backing, including the Archbishop of Canterbury's support, when it protested agaist sending anti-personnel carriers to El Salvador in 1978, and the delivery was cancelled.[13] Although cruise missiles became a higher-profile issue than arms sales in the early 1980s, protests about export of arms clearly retained their relevance. The Methodist Church passed a resolution at its July 1988 Conference urging the Government to stop sponsoring exhibitions of military equipment and to close down the specialized Defence Sales Organization.[14] When the Campaign picked up news of a proposed sale of Hawk jet 'trainer' planes to Iraq in February 1989, it prompted its supporters to protest to the Government on the grounds that the trainers could easily be converted to combat aircraft. The Foreign Office did later refuse an export licence.[15]

Opposition to arms sales has prompted protest in many countries. The Fellowship of Reconciliation in the USA coordinated a demonstration of hundreds outside an Exhibition of Defence Technology in Chicago in February 1979. Advance publicity about the planned protests led seventy-three companies to withdraw and the Exhibition organizers restricted entry to the hall. West Germans staged a similar protest, when over 500 demonstrators picketed a Defence Electronics Exhibition in Hanover in May 1982, handed out leaflets and tried to block entry.[16] The Latin American religious organization, Service for Peace and Justice, has opposed trade in arms which, it argues, sustains dictatorships and makes border conflicts more likely to escalate into war.[17] Campaigns in Latin America included protests in 1988 by the Chilean Committee for Denuclearization and Demilitarization, which persuaded members of the Organization of American States to withdraw from an arms fair. When the Thai Ministry of Defence promoted the first arms exhibition in Bangkok at the same time as the 'Defence Asia '87' conference, the Peace Action Group of the Coordinating Group for Religion and Society in Thailand protested outside, using street theatre to demonstrate alternatives to military defence.[18] Australian peace groups, which had prevented a defence equipment exhibition in 1986, came together in 1989 to create Stop Arms for Export and to demonstrate at the arms fair planned for Canberra in November 1989. They were trying to counter the Labour Government's decision to double its arms exports.[19]

Possible curbs on the arms trade have received attention at international governmental level. The International Fellowship of Reconciliation had decided in 1980 to back its French section in urging the European Parliament to consider arms exports. Then the Swedish Peace and Arbitration Society, which had uncovered the scandal of illegal arms sales to the Middle East by Bofors in 1984, urged international action.[20] The International Peace Bureau convened a conference of groups working against the arms trade in 1987 to draw up a list of proposals for the European Parliament and the United Nations. The Security and Disarmament Sub-committee of the European Parliament did in 1988 look at the possibility of common Community policies, including a register of arms exports. The Third Session of the UN Special Session on Disarmament in 1988, which was intensively lobbied by the Bureau and others on the arms trade, also addressed itself to this topic. A number of countries, including Britain, supported a register of arms exports and some constraints; but others building up their own arms industries opposed all controls and no agreement was reached.[21]

TAX REFUSAL

Pacifism now implies individual refusal to support the military policies of the state, so non-payment of taxes has emerged as an appropriate method of protest and non-cooperation. There is a long tradition of pacifists refusing to pay taxes on grounds of conscience, especially in the USA. Since the 1970s, however, tax refusers in the USA and elsewhere have adopted a more sophisticated political campaign by withholding the proportion of tax equivalent to the proportion of the national budget going on defence, paying this portion of their tax into a fund for Third World development or constructive peace-making, and calling for a legal right to conscientious exemption from military taxes. For example, Senator Jo Vallentine of Australia held back 10 per cent of her taxes in 1988 and paid the money into the Melbourne Peace and Development Foundation. She also explored the possibility of amending the Taxation Act to make it legally acceptable for individuals to divert their taxes from military to peaceful purposes.[22]

Tax refusal, unlike objection to military service, could in principle be open to almost all citizens. In Britain, however, the PAYE system of employers deducting income tax from wages has restricted tax refusal to the self-employed. The Peace Tax Campaign launched in 1978 tried to bypass this obstacle and to establish a general principle by calling for a legal right to pay defence taxes into an alternative fund. A number of individual pacifists withheld part of their taxes in the 1980s, and in addition the Peace Pledge Union and the Quakers deducted the military portion of the PAYE taxes they paid for their employees. The case of thirty-three Quakers working for the Society of Friends went before a series of courts between 1983 and 1986, including the House of Lords and the European Court of Human Rights, but they lost their claim to a conscientious right to refuse defence taxes.[23]

Pacifists in Western Europe stepped up campaigns against war taxes in the context of the heightened peace consciousness of the 1980s. In

Switzerland, for example, organized resistance began in the 1970s – there were 120 tax refusers by 1975 – but a new initiative in 1983 resulted in 250 resisters pledged to pay 20 per cent of their taxes towards a peace research institute. The authorities usually distrained goods to cover the unpaid taxes, but in some cases also sentenced tax refusers to brief prison spells for failing to perform their military duty, so accepting a parallel with conscientious objection to military service. One protester, who had paid no military taxes since 1977, eventually sought asylum abroad after repeated prison terms and distraint of his tools.[24] Militant anti-militarism in Spain was reflected by around 1,000 tax resisters who, in 1985, were claiming the right of freedom of conscience and a constitutional right to refuse military service, and were keeping back 10 per cent of their taxes. The campaign had started in Andalucia in 1981, spreading to other regions three years later, and was backed by the Greens, the Christian Justice and Peace organization and the trade union federation, the CNT.[25]

A lively and controversial campaign arose in Italy, where pacifists called for official recognition of conscientious tax objection on the same basis as objection to bearing arms. Numbers who registered as objectors and refused to pay military taxes rose rapidly from 400 in 1982 to almost 3,000 by 1986. A cheque for the total sum withheld was sent each year to the president, asking him to put it to constructive use; when he refused to accept it, the money was given to a centrally administered fund for peace and development. The campaign's 150 local groups, who encouraged tax resistance by letters to the press, posters and by distributing a guide to non-payment of military taxes, frequently found themselves in court for 'inciting' others to break the law. Local courts generally acquitted them; nevertheless, when the Mayor and Council of Fidenza passed a resolution supporting the principle of war tax resistance they were brought to trial. The Catholic Church became involved in the campaign when 2,500 north Italian clergy issued a statement 'Blessed are the Peacemakers', which endorsed refusal to pay military taxes. A hundred clergy personally committed to withhold tax wrote to the Vatican in February 1988, noting the Pope's frequent pleas that funds should be diverted from arms to development, and asking that the Church should not discipline tax resisters. The Vatican began a study of the moral issues involved.[26]

By the end of the decade the tax resistance campaign was strengthening its transnational links. The first conference of tax refusal groups took place in West Germany in 1986, and a second in The Netherlands in 1988 drew campaigners from over a dozen countries. A world peace fund, proposed in 1986, appeared on examination to be over-ambitious. The Second Conference did, however, designate 1st September as International War Tax Day, and made plans to raise the issue of conscientious tax objection at the European Ecumenical Assembly and in the 1989 European parliamentary elections.[27] The British Peace Tax Campaign agreed a statement on the right to tax objection with Belgian, Dutch and West German groups, and reported that as the result of lobbying it had the backing after the elections of ten reselected MEPs and six newly selected MEPs. In addition eighty-six MPs in the British Parliament backed the campaign. Bills proposing a conscientious right to tax objection were introduced in Australia, the USA, Netherlands and Italy in 1989.[28]

CONSCIENTIOUS OBJECTION TO MILITARY SERVICE

The tax resistance campaign has built on the fairly widespread recognition in the West of an individual's right to refuse to bear arms on grounds of conscience. This right has not, however, been easily won. Campaigns to extend acceptance of conscientious objection preoccupied many pacifists in Europe for much of the post-war period, and interpretation of CO rights remains an important issue. CO provisions are of primary importance when governments impose universal conscription, though the existence of laws recognizing COs can of course help professional soldiers who change their views on war while serving in the armed forces. Conscientious objection has continued to preoccupy European pacifists because almost every Western European country has maintained compulsory military service into the 1990s. The major exception has been Britain, where conscription ended in 1961, and where pacifists have diverted their energies from supporting COs to counselling service personnel, in particular boy soldiers, about their rights.[29] Eire, Iceland and Luxemburg were the only other West European countries which had dispensed with conscription by 1990. (For the Soviet Union and Eastern Europe see Chapter 7).

The willingness of governments to recognize CO rights has reflected the strength of their adherence to parliamentary democracy, and the degree of cultural respect for liberal principles and for the individual conscience. So the USA, Canada, Australia and New Zealand made laws for COs between the two world wars, as did the

Netherlands, the Scandinavian countries and Britain. When Austria and West Germany began to create their own military forces again in 1955, both incorporated CO provisions in their legislation. However, pacifists have had to protest vigorously, and individuals refusing to join the armed services have suffered very severe penalties, before France and Belgium would recognize COs in the 1960s, and before Italy did so in 1971. After Spain, Portugal and Greece had emerged from dictatorships in the 1970s they began to move gradually towards some provision for CO status. Switzerland has refused to give COs legal recognition, though military tribunals may allow religious objectors to do non-military work during their call-up, because of its 'nation in arms' tradition of republicanism. Not surprisingly, Turkey, which has an abysmal human rights record and has suppressed any form of peace protest (see Chapter 5), has not recognized COs. (Turkish Greens who called for a CO law in 1988 were vilified in the press.)

The scope for provision for COs varies considerably, even when states do legislate for objectors to military service. Grounds for conscientious objection may be narrowly defined to cover only those who hold specific religious beliefs, or they may take into consideration wider ethical and social beliefs. How easy it is to become a CO depends on whether objectors have to satisfy a military or civilian tribunal, whether they can readily learn about their rights and on what the appeal procedures are if a tribunal's decision is negative. COs have also been very concerned about the nature of alternative service open to them: whether it is under military control or indirectly assists the military; whether it is punitive or socially constructive; and whether it is the same length as military service or longer. The penalties for those who refuse to serve but are denied CO status also remains an important issue.[30] Therefore, even after war resisters have won their initial campaigns for recognition of COs, as in France, they have pressed for further reforms of the law. While in countries like West Germany COs have reacted to measures which they saw as restricting their rights, helping the military or undercutting trade unions by using conscripts as cheap labour.

Pacifist bodies have campaigned for CO rights in order to gain social recognition that refusing to bear arms is a legitimate moral and social stance, and out of an urgent need to support young men suffering for their beliefs, including some, like Jehovah's Witnesses, whose position is wholly apolitical. The War Resisters' International (WRI), which had in the inter-war years seen compliance with CO regulations as unacceptable compromise with the armed forces, decided after 1945 that it should back campaigns for CO rights, despite occasional criticism from supporters.[31] The WRI has, however, also continued to give strong support to those war resisters who do decide that only total non-cooperation is consistent with their goal of abolishing the military.

Belgian pacifists campaigned vigorously, and 600 COs served over 1,000 years in prison, to get an initial CO law allowing alternative service passed in 1961.[32] Pacifists had to wage an even harder struggle for CO rights in France. The initial focus was the case of Jean Bernard Moreau, who had already served a year in prison for refusing to bear arms when he was rearrested late in 1949 and sentenced to another year's imprisonment in January 1950. Moreau had impressed the judges at his military tribunal, who expressed the view that there should be a law on conscientious objection, and his case received publicity in France and abroad. The Abbé Pierre, a former MRP deputy who left the party over foreign and social policy and became well known for his work with the poor and homeless, launched a petition calling for a law on COs. The papers *Canard Enchaîné*, *Franc-Tireur* and *Combat* backed this call. The Pacifist Action League and Committee for Legal Recognition of COs lobbied deputies, and in 1953 secured an initial vote in the National Assembly in favour of an amnesty for COs; but the vote was overruled by the Council of the Republic and lost in a second vote in the Assembly. By 1955 there were fifty-four objectors serving prison sentences, some in their third, fourth or fifth term.[33]

The veteran pacifist Louis Lecoin, editor of the weekly *Liberté*, initiated an appeal to de Gaulle in 1958 for clemency for COs in prison, and de Gaulle decided to release those who had served over five years. Nine men qualified for release immediately, and over 140 objectors gained eventual release under this policy by June 1962. Lecoin forced the Government to bring forward a bill making provision for COs when at the beginning of June 1962 he began to fast to the death. After the seventy-four-year-old Lecoin had fasted twenty-one days, de Gaulle promised to introduce legislation into the Assembly that session. French pacifists lobbied desperately to persuade members of the National Assembly to outvote an attempt by the Defence Committee to quash the bill that summer. The bill eventually passed its fourth reading in the National Assembly by 344 votes to 94, and became law in 1963.[34]

The French CO law, when achieved, was restrictive. A ban on publicizing CO rights meant that potential objectors did not always know about the law's existence. Moreover, objectors had to do alternative service for double the length of time of military service, and were drafted to hard physical labour in remote rural areas. Many objectors were refusing by the early 1970s to do this work and were sent to jail.[35]

A prolonged struggle to secure the rights of COs in Italy began about the same time as the campaign in France. Political debate was aroused in 1949–50 by the case of pacifist Pietro Pinna, who challenged the principle of universal military service by appealing against his original prison sentence to the Supreme Military Court. He received publicity in France and Britain and backing from twenty-three British MPs. The first bill proposing recognition of COs was introduced in the Assembly in 1950.[36] Public interest in the issue then lapsed in Italy until it was revived in 1961, when the French director Claude Autant Lara produced a film about a French CO for an Italian company. Both France and Italy refused to allow shooting of the film on their territory and both governments banned it from being shown. The Italian ban on 'Thou Shalt Not Kill' was imposed by the censor under security laws made under the fascists, and immediately became a civil liberties issue. The European Community of Writers arranged a private showing in Rome in October 1961, and when it was banned many of those invited including Italian film stars sat down in the street in protest. The Mayor of Florence defied national censorship and authorized screening of the film, and a new centre-Left Government lifted the ban in the spring of 1962, when the film bwas shown all over Italy.[37]

Political opposition to recognizing COs was due partly to fears that the Communists would use a CO law to undermine acceptance of military service. The Catholic Church was also initially strongly opposed: the Jesuits' paper, *Civiltà Cattolicà*, denounced the 1950 CO bill. The COs themselves were unable to bring significant pressure to bear, mainly because they were few in number and had in their ranks a high proportion of Jehovah's Witnesses, who did not in any case publicize their stand. It was therefore very important when the first CO to claim specifically Catholic grounds for his views came forward in 1963. He sparked off a major debate among Catholics. Two priests wrote publicly defending the principle of conscientious objection, and in the ensuing controversy (both priests were taken to court for their subversive views) the official Vatican newspaper declared the Church's neutrality on conscientious objection. The article made clear that Catholic COs could not appeal to the Church's teaching, but only to their own subjective interpretations. At this stage three more bills to make conscientious objection legal came before the Assembly, but despite support among Communists, socialists and some Christian Democrats, they were shelved. Another five bills were tabled between 1967 and 1970.[38]

When a CO law was finally passed in 1971, pacifists denounced it as extremely restrictive. It gave the Ministry of Defence the power to decide who should qualify as a CO, left COs under military jurisdiction and required them to do alternative service for longer than their military counterparts.[39] The Assembly passed an amendment to the law in January 1989, which recognized CO status was not a concession, but a right flowing from freedom of thought, conscience and religion.[40]

International pacifist groups were especially concerned about the position in Greece, where two Jehovah's Witnesses were shot in 1949 for refusing military service, and six others had their sentence commuted to life imprisonment. There were no further executions of COs – a death sentence passed by an Athens Court in 1966 was commuted – but as late as 1989 WRI reported there were about 400 Jehovah's Witnesses serving about four years in prison.[41] A 1977 law providing for unarmed service within the armed forces in practice made no difference. A political campaign inside Greece for proper recognition of CO rights began in December 1986, when Michalis Maragakis refused to obey his call-up and went on a public speaking tour. He also canvassed for support at a peace conference opened in Athens by Prime Minister Papandreou. He was subsequently sentenced to four years in prison, reduced on appeal to two years. Athens student Thanassis Makris was sentenced to five years by a military court in May 1988 for refusing military service, despite the fact that the Government had just undertaken to introduce a bill on CO rights. The Government had made this promise on 1 May in response to a hunger strike by Maragakis (seriously ill after fasting for over two months) and by Makris, who had been fasting since his arrest for three weeks. Socialist deputies in the European Parliament had pressed the Papandreou Government to improve its treatment of COs, and representatives of Green and anti-militarist parties offered strong support to the Greek COs. But the Greek armed forces were thought to be demanding very restrictive provisions. The Greek Parliament did begin to discuss a CO bill, but by the end of 1989 there were twenty-two pacifists, who had publicly announced they would refuse military service, facing imprisonment.[42]

As in Greece, resistance to conscription in Spain began with Jehovah's Witnesses, who were repeatedly sentenced for disobedience under the military code. Political interest in conscientious objection began in the late 1960s, when students in cooperation with French pacifists began to discuss the implications of conscientious opposition to military service, to write to the Government asking for a law on CO rights and to publicize their views through leaflets and pamphlets. A real campaign started in 1971 when a student activist and WRI member, Pepe Beunza, became the first Catholic CO. Beunza had the backing of international pacifist groups who protested on his behalf, and won internal publicity for his first prison sentence, and his subsequent rearrest and one-year jail term in 1972. A second student objector was condemned to six years in prison for 'sedition' in 1971, after spending a month in a mental hospital, while a young trade unionist received a three-year sentence to be followed by a spell in a disciplinary battalion in the Sahara.

The Franco regime responded to growing internal awareness of COs and to international pressure by passing a law recognizing the existence of COs in December 1973. It was not a strikingly liberal measure, since it provided that COs should be imprisoned for between three and eight years, lose all their civic rights and be debarred from a range of jobs, including teaching.[43] After Franco's death and the transition to parliamentary democracy the armed forces retained considerable power, and although the campaign for CO rights grew it had no immediate results. A CO law did not get passed until 1984, when a socialist government was in power and there was widespread popular opposition to NATO and to militarism. The now powerful Movement of Conscientious Objectors immediately rejected the new law and tried through the ombudsman to have it declared unconstitutional, so delaying it from coming into force until January 1988. Although the law provided wide moral grounds for objection, it excluded specifically political or anti-militarist beliefs, and allowed tribunals to enquire into individuals' personal lives, which was seen as a breach of civil liberties. COs also objected to the length of alternative service and military-style regulations governing it, and to the fact that those already doing military service could not apply for CO status.

When the CO law finally came into force in 1988 the National Council for Conscientious Objectors, set up under the 1984 law, had recognized over 24,000 COs. Applicants had adopted the tactic of making collective statements of the grounds for their objection to obviate personal investigation, and the National Council had accepted about 10,000 of these; but in February 1989 the Council refused to accept any more collective statements. At this point some Spanish war-resisters launched a campaign of total resistance to the draft (see below).[44]

Portugal, like Spain made no provision for COs until a parliamentary regime had been established for some years. It operated its military code rather more flexibly however, simply avoiding the conscription of Jehovah's Witnesses who would have refused to obey orders. When a Catholic CO made an issue of his refusal to be conscripted, but offered to do alternative service in the community, the military authorities tried threats and prevarication, and then resorted to declaring his eyesight was too poor for military service.[45]

States with universal military service can satisfactorily combine respect for individual conscience with military requirements so long as CO rights are only claimed by a small minority. If social change promotes widespread resistance to conscription, then tension between the demands of COs and the demands of the armed forces may provoke more restrictive interpretation of CO rights and defiance by objectors. Developments in West Germany illustrated this pattern. The Federal Republic wrote CO rights into its 1949 Constitution and interpreted them quite liberally when it imposed conscription in 1956. COs choosing alternative service could do a variety of social or medical work in the community free from military jurisdiction and initially only served for the same period as military conscripts. Between 1957 and 1971 about 75 per cent of applicants gained CO status, in 1972 only 52 per cent. The number of applicants rose from 4,431 in 1966 to 11,952 in 1968 – the year of student protest – and to 32,482 in 1972.[46] The Social Democratic Government accepted rising numbers of aspiring COs, but when the Christian Democrats returned to power in 1983 they decided that increasing CO applications (68,000 in 1983), combined with the fall in total numbers available for the draft, required action. A new law passed in July 1983 extended alternative service to two years, envisaged employing COs in heavy manual labour, tightened up application formalities and lifted the previous provision that application for CO status automatically postponed compulsory entry into the armed forces until the draft board had reached a decision. The government proposals prompted a token protest strike by about 10,000 COs on 27 January 1983, and opponents of the law began court action to have it declared unconstitutional.[47]

The WRI expressed concern at the end of 1984 that despite increased formal recognition of CO rights, many West European governments were tending to make it harder to gain CO status. In Finland, for example, rising numbers were claiming the fifty-year-old right to conscientious objection, the Government was tightening the rules, and the Finnish Union of COs was demanding a truly civilian peace-

orientated alternative service.[48] Governments have, however, been
constrained not only by opposition to conscription based on moral
and political beliefs, but by a much more widespread unwillingness
of young men to take time out of their lives for uncongenial military
discipline and training. The West German Government abandoned
plans in 1988 to extend military service from fifteen to eighteen
months because of popular hostility. The reluctance of conscripts in
some countries is intensified by harsh and dangerous conditions. The
Greek armed services have a record of military accidents, but the
Spanish forces too received unfavourable publicity in 1989 for a high
rate of deaths both in military training, and in car accidents and by
suicide. The total number of deaths was over a hundred a year, the
estimate of suicides for six years was over 160.[49]

TRANSNATIONAL ACTION FOR CO RIGHTS

Transnational protests on behalf of Spanish COs in the early 1970s
illustrated the growing strength of anti-militarist groups and increasing concern about human rights. Pacifists have always tried to
publicize the plight of imprisoned COs and to express solidarity:
American pacifists had, for example, protested on behalf of Jean
Bernard Moreau. WRI inaugurated Prisoners for Peace Day on 1
December 1956, and every year since has published a list of COs and
other war-resisters jailed for their beliefs and actions, and urged
sympathizers to send greeting cards. The scale of protests and the
degree of cooperation between national groups increased markedly
however in the 1970s.

Immediately after Pepe Beunza was jailed in January 1971, WRI
and an *ad hoc* committee in Geneva launched a campaign on his behalf.
An international march set off from Geneva in February with the aim
of reaching Beunza's prison in Valencia. When they reached the
Spanish border the 500 protesters were stopped by the Spanish police
and the Spaniards among them briefly arrested. Pacifists pursued the
campaign with protest fasts and occupation of several Spanish embassies. WRI and the Geneva Committee cooperated with the International Fellowship of Reconciliation and Pax Christi in October that
year to demonstrate in Rome where the Synod of Bishops was
meeting. The 300 marchers, many in mock prison uniforms, walked
to St Peter's Square to draw attention to COs imprisoned in twelve
countries, including Spain and Italy.[50]

The Spanish Government faced condemnation for its treatment of COs on human rights grounds. Amnesty International had success-fully lobbied the Council of Europe to recognize conscientious objection as a human right, and now combined with the Assembly of the Council of Europe and the International Commission of Jurists to press for a CO law in Spain. Increasing acceptance of human rights arguments for CO status has meant that by 1989 Greece was the only member of the EEC which did not have a CO law. The European Parliament passed a resolution in favour of CO rights in 1983.

Achieving real world-wide recognition of COs has posed even greater problems than progress in Western Europe. The WRI first took an international petition for CO rights to the United Nations in 1949. Peace and human rights organizations began to coordinate pressure when the International Peace Bureau called a conference in 1968, attended by Quakers, International Voluntary Service, WRI and Amnesty International, to consider how to promote recognition of COs. At a follow-up conference in 1969 they agreed a draft resolution suited to the UN General Assembly. The UN Commission on Human Rights passed a resolution asking the UN Secretary-General to report on treatment of COs in 1971, and peace organiz-ations lobbied for a resolution favouring CO rights throughout the 1970s. WRI presented a petition with 40,000 signatures from twenty-seven countries to the 1973 session of the Commission, when some Western countries and India tried unsuccessfully to get the issue of CO recognition referred to all member states via the Economic and Social Council. The Soviet Union, which did not concede any CO rights, blocked progress. The United Nations finally passed a resolu-tion recognizing conscientious objection in 1987. It agreed without a vote in 1989 on a stronger resolution, which urged states practising conscription to allow genuinely civilian and non-punitive forms of alternative service. The resolution had importance as an interpretation of the Declaration of Human Rights, although it was not legally binding. Spain was one of the sponsors of the resolution, as was Hungary, the first East European state ever to give such support, and a sign of changing policies in Eastern Europe.[51]

Since most countries do not recognize COs, and often impose very harsh penalties on objectors to military service, many draft resisters have escaped abroad before they could be called-up, or have deserted from the armed forces. Objectors seeking asylum in other countries have inevitably raised questions about their legal status and prompted pacifists to organize support. Many young Portuguese left their country in order to avoid fighting in a colonial war in Africa in the early 1970s, for example, and a British Committee for Portuguese War-Resisters tried to clarify their status with the Home Office.[52] During the 1980s the war between Iran and Iraq prompted Iranian men and boys to escape abroad to avoid being drafted and raised the issue whether they should qualify for political asylum in Western Europe. Courts in West Germany reached different rulings on whether Iranian draft-resisters would face political prosecution if returned home. The Dutch Union of COs offered to coordinate international action on rights of asylum for war-resisters in 1989 and a Dutch lawyer acting for COs who had escaped to the Netherlands sought to develop the legal argument that the UN Commission on Human Rights resolution recognizing CO rights should qualify war-resisters for political refugee status.[53]

As transnational action on behalf of COs intensified in the 1970s, some European objectors decided to launch a campaign for total non-cooperation with military conscription. The campaign drew on anarchist and socialist traditions of war resistance, as well as being influenced by the mass protests against the draft in the USA during the Vietnam War. The organizers of International Collective Resistance announced their aims at a press conference in October 1975, and demonstrated these intentions through follow-up protests in Strasbourg, where resisters from seven countries handed in their call-up papers at the Council of Europe headquarters or burned them. By the end of the year several organizers were in prison and others had gone underground to elude the police. Individual objectors took an absolutist stand in France, Italy and the Netherlands, where two young men called for a hundred others to follow their example.[54]

The Spanish Movement of Conscientious Objectors renewed the call for transnational resistance to the call-up in 1989 and members travelled round Europe urging support for this campaign. Total resistance to the draft had taken three forms in Spain. Those who already had gained CO status refused to do their alternative service and objectors refusing to recognize the CO tribunal presented themselves in groups to the military authorities a few days late, when they had technically become deserters. Sympathizers with the strategy of total resistance not liable to call-up adopted the third tactic of self-incrimination, signing letters to the military courts indicating they had urged disobedience, an act itself punishable under the military code. A range of social groups expressed solidarity through self-incrimination and publicized their stand. The International Conscientious Objectors' Meeting in the Basque country in July 1989, where ten countries were represented, responded to the Spanish campaign by deciding to make total resistance the focus for protests on International COs' Day on 15 May 1990.[55]

WAR RESISTANCE IN SOUTHERN AFRICA

Organized campaigns against specific wars have often combined use of CO rights (if they exist), open defiance of the draft and support for draft evasion and desertion. Evasion and desertion may attract individuals for many reasons, not all of them admirable, but political opposition to maintaining white supremacy by force did motivate many conscripts in Southern Africa in the 1970s and led to organized war resistance.

During the guerrilla war in Rhodesia (now Zimbabwe) a group of young white conscripts at a Bulawayo barracks founded the Zimbabwe Democrat organization in 1977, and began to circulate a newsletter inside the army to persuade other conscripts to think about their political role and to encourage desertion. The group also offered practical advice and help to political deserters and made contact with South African war-resisters living abroad.[56]

All white men in South Africa were obliged to serve in the armed forces, initially for two years followed by further spells of duty, and there was no right of conscientious objection. The Government's own figures showed over 3,000 men ignored call-up papers each year between 1975 and 1978. Many South Africans evading service in the Defence Force went abroad, and their increasing numbers in the 1970s meant draft evasion became part of a movement of resistance to the Government's policy and a refusal to take part in oppression of neighbouring African countries and of the black townships in South Africa. Draft-resisters abroad began to organize themselves in 1978, when Committees on South African War Resistance were set up in Britain, The Netherlands and the USA, to offer advice to potential draft evaders and to promote possibilities of asylum. UN Resolutions against apartheid and favouring such asylum created international legitimacy for the campaign. Bishop Trevor Huddleston launched a register of resisters in exile in 1989, asking individuals to sign a declaration stating their own refusal to serve in the South African Defence Force and expressing solidarity with those publicly resisting inside South Africa.[57] This was a counterpart to the register already set up inside the country.

The internal opposition to serving in the armed forces grew during the 1980s. The campaign began when in the late 1970s several pacifists (other than Jehovah's Witnesses) were jailed for conscientious objection. The case of Richard Steele, a Baptist, who told his tribunal that military service upheld 'a fundamentally unjust society' aroused particular interest.[58] CO support groups arose in 1979 and churches and universities took up the arguments for a right to conscientious objection. The Government responded with the April 1983 Defence Amendment Act, which granted recognition and a right to alternative service to strictly religious pacifists, but sought to deter political objectors by raising the sentences for resistance to six years, one and half times the total period of military service required.

The End Conscription Campaign, which began in mid-1983, criticized the Act and declared its determination to oppose use of the Defence Force in Namibia and the black townships. The campaign had backing in universities, churches, community groups and women's groups – women were indeed prominent in it.[59] The campaign first came up against the Government in 1985, when police raided offices and homes and detained several of the organizers, but it continued to promote resistance to conscription until August 1988, when it was banned under the Emergency regulations, and some of its leaders jailed. The CO support groups, which had been largely superseded by the End Conscription Campaign, then stepped into the breach and launched their own nation-wide campaign in May 1989. It included public meetings, a prayer service in Soweto, a petition to Parliament calling for release of COs and demonstrations in Cape Town and Johannesburg by the Black Sash women. A year after it had been banned, the End Conscription Campaign defied the Government and held public protests in Natal University and Durban.

There were two categories among those who refused to do military service on the grounds that it upheld apartheid: those who resisted when first conscripted, and those who rebelled after initial service with the Defence Force. David Bruce, a university student whose mother was a Jew who had escaped to South Africa from Nazism, represented the first category. He refused the call-up in July 1988 and was sentenced to six years in prison. David Bruce acted alone, but in August 1987 twenty-three men made the first collective public commitment not to serve in the Defence Force. Ivan Toms, who was one of the twenty-three, fell into the second category. He was a doctor who had been in the Defence Force in Namibia and found that his medical work was an adjunct of military intelligence. Toms, a committed Anglican, then worked for eight years as a doctor in the black townships round Cape Town. When called up in March 1988 he returned his uniform to ensure that his defiance would not be ignored and was sentenced to twenty-one months in prison, but later released on appeal. The End Conscription Campaign organized a nation-wide speaking tour and a number of vigils, one joined by Bishop Tutu, on his behalf.

Draft resistance mounted at the end of the 1980s: 143 collectively declared they would not serve in the Defence Force in August 1988, and 771 took the same stand in September 1989. Church leaders initiated a register of COs. The majority of objectors stressed their rejection of apartheid, but religious pacifists began to challenge this distinction between political and religious motives. One Christian pacifist left his community service in 1989 for this reason and sixty-eight religious COs already doing community service were among the 771 taking a public stand against the role of the Defence Force.[60]

The resistance to conscription prompted calls for a non-punitive and constructive form of alternative service, instead of six years of unskilled labour. Women Against War mobilized about 1,000 mothers of former or potential conscripts to urge, in February 1989, that COs should have the right to work in religious or welfare organizations, and their proposal was endorsed by the South African Council of Churches. Sections of the business community, influenced by the arguments of a twenty-eight-year-old career development officer refusing further military service, also supported proposals for a better form of alternative service to stop talented men leaving the country.

Pacifists as well as anti-apartheid groups abroad gave publicity and support to the campaign against conscription in South Africa. WRI responded to an invitation to send a delegation to South Africa in May 1989. The WRI Secretary, together with a black American, a former GI in Vietnam, and a pacifist from the Netherlands, where there is a liberal form of alternative service, spoke at public meetings and the team visited COs in prison. International CO's Day on 15 May 1989 became a focus for expressing solidarity with South African resisters. The new Greek Union of COs picketed the office of a South African airline and Finnish COs doing alternative service went on strike. In Israel a Tel Aviv meeting celebrated both South African COs and Israelis imprisoned for opposing their own forces's suppression of the Palestinian *intifada*.[61] The connection had already been personified by the case of David Neuhaus, who emigrated to Israel to avoid military service in South Africa, and then found he felt obliged to resist conscription into the Israeli Defence Force.[62]

Draft evasion by South African whites was only one strand in the major struggle by blacks, Indians, coloureds and some whites over many years against apartheid. The open defiance of conscription that began in the 1980s did have considerable symbolic significance, but it was simply one element in the growing internal resistance to the regime and took on international importance partly because of the strength of popular and governmental opposition to the South African Government throughout most of the world. Peace activity in Israel, and in particular resistance to joining the armed services, has by contrast been a strictly minority tendency, with little outside support, though Western attitudes to Israeli Government policies were changing by the end of the 1980s.

PEACE PROTEST AND RESISTANCE IN ISRAEL

The socialist idealism which was influential among early Jewish settlers in Palestine, and in the founding of the Jewish state, might in other political contexts have been sympathetic to traditions of pacifism and war resistance. But in the Israel that emerged out of the war of 1948, which remained in a permanent state of siege threatened by its Arab neighbours, the idealism of the kibbutz merged with Jewish nationalism, and armed service for the state became a basic civic duty. In these circumstances organized peace activity was for a long time minimal, although WRI did have a small Israeli section, which supported individual COs. Israel conscripted both men and women, but only allowed women to claim conscientious grounds for refusing military service. Although some men were imprisoned for resisting the call-up, the authorities tended to exempt pacifists as 'unsuitable' for military service: between 500 and 1,000 pacifists were thought to have been exempted by 1975, when the military authorities were reviewing exemptions.[63]

Peace protest drew in broader sections of Israeli society from the late 1970s, and expanded in response to three major issues: the 'occupied territories'; the 1982 invasion of Lebanon and the *intifada*. Peace action began with opposition to Israel's long-term occupation of the territories captured in the Six-Day War (June 1967). Support for returning the occupied territories through negotiated peace settlements with neighbouring Arab states grew after the November 1977 visit by President Sadat of Egypt to Jerusalem, which led to the 1979 Peace Treaty giving Sinai back to Egypt. It was in this context that twenty-seven high school students declared in July 1979 that they would not agree to serve in the occupied territories. The authorities responded with a one-year prison sentence on one of the leaders of the 'Group of 27' in January 1981.[64]

The Israeli invasion of Lebanon in June 1982, allegedly to force the Palestine Liberation Organization out of the zone north of Israel's border, and so prevent PLO incursions, created an unprecedented surge of public protest. The moderate Peace Now organization, set up in 1977, held a rally of 100,000 in July, but protests had begun in June when the Committee to Stop the War mustered 20,000. Even more significantly, many army reservists, including some who had fought in the Lebanon, demonstrated their opposition to the war outside the Knesset. A colonel ordered to attack West Beirut had preferred to give up his command. Reservists launched their own movement 'There is a Limit' querying the legality of the Lebanon War and claiming the right to refuse to obey illegal orders. Over 2,000 reservists signed a petition asking that they should not be ordered to the Lebanon and 150 were court-martialled.[65]

Intensity of opposition to the Lebanon War did not denote that there was widespread public revulsion in the first few months of the war. The Labour Party backed the Likud-dominated Coalition Government, which drew 300,000 to its own rally in favour of the war. A public opinion poll in August showed that 90 per cent of those asked were behind the Israeli incursion into the Lebanon, although only half of them favoured occupying West Beirut. Public opinion altered after Israeli forces entered Beirut and allowed the massacre in the PLO camps of Sabra and Shatila. There were larger demonstrations, the Labour Party attacked the Government and leading members of the Government called for a public inquiry, which was eventually held.[66]

The Palestinian uprising in the occupied territories of Gaza and the West Bank, which began in December 1987, marked the third phase in peace activity in Israel. The *intifada* involved a campaign of non-cooperation and open defiance, often developing into spontaneous popular violence, and was therefore quite different in character to the organized armed attacks on Israel previously adopted by the PLO. The *intifada* drew on the old and the very young, women as well as men, and the role of the Israeli forces in trying to quell the revolt became increasingly controversial.

The 'There Is a Limit' campaign had continued after most Israelis had been withdrawn from the Lebanon and had, after some debate, decided to extend its opposition to service in the occupied territories. So for example 350 reservists signed a petition, published in the press in June 1986, asking not to be sent to these territories. The petition argued that Jewish settlement and Israeli measures in the occupied territories were making peace with Arab states impossible and corrupting Israel's own values, declared that the signatories would honour their oath 'to defend the integrity and security of the State of Israel', but asked not to have to take part 'in the suppression and occupation in the territories'.[67] The 'There Is a Limit' campaign launched a new declaration in December 1987 in response to the *intifada*, issuing a more unequivocal statement of refusal to join in suppressing the uprising. Nine months later 600 had signed, forty-two had been court-martialled and a hundred excused from service in the territories. The campaigners had circulated booklets stating why they were refusing to serve, and giving advice on procedures and rights for those who chose to join the campaign within the armed forces. A parallel campaign began among high school students, one of its organizers being sentenced to several consecutive prison terms in 1989. He was only the seventh conscript to be jailed, though about seventy reservists had been imprisoned by late 1989 for refusing to serve in the occupied territories.[68]

The scope of opposition to the Israeli suppression of the *intifada* was demonstrated when the Council for Peace and Security emerged in spring 1988, representing 200 generals and officers on the reserve list. The Council argued that Israel would be more secure if its forces did not have to hold down the occupied territories, if Israel was not politically divided over the territories, and if peace could be negotiated with other Arab states. The generals took out full-page press advertisements to state their views during the 1988 election campaign.[69]. By 1988 around ninety peace groups existed in Israel, many of them small and localized. End the Occupation Now was an umbrella organization for a number of groups, including Women in Black, which held a weekly vigil in West Jerusalem. Peace Now remained the best known and most respectable of the campaigning peace bodies.[70] Sections of the Labour Party supported giving up at least part of the occupied territories. Despite the role of a Labour Defence Minister in trying to crush the Palestinian uprising when it began, the Labour leader, Simon Peres, argued during the elections that holding on to all the occupied territories, with their rapidly growing Palestinian population, was incompatible with maintaining a truly Jewish and democratic state.

The PLO's major decision at the end of 1988 to reverse its previous policy and to recognize the right of the state of Israel to exist alongside an independent Palestinian state, and to abandon the armed struggle against Israel, strengthened the case of those calling for negotiations.

Some Israeli peace activists had, however, established links earlier with the PLO, despite a law passed in January 1986 making such contacts illegal. Four Israelis, who met with the PLO in Romania, were put on trial in June 1987. But the first to be jailed for flouting this law was a sixty-two-year-old activist, who ran his Voice of Peace radio station off-shore from Tel Aviv, and was sentenced to six months imprisonment in October 1989.[71]

Many of the small Israeli peace groups were committed to fostering understanding and cooperation between Israelis and Palestinians. One such group was the Israeli Women's Alliance Against the Occupation, set up in January 1988, which began to meet with Palestinian women and to hold public meetings addressed by them. The Middle East section of the International Fellowship of Reconciliation, which brought together Jews, Christian Arabs and Muslims, cooperated with the Palestinian Centre for Non-violence, based in East Jerusalem, in a number of acts of solidarity with the Palestinians. One of their better-publicized actions was to plant several hundred olive trees along the Green Line, the frontier between Israel and the West Bank, after the Israeli Government had taken over this land in January 1986 and uprooted olive trees on land previously belonging to Palestinian villagers. Thirteen of those involved were later taken to court.[72]

Joint action between Palestinians and Israelis was combined with a major international presence at a large demonstration in Jerusalem in December 1989. The initiative for a European expression of solidarity with Middle East peace activists arose out of the END Convention in Spain in 1989, and the Italian Peace Association played a major part in bringing 1,300 Europeans to Jerusalem to join in demonstrations calling for an Israeli and a Palestinian state, respect for human and civil rights and peace negotiations. Israeli and Palestinian women's organizations arranged a Woman's Day on 29th December, which included a conference in Israeli West Jerusalem, joining the Women in Black vigil, and a march into East Jerusalem. When 5,000 Palestinian, Israeli and European women walked through East Jerusalem they were taking part in the first legal demonstration since the 1967 occupation. The police arrested over twenty women when a Palestinian flag was unfurled, but did not hold the five Italians among them. The next day Peace Now had sponsored a human chain round the old walls of Jerusalem, stretching from West to East. Up to 30,000 people took part in a highly charged atmosphere, which was created by hostile Israeli counter-demonstrations and tense Israeli police, who launched attacks with clubs, tear gas, rubber bullets and water cannon on demonstrators. Most police violence was directed against Palestinians and peaceful displays of Palestinian nationalism. The presence of members of the Israeli Knesset and a large international contingent simultaneously helped to curb police attacks and ensured international publicity for habitual police behaviour towards Palestinians.[73]

The Jerusalem demonstration illustrated how even a strictly non-violent public protest based on a moderate programme can be interpreted as provocative in a context of prolonged and bitter conflict. The Israeli peace campaigners faced the dilemma that acts of reconciliation and solidarity with moderate Palestinians threatened to deepen the divisions within Israeli society, which by the end of the decade had polarized over the issue of the occupied territories.

NORTHERN IRELAND: RESISTANCE OR RECONCILIATION?

Bitter historically based social divisions, political extremism and major obstacles to any resolution of the conflict have also been characteristic of the troubles in Northern Ireland. Many peace activists in Britain and Eire have avoided trying to tackle the conflict. Those who have felt obliged to act have adopted very different strategies depending on their political analyses of the situation and beliefs about peace. Some radical pacifists have seen British rule in Northern Ireland, and in particular the role of the troops in Northern Ireland since 1969, as the primary obstacle to a just and peaceful resolution of the conflict. Others have concentrated on local work in the community designed both to meet some of the problems of poverty and deprivation in Northern Ireland and to bring Catholics and Protestants together. Christian peace groups in the North and South of Ireland and in Britain have tended to focus on these activities, which have sometimes extended to creating opportunities for unpublicized dialogue between opposed political groups. The third approach, which has been initiated spontaneously by individuals caught up in the violence of life of Northern Ireland, tried to mobilize inter-communal opposition to deliberate and random use of violence by the paramilitaries or by mobs.

Pressure for British troops to leave Northern Ireland has come primarily from supporters of the Republican cause of a united Ireland and from the socialist Left. But pacifists have argued a pacifist case that the British troops, officially sent into Northern Ireland to protect Catholics menaced by Loyalist mobs, rapidly became an instrument of Protestant rule and an occupying force in Catholic areas. Moreover, it was argued, they often resorted to unacceptable tactics and levels of violence. In addition some pacifists believed that the presence of British troops strengthened the Provisional IRA and blocked any solution to the conflict by enabling politicians to pursue sectarian policies without taking real responsibility for the future of the province.

A group of radical pacifists in Britain launched the British Withdrawal from Northern Ireland Campaign in July 1973, with the aim of arguing the case for troops leaving Northern Ireland among soldiers who might be sent to serve there. One campaigner was arrested twice for giving out leaflets at barracks and the second time sentenced to eighteen months in prison under the Incitement to Disaffection Act. The group then reworded the leaflet and distributed it at several barracks. The authorities responded by arresting fourteen of the group and putting them on trial for conspiracy under the Incitement to Disaffection Act. The arrests prompted prominent peace activists and Young Liberals to give out the leaflet as an act of solidarity and a petition upholding the right of civilians to communicate with servicemen. The trial of the fourteen opened at the Old Bailey in September 1975 and ended after several weeks with the jury acquitting the defendants.[74]

Long-established peace organizations working in Northern Ireland included the Fellowship of Reconciliation, which from 1969 began to run play schemes in Derry and then Lurgan, and International Voluntary Service, which began in 1971 to organize joint holidays for Catholic and Protestant children and later switched to running teenage work camps. A new initiative for peace and reconciliation was launched in 1965 by a chaplain at Queen's University, Belfast. The Corrymeela Centre offered its resources to youth groups, old people's groups and work camps, but laid increasing stress on reconciliation between Protestants and Catholics. In 1988 Corrymeela called a conference of almost all the political parties, and repeated the exercise the following year. The dialogue excluded only Sinn Fein, which many could not afford to meet in any open forum, and those Unionists favouring total integration with Britain. A Southern Irish equivalent to Corrymeela was set up in 1974 by a Dublin group. The Glencree centre in County Wicklow organized seminars and conferences, sometimes in conjunction with Corrymeela, and offered holidays to individuals escaping from the tensions of the North. Glencree also owned a house in Belfast which was used for meetings.[75]

Reaction against the violence and deaths caused in Northern Ireland was represented by Witness for Peace, created by a Protestant clergyman after his son was killed by a bomb in 1972, which tended to concentrate on symbolic reminders of the number of violent deaths – planting crosses, keeping a public scoreboard of those killed and annual remembrance services. A more ambitious attempt to stop violence was made by a retired cleaner who hoped to unite women to act against youths throwing stones, gang fights and attacks on individuals. Women Together, which started in 1970, found increasing difficulty in intervening when the number of people carrying guns increased, but continued in existence. Its office was burned down in 1976.[76]

By far the best-known and most controversial peace venture in Northern Ireland in the 1970s was the campaign launched by the Peace People to stop the violence by Republican and Loyalist paramilitary groups, which for a time won significant popular support. Peace People grew out of a tragic incident in which three children were killed on the street after an IRA car, whose driver had been shot by the army, went out of control. A woman who had seen the deaths immediately joined with other women to collect signatures for a petition against the violence of the paramilitaries and the next day, 11 August 1976, met the children's aunt. These two women, from the Protestant and Catholic communities, were thereafter seen by the press as the leaders of the movement, and they were later given the Nobel Peace Prize.

Peace People represented a surge of feeling against the levels of paramilitary violence in the previous year and a half, which had seen random killings of Catholics by Loyalists, Protestants by Republicans and internecine strife between opposed Republican paramilitary groups. The first peace rally in the road where the children had died brought 10,000 out on 14 August, a week later 20,000 came to a rally in a Belfast park; and on 6 September 25,000 turned out in Derry. By November 1976 Peace People had over eighty active local groups, offices in Belfast and Derry, its own journal *Peace by Peace*, and could mount twenty-one peace rallies on 6 November.

The Peace People attracted a range of responses from the political parties in Northern Ireland. Ian Paisley's *Protestant Telegraph* criticized them for being a Roman Catholic Front, but at the end of October prominent Unionists joined the Peace People leadership. Gerry Fitt, then leader of the Catholic SDLP, declared support but some members of the Party attacked the Peace People and feared it was in the process of becoming a political party. Official Sinn Fein, which was opposed to the 'armed struggle' being waged by the Provisional IRA since 1970, issued a statement in November 1976, which stressed the need to overcome the sectarian divide in the North and backed the Peace People. Provisional Sinn Fein was predictably worried by the extent of popular support for the Peace People and extremely hostile to its policies. It took banners to the Peace People Rally in Derry in September, where Derry Socialist Women gave out a leaflet asking why Peace People did not attack killing of children by the British troops (a twelve-year-old girl had been shot dead on 14th August by Paratroopers). Provisional Sinn Fein stepped up its campaign against the Peace People in October, when it published a booklet claiming Peace People were being manipulated, and organized a counter-demonstration to a Peace People March in the Falls Road, Belfast. Provisional IRA supporters threw bricks and stones at peace marchers.[77]

The Peace People had not been helped in the early days by the British government response, which sought to use them against the Provisional IRA and which issued a poster widely interpreted as a Peace People poster. Moreover, as the two women leaders were swept along by the momentum of the campaign and as Peace People groups sprang up and began to issue their own statements, public utterances did give the impression that Peace People were very uncritical of the role of British troops. By October, however, the leadership, now expanded to include an articulate exponent of non-violence and the ideal of political decentralism, had reached a more considered position. They maintained their primary opposition to the illegitimate inter-communal violence of the paramilitaries, and argued that the British army and Royal Ulster Constabulary did have a legitimate interim role in trying to uphold the rule of the law. Indeed, while they urged an amnesty for those holding arms, they also urged people to inform on paramilitaries to the security services. But they were also prepared to criticize excesses by the security forces. Later Peace People gave greater weight to helping people assert their rights in relation to the security forces. The Peace People also began to invest some of the large sums of money flowing into their cause to undertake constructive projects – they announced the setting up of a factory in an area of high unemployment in November 1976 – and also passed on funds to community projects which applied to them. A year later a Peace People Assembly engaged in a serious debate about its role and aims, a debate which included attempts to define more clearly the implications of the 'community politics' the movement had embraced. The Assembly adopted guidelines which clarified that its aim was not to become a political party, that as a non-sectarian body members of any political party could belong to it, and that economic, educational, cultural and other issues which could promote conflict fell within Peace People's concerns. The Assembly did not agree on a proposal stressing the need to develop a Northern Irish identity separate from both British and Irish nationalism, but deferred final decisions to a later Assembly.[78].

The Peace People drew in numbers of people already concerned about active peacemaking and had a strong middle-class appeal. But observers at demonstrations and the 1977 Assembly confirmed that significant numbers of working-class women took part. Peace People predominantly attracted middle-aged women, and had little appeal to the young working-class men who were the recruiting ground for both Catholic and Loyalist paramilitaries. This was a crucial weakness in a strategy of mobilizing effective grass-roots public opinion to stop the violence, but inherent in the local culture. The Peace People also suffered to some extent from their own initial success, which catapulted the two women to media fame, took them on speaking tours abroad and led to the Nobel Prize. They were vulnerable to a good deal of jealousy and a target for criticism for organizational mismanagement. Ironically the Peace Prize did more harm than good, leading to allegations that the women had misused the prize money (one of them did keep it for herself) and further isolating the leaders. So although the Peace People continued to exist for years, operating at a lower key in community and reconciliation projects, the high hopes it had raised faded by the end of 1978.[79]

Peace activists in Britain divided in their responses to the Peace People. Many felt they should be strongly supported, both because of their aim of ending sectarian violence and because of the nonviolent approach and community politics they endorsed. A rally in Trafalgar Square in November 1976 called to demonstrate in favour of the Peace People drew 15,000 and a counter-demonstration by the Troops Out campaign. Some radical pacifists were alienated by the efforts of the Peace People to enlist establishment support from churches and from all political parties, including the British Conservatives. But the crucial disagreement was over the role of British troops. The Peace People Movement illustrated the extreme difficulties of high-profile peace action, as opposed to smaller-scale and little publicized attempts at reconciliation and practical aid.

TRANSNATIONAL INTERVENTION

Despite the complexity of many political conflicts, pacifists have often tried to intervene in other countries in order to offer solidarity and political or practical aid, or in the hope that outsiders may be able to play a mediatory and reconciling role. These aspirations lay behind the decision at a WRI Conference in India in 1961 to set up a World Peace Brigade, bringing together Western pacifists and the Gandhian movement in India. The Gandhian movement had its own peace brigade which combined various forms of local community work with direct non-violent intervention when needed to calm rioting between Hindus and Muslims. The World Peace Brigade was intended to provide teams of experienced volunteers to work with local groups striving for peace or justice. At its inaugural conference in January 1962 the World Peace Brigade decided to offer its services to liberation movements in Southern Africa, and a team based in Dar es Salaam cooperated with Kenneth Kaunda in plans to organize a march into Northern Rhodesia to coincide with a general strike. Political developments made the march redundant and plans for a permanent non-violent centre in Tanganyika (now Tanzania) fell through.[80]

The Brigade attempted to play a conciliatory role in a conflict between states after the border war between India and China in late 1962. The Delhi–Peking Friendship March in 1963 was jointly sponsored by the Peace Brigade in India and the World Peace Brigade, and illustrated the pitfalls as well as the possible advantages of an international group publicly challenging nationalist sentiments.

The definition of the border between India and China had been a source of uncertainty and dispute throughout the 1950s, exacerbated by the Chinese occupation of Tibet and the Chinese building of a road for military transport in an area claimed by India. An uneasy truce, which allowed both the Chinese and the Indians to occupy parts of the disputed territory, was broken by armed clashes in 1959. But the 1962 border war brought the two countries into open enmity. China was on the verge of totally breaking with the Soviet Union, which had been arming India, and was adopting an increasingly intransigent foreign policy stance. India was, however, arguably responsible for provoking the border war, when Nehru proclaimed publicly in October 1962 that India would occupy all the disputed territory, after Indian forces had already moved forward. China started the fighting when it launched an attack on Indian troops, but ended hostilities after it had reclaimed its 1959 positions. The Indian

Government and media portrayed the Chinese as clear aggressors and in the resulting mood of nationalism and hostility to China even many members of the Gandhian movement endorsed India's war effort.

The Friendship March left Gandhi's memorial in Delhi in March 1963 with the aim of walking 4,000 miles to Peking, with a core of thirteen marchers which included Indians, two experienced American pacifists, and volunteers from Japan, Burma, Ceylon and Austria. The march did not adopt any specific political proposals, but stressed the need to create friendship and promote understanding between the Indian and Chinese people.[81]

The march organizers had approached the official Chinese Peace Committee to ask for the right to enter China, but it soon became clear that the Chinese authorities viewed the action with extreme hostility. The fact that the march began in India and was sponsored by the Indian Peace Brigade movement was probably in itself cause for suspicion. Chinese antagonism was particularly focused on the figure of J.P. Narayan, a key figure in the Gandhian movement, a co-chairman of the World Peace Brigade and a sponsor of the march. Narayan had alienated the Chinese by his criticism of their role in Tibet, but in addition he had in the early days of the border war made anti-Chinese statements, though he soon moved towards opposition to the war and to Indian military preparations. The official Chinese view of the march was purveyed by the New China News Agency: 'A group of Indian reactionaries in collusion with US imperialists are on a so-called "Delhi–Peking Friendship March."'[82] The Chinese Government underlined its determination not to let the marchers near its borders by putting pressure on both Burma and East Pakistan to refuse to allow the group into their own territories.

Although the march failed early on to make headway with the Chinese authorities, it did spend six months traversing India where – after initial difficulties – it began to achieve a more positive response. The Government of Uttar Pradesh (the first state the marchers passed through) considered putting the marchers in prison, but were persuaded that they could not stop people advocating non-violence 'in the land of Gandhi'.[83] The marchers also met early on with hostility from Orthodox Hindu counter-demonstrators, and had even had a very mixed reception from the Gandhian movement. However, by the time they reached Bihar the marchers were drawing crowds of over a thousand to their nightly meetings and had better press publicity.[84] The marchers had by then resolved some of their own internal differences, and they were also assisted by a slackening in the popular hostility to China. One of the achievements of the march was to challenge the majority in the Gandhian movement to consider their own attitudes to the border war. The Indian Peace Brigade had, however, already started work in border areas to calm local fears, combat the extreme poverty there, and later set up a peace centre near the border.[85]

The World Peace Brigade, set up in 1962, proved too grandiose in its ambitions, too lacking in resources and too reliant on key personalities in the USA and India (who had many other demands on their time): consequently, it faded away. *Ad hoc* groups continued, however, to initiate transnational action. When the Pakistani army occupied East Bengal (later Bangladesh) in 1971 to repress popular unrest, a group of British pacifists launched Operation Omega, which had the dual aim of making an outside protest against the oppressive role of the Pakistani army and of taking a small amount of high-protein food to assist the thousands of refugees fleeing from the army. The team went with two trucks and without visas to the East Bengal border where, at a second attempt to enter East Bengal, one group was arrested by the Pakistani army and the other got through with its relief supplies ahead of the established aid agencies working through official channels. Some Omega volunteers stayed in Bangladesh engaging in local relief work until 1973.[86] The Omega team managed to overcome the hazards facing this kind of venture, volunteers falling ill and breakdown of transport on the one hand, and serious cultural or political misunderstandings with local people on the other. The team had a friendly reception from Indian border guards and established links with Bengali guides to help in distributing food supplies. It also had organizational backing from the WRI and from *Peace News*. By contrast, Operation Namibia, which meant to test the intentions of the new Government (installed by South Africa in 1977) by delivering a boatload of books banned by South Africa, suffered numerous problems. Their ship, the *Golden Harvest*, ran onto rocks off Gambia and after long delays sailed on round the West African coast. After a good reception in Ghana the crew ran into serious difficulties, first with the Nigerian authorities and then in Togo. Because of the time taken to launch and carry out the voyage the situation in Namibia itself was also changing,[87] so making it more difficult for the team to maintain coherent aims.

The idea of organizing transnational teams to intervene non-violently in areas of conflict was revived by Indian Gandhians in 1981 and Peace Brigades International came into being. The new body made Central America its primary focus and engaged in careful preliminary work to establish where local groups might welcome the presence of an international team, visiting Costa Rica, Nicaragua, Honduras and El Salvador in 1982. The Peace Brigades decided to put a core group into Costa Rica to work on training for non-violence, and in 1983 sent a team of nine Americans to the border between Nicaragua and Honduras, with the aim of monitoring violence by the Contras and doing practical work in the area, such as planting a peace garden on Catholic Church ground and helping with coffee picking.[88] The group went to prepare the way for a permanent presence on Nicaraguan borders by American Christian pacifists who formed Witness for Peace. This body received world-wide publicity in September 1985, when some of its members, who were travelling together with journalists along the San Juan river where it borders Costa Rica and Nicaragua, were kidnapped by the Nicaraguan Contras.[89]

The Central American Peace Brigades adopted a rather different form of action when they sent a team of volunteers into Guatemala to assist the Group for Mutual Support, which has campaigned for members of their families who have 'disappeared'. Peace Brigades' volunteers acted as escorts for group members, staying in their homes, walking by them on the street and sitting with them in public places, in the hope that the presence of international observers would provide some protection against assassination. The Peace Brigades remained in Guatemala from 1983 into 1990, although in 1989 the international volunteers themselves were seriously menaced, receiving death threats in May, having their house in Guatemala city blown up by a grenade in August, and three volunteers being badly hurt in a knife attack in December.[90] A Peace Brigades' presence in El Salvador from 1987 to 1989 to help protect Christian opposition groups and trade union leaders found itself under even greater pressure. Volunteers were frequently arrested and interrogated by the military police and they were all expelled in November 1989 as a threat to 'the security of the state.'[91]

Peace Brigades International did engage in some more specifically pacifist activity in Central America, providing materials for teachers interested in peace education in El Salvador and sending a team to Indians in Guatemala who were resisting military service. The primary emphasis was, however, on promoting human rights in these two countries and working with international bodies which publicize kidnapping and assassination of opposition figures. This policy reflects the belief that peace must be based on social justice and democratic freedom. It was also a response to the fact that in Central and Latin America the primary role of the armed forces and security services has not been defence against outside attack but suppression of internal opposition, non-violent as well as violent. The Peace Brigades decided, however, to maintain an emphasis on human rights when the organization began towards the end of the decade to extend its activities to other parts of the world. A team went to Sri Lanka in 1988 to provide a non-violent escort for lawyers trying to assist people detained without trial.[92] This strategy provided a practical means for Western pacifists to associate themselves with non-violent activists in Third World countries struggling for basic rights.

OPPOSITION TO THE GULF WAR

When the USA and its allies agreed upon armed intervention in the Gulf to liberate Kuwait from Iraq, people from diverse ideological positions came together to oppose the war and peace groups adopted many of the tactics outlined above.

The great majority of those who opposed the war agreed with their governments that Iraq's occupation of Kuwait and its plan to integrate it into Iraq was an unjustified act of aggression. They also welcomed the UN Security Council decision in August 1990 to impose economic sanctions on Iraq and agreed that Saddam Hussein ran a brutal dictatorship and was abusing human rights in Kuwait as well as in Iraq itself. They did not agree that it was either necessary or desirable to move from sanctions to launching an attack on Iraq in January 1991.

Before the war started there was widespread resistance to the prospect of the United States leading a military coalition into a war in the Middle East. The governments of Saudi Arabia (threatened by Iraq) and of Egypt were prepared to cooperate in military action, but popular sentiment in these countries and elsewhere in the Arab world was in varying degrees hostile to what was seen as American imperialist intervention in the Middle East. The PLO gave unequivocal backing to Saddam Hussein (whilst making some attempt to mediate in order to avoid war) thus throwing the Israeli peace movement into disarray. In the West political figures on the moderate right or centre of the political spectrum, as well as on the left, voiced anxiety that war would draw Israel into conflict with Iraq. They feared that Iraq would use chemical weapons and that the United States might retaliate with nuclear weapons, and that the war would therefore precipitate disastrous political conflicts in the Middle East and have appalling environmental consequences. Once war had begun popular opposition remained strong in Germany (with historic reasons to distrust resort to arms) and in Italy, where the Pope had made vehement pronouncements against the use of force. But in the USA and Britain, the two countries most heavily committed to the war, the political establishment closed ranks once war had begun. The US Congress, deeply divided in advance over committing American troops to fight in the Middle East, united behind President Bush in voicing support for American servicemen and servicewomen. The Labour and Liberal Democratic Parties in Britain rallied behind Mr Major's government, with only a few dissentient left wing MPs publicly airing their doubts about the desirability of the war, or the conduct of it once started.

During the pre-war period the peace groups in the West appeared to be enjoying a revival of support and influence. Veterans of the Vietnam War and established peace organizations in the USA began to mobilize teach-ins and public protests, drawing on some of the tactics and slogans of the Vietnam era, but exercising more political tact and self-discipline in presenting their views to the public.[93] Some families of reservists called up to fight campaigned bitterly against resort to war. In Europe a wave of demonstrations early in 1991, using the slogan 'No Blood for Oil', roused memories of the END movement ten years earlier.[94] The issue of arms sales to dictatorial and repressive regimes was high on the political agenda, with revelations about the role of companies in West Germany and in Britain (which officially had debarred selling weapons to Iraq) helping to arm Saddam Hussein making the headlines. Conscientious objection and draft resistance became prominent in the campaign against war in the USA and Britain. The pacifist advice service in London, At Ease, was approached by scores of soldiers and reservists trying to avoid going to the Gulf on political or personal grounds, and received unusual publicity in the popular press and on the BBC.[95] The American Central Committee for Conscientious Objectors was also inundated with enquiries. A US marine refused to board a plane to Saudi Arabia, declaring that the USA had supported Saddam Hussein in the war against Iran and helped to arm him with chemical weapons. An Australian sailor refused to join his ship bound for the Gulf, saying he was not prepared to fight to defend American oil; and several other members of the Australian navy took the same action.[96] As an indirect result of the war there was a fifty-four per cent increase in Germans applying to become COs.[97]

The months before the official UN deadline of 15 January 1991 for Iraq's withdrawal from Kuwait also saw an unprecedented degree of unofficial diplomacy and transnational action designed to secure release of the western hostages seized by Hussein and to find ways of avoiding war in the Gulf. Peace groups discussed the possibility of sending voluntary hostages to replace those being held and made plans for peace ships to sail towards the Gulf calling in at ports along the way to publicize the case against war.[98] The Gulf Peace Team, initiated by an *ad hoc* group in London, decided to revive the aims of the World Peace Brigade to deter war by placing an international team of non-violent volunteers between the opposing armies. Saudi Arabia refused to admit the team, but a group was allowed into Iraq and established a camp in a traditional place of pilgrimage near the Saudi Arabian border. The team negotiated conditions to secure their impartial political stance and were allowed to remain in the camp for ten days after war began. However they were inevitably dependent on the goodwill of the Iraqi authorities and were forced to leave the camp and deported from the country in February. It was more ambitious and attracted wider support than previous attempts at transnational intervention – 86 volunteers from 16 countries were in the camp on 15 January – and achieved publicity in many parts of the world.[99]

The outbreak of war did not immediately undermine the peace movement developing to oppose it. On Saturday 19 January an estimated minimum of 30,000 demonstrated across the USA; up to 60,000 in Sydney and thousands in other major Australian cities, and several thousand in different towns in Britain. Protests were reported from India, Canada, France, Belgium, Norway, Turkey, Spain and above all Germany, where students went on strike in almost all the main universities. A week later up to 100,000 demonstrated in Washington and many thousands in Europe. Peace campaigns did, however, have problems in maintaining the momentum of protest into February. In Britain, CND, which had been forging a new anti-war role and identity for itself, also ran into policy difficulties in its uneasy coalition with far left groups opposing the war on anti-imperialist grounds.[101] Because the war was brief, the Allies proved to have overwhelming military superiority and allied casualties were extraordinarily light, the war was over before public disillusion or revulsion set in. The Allies also took pains to present the war as not only having a just cause but as being waged by just, discriminate, means avoiding unnecessary civilian casualties. Although this image was undermined by pictures of dead families being brought out of a

Baghdad bunker (which the Allies claimed was a military command post) only opponents of the war expressed serious reservations about the bombing policy which destroyed the infrastructure of Iraqi society. The peace movement also found that many of its worst prophecies were not realized. Despite Iraqi missile attacks on Israel, the Israeli government did not retaliate, and Iraq never used chemical weapons. Although many of the peace movement's advance fears had been shared by the Allied governments and their military staffs, the end of the war left peace campaigners looking – at least in the short term – discredited for their warnings of disaster.

The widespread peace protest in response to the Gulf War suggested the comparative strength and potential of peace groups in the West at the beginning of the 1990s, although the peace groups which had developed in Eastern Europe found themselves weak and socially isolated when attempting small scale action against the Gulf War.[102] The experience also indicated, however, the continuing difficulties of maintaining mass opposition in countries at war (unless the war is seen to be going badly), and the danger of exaggerating the risks involved.

NOTES AND REFERENCES

1. *Fellowship*, August 1965, p. 2; December 1965, p. 1.
2. *Fellowship*, September 1985, p. 26.
3. *Peace News*, 11 January 1985, p. 18; 13 November 1987, p. 20; *Sanity*, August 1985, p. 28.
4. *Peace News*, 20 February 1980 and 28 November 1986, pp. 16–17. *Sanity*, August 1980, p.28.
5. *War Resister*, **56** Winter 1949, p. 16; and information from WRI.
6. *WRI Newsletter*, **223** March–April 1989, p. 7.
7. War Resisters' International, *Prisoners for Peace*, December 1986, p. 5;
8. *Peace News*, 3 October 1986, p. 20; *Sanity*, December 1986, p. 5.
9. *War Resistance*, 3rd and 4th Quarters 1974, pp. 18, 23.
10. *Peace News*, 22 March 1985, p. 6; *WRI Newsletter*, **205** May–June, 1985, p. 1.
11. Bruno Kaufmann, 'Towards a Switzerland Without an Army', *WRI Newsletter*, **224**, May–June 1989, p. 4, *Peace News*, 8 December 1989, p. 2; *Keesings*, January 1988, p. 35667, November 1989, p. 37049.
12. *Peace News*, 29 May, 1981, p. 4; 14 May 1982, p.3.
13. Chris Smith, 'Disarmament, Peace Movements and the Third World', *Third World Quarterly*, **6**, 4, 1984, p. 900.
14. *CAAT Newsletter*, **92**, August 1988.
15. *Peace News*, 4 August 1989, p. 3; Russell Johnston, 'Curbing the Arms Trade', *Bulletin of the Council for Arms Control*, No. 48, February 1990,

pp. 1–2. Johnston suggests the Foreign Office decision was taken largely on human rights grounds in response to the pressure from public opinion.

16. *Disarmament Campaigns*, **1**, February 1980, p. 15 and No. 19, February 1983, p. 5.
17. *Disarmament Campaigns*, **12**, January 1987, p. 14.
18. *Reconciliation International*, November 1987, p. 21.
19. *WRI Newsletter*, **225**, July–August 1989, p. 5.
20. *Peace News*, 3 April 1987, pp. 10–11 carries an account of the Bofors affair from the point of view of an electronics engineer who worked fourteen years for the company and leaked evidence of illegal deals to the Swedish Peace and Arbitration Society.
21. *CAAT Newsletter*, **91**, June 1988 and No. 92, August 1988; Rainer Santi, Draft of Brochure on the History of the IPB, October 1989.
22. *WRI Newsletter*, **223**, October–November 1988, p. 18.
23. *Peace News*, 13 November 1987, p. 20 and *WRI Newletter*, No. 217, October–November 1987, p. 14.
24. *WRI Newsletter*, **219**, March–April 1989, p. 7.
25. *WRI Newsletter*, **206**, July–August 1985, p. 11.
26. *Disarmament Campaigns*, February–March 1986, p. 2; *Reconciliation International*, February 1987, p. 29, and *WRI Newsletter*, **220**, April–May 1988, p. 14.
27. *WRI Newsletter*, **223**, October–November 1988, p. 17.
28. British Peace Tax Campaign, Annual Report 1989.
29. At Ease is a group offering free advice to members of the armed services, and was formed by pacifists from the Central Board for Conscientious Objectors to offer help to those who do not fall into the category of COs.
30. Colin Mellors and John McKean, 'Confronting the State: Conscientious Objection in Western Europe', *The Bulletin of Peace Proposals*, **13**, 3, 1982, pp. 227–39.
31. *The War Resister*, **78**, 1st Quarter 1958, pp. 10–12 carried a letter from a Belgian member reminding WRI of its original stance.
32. *Ibid.*, **94**, 1st Quarter 1962 p. 3; **6**, 11, 3rd Quarter 1963, p. 11. CO rights were not properly recognized until 1964.
33. *Ibid.*, **56**, Winter 1949, pp. 27–8; No. 57, Spring 1950, p. 19; No. 82, 1st Quarter 1959, p. 5.
34. 'Louis Lecoin Has Won', *Peace News*, 29 June 1962, p. 1; and Pierre Martin, 'Slow Progress for French Conscience Bill', *Peace News*, 10 August, 1962, p. 12; *Fellowship* **2**, February 1964, p.2.
35. Joe Gerson, 'Draft Resistance in Europe', *War Resistance*, **3**, 10, 1975, p. 11.
36. *The War Resister*, **56**, Winter 1949, p. 25.
37. *Peace News*, 27 October 1961, p. 1; 11 May 1962, p. 3.
38. Pietro Pinna, 'Conscientious Objection in Italy', *War Resistance*, **2**, 14, 3rd Quarter, 1965, pp. 3–8; *War Resistance*, **2**, 35, 4th Quarter, 1970.
39. *War Resistance*, 3rd Quarter 1971.
40. *WRI Newletter*. **223**, March April 1989.
41. *The War Resister*, Winter 1949, pp. 23–4; 'COs in Greece', *The Pacifist*, December 1979, **18**, 2, pp. 7–10.

42. *WRI Newsletter*, **220**, April–May 1988, p. 2; **223**, March–April 1989, p. 5; and **227**, November–December 1989, pp. 2, 6.
43. 'The History of Conscientious Objection in Spain', *War Resistance*, November 1975 (Special Issue), pp. 10–15.
44. *WRI Newsletter*, **219**, February–March, 1988, p. 15; **227**, November–December 1989, p. 3.
45. *War Resistance*, **2**, 39, 4th Quarter 1971, p. 14; November 1975, pp. 15–16.
46. *War Resistance*, **3**, 3, p. 7.
47. *Fellowship*, March 1985, p. 17; and John March, 'German Objectors on the Front Line', *Peace News*, 1 April 1963, pp. 8–9.
48. *Peace News*, 30 November 1984, p. 10.
49. Howard LaFranchi, 'Spain's Youth Ask: "Why Compulsory Military Service?"'; *Christian Science Monitor*, 1 November 1989; Andy Robinson, 'Voices of Protest Rise Against Death in the Afternoon', the *Guardian*, 1 November 1989, p. 44.
50. *War Resistance*, November 1975, pp. 10–15.
51. *War Resistance*, 2nd and 3rd Quarters, 1968, pp. 33–4; 3rd Quarter 1973, pp. 2–4; *WRI Newsletter*, **223**, March–April 1989, p. 4; Santi, *Draft History of the IPB*.
52. *War Resistance*, 3rd and 4th Quarters 1974, p. 24.
53. *WRI Newsletter*, **227**, November–December 1989, pp. 9–10.
54. *War Resistance*, **3**, 10, 1975, pp. 10–11.
55. *WRI Newsletter*, **225**, July–August 1989, p. 2; **227**, November–December, 1989, p.3.
56. *Peace News*, 3 August 1979, p. 5.
57. *Peace News*, 7 December 1979, pp. 6–7; *WRI Newsletter*, **227**, November–December 1989, p. 11.
58. *Peace News*, 4 April 1980, p. 4.
59. *Peace News*, 9 August 1985, pp. 8–9.
60. *WRI Newsletter*, **219**, February–March 1988; **223**, March–April 1989, pp. 10–11; **224**, May–June 1989, pp. 7–10; **226**, September–October 1989, p. 2.
61. *WRI Newsletter*, **224**, May–June 1989, p. 2.
62. *WRI Newsletter*, **223**, March–April 1989, p. 12.
63. *The War Resister*, **67**, Spring 1955, pp. 12–13; *War Resistance*, **3**, 9, 1st Quarter 1975, p. 23.
64. *WRI Newsletter*, **181**, March 1981, p. 14. On the origins of the peace movement and the rise of Peace Now see: David Hall-Cathala, *The Peace Movement in Israel, 1967–87* (London, Macmillan, 1990).
65. Gideon Spiro, 'There Is a Limit to the Oppression', *WRI Newsletter*, **222**, October–November 1988, pp. 14–15; 'Israel and the War in the Lebanon', *Strategic Survey 1982–1983*, (London, IISS, 1983), pp. 69–75.
66. *Strategic Survey 1982–1983*, p. 74.
67. *Peace News*, 14 November 1986, p. 13.
68. *WRI Newsletter*, **223** October–November 1988, pp. 14–15; *Peace News*, 1 September 1989, p. 3.
69. Jonathan Marcus, 'The Politics of Israel's Security', *International Affairs*, **65**, 2, Spring 1989, p. 235; *Pax et Libertas*, December 1988, p. 13.
70. Diana Shelley, 'A Time When People Can't Sleep', *Sanity*, June 1988, pp. 20–1.

71. END Newsletter, **8**, June 1987, p. 1; *WRI Newsletter*, **226**, September–October 1989, pp. 13–14.
72. *Sanity*, June 1988, pp. 20–1; *The Gandhi Foundation Newsletter*, **12**, Summer 1987, p. 8; *Reconciliation International*, November 1987, p. 20.
73. Women's International League for Peace and Freedom, *International News*, December 1989; Howard Clark, 'Peace Activists Encircle the Heart of Jerusalem', *Peace News*, 12 January 1990, pp. 1, 4; Ian Black, 'Water Cannon Swamps Jerusalem Peace Rally, the *Guardian*, 1 January 1990, p. 20.
74. *War Resistance*, November 1975, pp. 8–10.
75. 'Nonviolence in Irish History', *Dawn*, **38**, **39**, April–May 1978; *Peace News*, 7 August 1981, p. 14 (on Glencree); 10 November 1989, p. 8 (on Corrymeela).
76. *Dawn*, April–May 1978.
77. Extended and thoughtful analysis of the Peace People was provided by articles in *Peace News* on 10 September 1976, pp. 3, 6, and 9–13; 5 November 1976, p. 6; 11 February 1977, pp. 8–10; 25 February 1977, pp. 12–14.
78. *Peace News*, 4 November 1977, pp. 7–8.
79. Bob Overy, *How Effective Are Peace Movements?* (Bradford School of Peace Studies and London, Housmans, 1982), pp. 30–8 gives a sympathetic and extended analysis of the Peace People's policies and problems.
80. Charles C. Walker, 'Nonviolence in Eastern Africa 1962–4: the World Peace Brigade and Zambian Independence', in A. Paul Hare and Herbert H. Blumberg (eds), *Liberation Without Violence* (London, Rex Collings, 1977), pp. 157–77.
81. *Peace News*, 8 March 1963, p. 9.
82. Quoted in *Peace News*, 19 April 1963, p. 3; see also *Peace News*, 3 May 1963, p. 3; and *Liberation*, May 1963, p. 9 on Chinese reactions and on J.P. Narayan.
83. *Peace News*, 5 July 1963, p. 3; *Gandhi Marg*, 7, 3, July 1963, p. 210 elaborates on political attacks on marchers in Uttar Pradesh.
84. *Liberation*, April 1963, p. 5; *Peace News*, 5 July, 1963; 4 October 1963.
85. *Gandhi Marg*, **7**, 2, April 1963, Editorial; *Peace News*, 13 December 1963, p. 3.
86. *Peace News*, 'Operation Omega', in Hare and Blumberg (eds), *Liberation Without Violence*, pp. 220–38.
87. *Peace News*, 17 June 1977, p. 7; 15 July 1977; 17 November 1978, p. 5.
88. *WRI Newsletter*, **191**, December 1982, p. 16; *Peace News*, 30 September 1983, p. 6.
89. *Fellowship*, September 1985, p. 24; *Peace News*, 20 September 1985.
90. *Reconciliation International*, **1**, 1, February 1986, pp. 9–11 prints letters from an IFOR staff member joining the Peace Brigades in Guatemala. See also *Peace News*, 1 September 1989, p. 2; 23 February 1990, p. 2.
91. *WRI Newsletter*, No. **217**, October–November 1987, p. 5; *Peace News* 23 February 1990, p. 2.
92. Peace Brigades International leaflet 'Nonviolent Action for Human Rights'.

Peace Movements

93. *The Guardian*, 24 September 1990, p. 19, and *Weekend Guardian*, 16–17 February 1991, pp. 12–13.
94. *The Guardian*, 14 January 1991, p. 3 reported up to a quarter of a million in Germany, 200,000 in France and 42,000 in London plus rallies in other British cities.
95. *The Guardian*, 24 December 1990, p. 1.
96. *Peace News*, October 1990, p. 6.
97. *The Guardian*, 6 February 1991, p. 3 and 7 February 1991, p. 2.
98. *Peace News*, October 1990, p. 7.
99. *Peace News*, 1 February 1991, p. 7 and 15 February 1991, p. 5.
100. *Peace News*, 1 February 1991, p. 3 covered protests on 19 January; *The Independent on Sunday*, 27 January 1991, p. 7 on 26 January protests.
101. *The Guardian*, 13 February 1991, p. 3.
102. *Peace News*, 1 March 1991, p. 4.

CONCLUSION
Assessing Peace Movements

Peace activity has increased significantly since 1945. Numbers of peace groups and a variety of peace campaigns have multiplied in North America and North-West Europe, where a tradition of peace action was already well established. Peace protest has in addition spread to other parts of Europe, and to other continents where previously independent peace groups were weak or nonexistent. Although many campaigns came and went, by 1990 transnational peace activity appeared to be permanently established on a wider scale than in the past. Indeed, the growth of peace protest can be seen as part of a more general growth in the numbers of voluntary citizens' groups – like Amnesty International – and a growing transnational consciousness fostered by the world coverage provided by television and radio.[1]

TRENDS ENCOURAGING PEACE ACTIVITY

Peace campaigns draw on a number of institutional and cultural influences which cross national frontiers, as we have seen in previous chapters. Liberal principles enshrined in international charters of human rights have been invoked to protect the right to dissent against war and military service. Expanding awareness of global environmental issues has overlapped with and strengthened peace protests in the 1980s. To a lesser extent feminist commitments and transnational networks have fostered peace activity and resistance to military policies. Since the 1950s young people have begun to identify themselves in opposition to established culture and often in protest against mainstream politics. Youth culture represented by music, dress and, in the 1960s in particular, by soft drugs, includes strands of violent nihilism and self-indulgent hedonism, and has to a considerable extent been purveyed by commercial interests. Nevertheless, youth culture and pop music have often been enlisted on behalf of global solidarity – for example the Band Aid concerts to combat famine in Ethiopia. Nuclear disarmament campaigns in the 1960s and 1980s gained impetus from an upsurge of youth rebellion, and expressions of protest often reflected youth culture. The movement against the Vietnam War was closely linked both to the transnational student militancy of the 1960s and the flowering of the hippy 'counter-culture'. In a more complex way young people in the USSR and Eastern Europe in the 1980s turned to Western music to express personal dissent and to provide a focus – in the songs of former Beatle John Lennon – for peace protest.

Given the strength of transnational influences on peace campaigns, and the consciously internationalist goals and attitudes of most peace activists, it is ironical that many campaigns have won support through an appeal to nationalism. Opposition in Canada to US-controlled nuclear warheads in their territory in the early 1960s, and strong popular backing in the 1980s in New Zealand for government resistance to US nuclear-armed ships visiting New Zealand ports were both examples of national pride reinforcing anti-nuclear attitudes. At a more subtle level, widespread Japanese peace sentiment has been interpreted as an acceptable expression of nationalism and of a new Japanese identity after the experience of defeat in the Second World War.[2] Similarly CND's emphasis in the late 1950s on Britain giving the world a moral lead towards nuclear disarmament has quite often been ascribed to a transmuted consciousness of Britain's claim to great power status – a form of moral imperialism.

CND's attempt to harness British nationalism to disarmament had in practice only limited appeal in challenging a much more deep-seated association between great power status and military might, which ensured continuing support for a British H bomb. Nationalist sentiments rooted in historical memories, cultural and political differences, and both economic and political resentments of central power have, however, ensured that within Britain there was much wider support for CND in both Wales and Scotland than there was in England. This was true of both phases of the nuclear disarmament movement, but became especially evident in the 1980s when the Thatcher Government projected a purely English nationalism and lost almost all Conservative support in Scotland. Scots reacted against both US Poseidon missiles and British Polaris and the projected Trident missiles being based in their country.[3] Local nationalism in Spain rejecting the policies of Madrid also lent support to various forms of anti-militarist protest.[4]

The most spectacular link between assertion of suppressed nationalism and opposition to central military policies has, however, occurred in Eastern Europe and the USSR. Chapter 7 described how in Slovenia anti-militarism became intertwined with growing pressure for the autonomy of Slovenia from Belgrade. In Lithuania resistance to conscription into the Soviet forces was one of the major elements in the nationalist movement, and in Estonia numbers of draft-resisters mounted rapidly as demands for independence encountered moves by Moscow to supress separatism.[5] On the other hand, peace groups sensitive to the chauvinist and intolerant elements often present in nationalism have tried to develop justified national opposition to foreign suppression into a broader transnational humanism – as Freedom and Peace did in Poland.

Nationalism as a label encompasses many variations of sentiment and belief, as the examples just given indicate, and can be associated rhetorically with very diverse policies. Peace campaigns can and do draw on desire to play an influential role on the world stage, desire for national control over domestic and defence policy, and hostility to great power pressure. Precise expression of nationalism may also vary between committed peace campaigners – whose policy statements tend to link an enlightened nationalism to international aims – and those who offer support on very specific issues.

These considerations are important when assessing the role of 'anti-Americanism' in fuelling many peace protests. There is no doubt that opposition to US military bases throughout Western Europe and the Pacific region has been intensified in most cases by the fact that they are American. Dislike of the bases has sprung from a sense of self-preservation – fear of being drawn into wars fought to promote US superpower interests – and anger at allowing a foreign power to control national destiny. Protests at US bases have in addition reflected antagonism to US political intervention and backing for dictatorial regimes, an element in Spanish and Philippine campaigns in the 1980s. Furthermore, American economic power and cultural dominance have encouraged in many parts of the world a wish to reassert a historic and cultural identity independent of the USA – attitudes which have underpinned opposition to US bases, US arms imports or the symbolic implications of American war toys. The

END movement drew on a European consciousness opposed both to US superpower influence and to the more direct Soviet domination of Eastern Europe.

Anti-Americanism within peace movements has usually been directed against the US political and military establishment, stressing the role of the 'military-industrial complex' and the CIA. Levels of distrust of Washington have also varied, depending on US foreign policy and the nature of the Administration. Alarm and hostility were more acute during the Nixon presidency and the first term of Reagan's incumbency. Non-aligned peace groups have usually established close links with American peace campaigners, so transatlantic solidarity in opposing military policies has mitigated anti-American attitudes. Nevertheless, peace campaigns have in practice touched on popular anti-American prejudices in the wider population. Communist parties have often linked peace issues to much more explicit anti-Americanism. Even in consciously non-aligned movements outsiders reading the literature or attending meetings have often been struck by the degree of suspicion and hostility directed against Washington.

Rejection of US power derives partly from ideological opposition to American capitalism, since many peace activists have been members or supporters of parliamentary socialist parties or groupings further to the Left. This association between peace movements and the political Left in the West has been a source of partial strength, but also in many cases a significant weakness. Where social democracy has widespread support, as in Scandinavia, peace movement goals have been partially adopted by strong political parties. Denmark was, for example, the only NATO country – apart from Greece then governed by the socialist Panhellenic Socialist Party – to refuse in December 1983 to endorse the NATO missile deployment. (Although a minority centre-Right government was then in power in Denmark, it was responding to strong pressure from the Social Democrats in Parliament.)[6] On the other hand, close identification between nuclear disarmament campaigns and socialist parties has left them vulnerable to electoral swings which may be rooted in other political and economic factors. Moreover, when peace campaigns have become part of the conflict between Right and Left it has been harder to achieve limited goals with the potential to attract wider support. During the 1980s the Belgian and Dutch movements against cruise missiles were the most successful in Western Europe in transcending the Left-Right divide, partly because of church opposition to cruise.

Whereas association between peace campaigns and socialist parties has tended to polarize public attitudes to peace issues, links between disarmament goals and environmental concerns often have had a unifying effect. People worry about pollution of the atmosphere and danger to health whatever their political beliefs, and the nature and danger of radioactive fall-out can be approached at the level of scientific analysis and debate as well as popular protest. It is not surprising that nuclear testing has evoked widespread public concern in many parts of the world. Indeed, the 1963 Partial Test Ban Treaty banning tests in the atmosphere and under water (but not underground) has sometimes been described as a public health measure. Nor is it surprising that there was a wider coalition in the Pacific in the 1980s to condemn all nuclear weapons tests in the area (when even underground tests were thought to be polluting the surrounding ocean), than to oppose nuclear bases or other strategic deployments.

Even environmental dangers do of course relate to political conflicts, and scientific debate can become entangled in ideology when there is room for doubt and disagreement. During the 1950s the arguments about nuclear testing were to some extent trapped in the politics of the East-West confrontation, and appeals to preserve the global environment had less resonance then than they do now. Moreover, states developing their own nuclear bombs were disinclined to give immediate weight to possible health hazards. Maximum opposition has been expressed when nationalism and anti-colonial attitudes combine with health and environmental fears. The outrage in Japan in response to the fall-out from the US Bikini bomb in 1954, widespread anger in West Africa against French atomic tests in the Sahara in 1960 and resistance in the Pacific to French testing in the 1980s all illustrated this potent combination.

Not only national but also local concerns can give strength to campaigns against military deployments, if these threaten people's local livelihood, or cause nuisance or potential danger. In fact local opposition, quite unrelated to peace group activity, has sometimes erupted in normally right-wing areas. In the early 1970s some US senators were startled to discover strong local resistance to the siting of anti-ballistic missile sites in their constituencies.[7] When organized peace groups have supported such local protests – as in Larzac in France – they have won some of their more notable victories. Local protesters have in addition chosen to identify themselves with wider peace movement goals, as in a number of campaigns in Japan.

In general, however, where military bases create a local hazard or environmental nuisance, people are more likely to tolerate the base when they feel under military threat. US air bases in Western Europe have inevitably created alarm about low-flying aircraft and dislike of the noise made by the planes. The tendency of West Germans to complain about these problems appeared to increase significantly in 1989, as the receding Cold War largely removed the sense of a possible military threat from the Soviet Union. Peace groups also looked likely to join forces on these kind of issues with local environmental campaigners in Britain.[8]

SPECIAL PROBLEMS FOR PEACE CAMPAIGNS

Comparison between Green movements and peace campaigns suggests interesting similarities, but also some important differences. Both claim to represent the interests of society as a whole, and both movements speak on behalf of an embryonic global community and for future as well as present generations. Both can draw on national or local concerns to resist external threats to their environment, but both also have to challenge strong state interests and economic interests which stand in the way of international action to resolve global crises. The Greens, however, look more successful than peace campaigners. The Green movement has numerous goals, some (for example the abolition of nuclear power) very controversial, and much of its public support is clearly superficial. Moreover, to make substantial progress on an issue such as protection of the ozone layer the Greens have to overcome vested interests in governments and the economy. So the success thus far of the Greens should clearly not be exaggerated. Nevertheless, as we have already noted, commitment to preserve the environment can transcend normal ideological divisions. The need to preserve the ozone layer, for example, is one of the few issues on which peace activists and their opponents would probably agree in principle. There is also quite a wide measure of agreement on the steps which need to be taken, and more willingness by governments to make some compromise, than in arms control negotiations with an adversary. Compromise is likely to be seen as statesmanlike and generous, whereas in arms control compromise is liable to be attacked as weakness and 'appeasement'. Environmental dangers to the world as a whole create perceptions of threat very different to those posed by armed confrontation.

Some of the particular problems facing peace campaigns have been indicated in earlier chapters. Peace movements challenge in varying degrees the principle of pursuing national defence and security by military means and, therefore, confront fundamental fears for national safety and identity. They also tend to appeal for internationalism in a context where national interest has always taken precedence, and for trust when distrust is dominant. Even at the level of rational debate, when it is possible to discuss precise interpretations of national interest or safety, and levels of threat, peace arguments are contested by much orthodox international relations theory. In actual peace campaigns the symbolic and emotional factors usually come to the fore, and peace activists have often been patronized as woolly-minded idealists or vilified as cowardly and unpatriotic. In some cases campaigners can find support in a tradition of neutralism – which buttressed opposition to NATO nuclear weapons in Norway and Denmark – or in fear of entanglement in foreign wars, which motivated some opponents of the Vietnam War in the USA and prompted Congressional doubts in 1991 about American military action in the Gulf. National interest and patriotism tend, however, to be defined by governments and propagated by the mass media. The Conservative Government in Britain managed, for example, in 1983 to polarize debate about new nuclear weapons and defence policy into an apparently simple choice between maintaining British defences and unilateral disarmament. The Government was helped in this instance by divisions in the Labour leadership over defence.

Peace protesters have often had to face not only the charge of being unpatriotic, but of assisting the enemy. During the period up to 1990 peace campaigns in the West were usually trapped by Cold War logic. Peace groups have necessarily had to argue against enemy stereotypes, to encourage awareness of legitimate concerns on the other side, and to challenge what they saw as military propaganda by their own side, such as exaggerations of the military strength of the Soviet Union. In the context of the ideological hostility engendered by the East–West conflict, and the deliberate attempts by the Soviet Government to make use of Western peace campaigns, opposing the Pentagon without becoming apologists for the Kremlin required a difficult balancing act. Campaigners often disagreed on details of policy, or on the extent to which they should publicly oppose Soviet military measures, bearing in mind the danger of reinforcing Cold War assumptions and their primary obligation to oppose their own governments' actions. Talking to the other side has also seemed necessary but contentious. The difficulties involved for Western peace groups in deciding how far to establish contact with official bodies in the Soviet bloc have been examined in previous chapters. Disagreements on this issue reflected not only varying degrees of distrust of the Soviet Union within peace movements, but also divisions between organizations committed to fostering trust, or encouraging nego- tiations, and campaigners deeply suspicious of military establishments and motives of governments on both sides. The opponents of nuclear disarmament movements, however, tended to dismiss such distinc- tions and to attack all protesters for being pro-Soviet.

When national security is seen to be very directly at stake, govern- ments tend to be more intolerant of peace activity and of contacts with the enemy. The Israeli Goverment, for example, made it illegal for Israelis to talk to representatives of the Palestine Liberation Organization – a prohibition which some peace activists deliberately defied. But Israel has tolerated significant debate and protest spon- sored by peace campaigns.

LIBERALISM, DEMOCRACY AND DEFENCE

Peace groups which challenge aspects of national defence policy, or query the whole concept of military security, raise in very concrete form the inherent tension between the requirements of military defence and the principles of liberalism and of parliamentary democ- racy. Previous chapters have shown how far peace campaigns have been dependent upon the existence and the spread of liberal democ- racy. Where autonomous peace groups have managed to emerge within one party states, or under military rule, their existence has been an indication of some measure of tolerance and pluralism, however precarious. Conversely, peace activists claiming the right to criticize the military, or conscientious objectors refusing to be con- scripted, have helped to extend the boundaries of free speech and the definition of individual human rights. Peace campaigns have, how- ever, gone further to challenge implicitly or explicitly the role of the armed forces and of the security services.

The role of the armed forces in any society is officially to defend the country against external enemies, but because of their tightly-knit organization and control over weapons, the forces pose a potential threat to civilian rule and have frequently seen their role also as destroying the 'enemy within', or restoring 'order'. In Latin and Central America in particular the frequency of military coups and military dictatorships has linked peace campaigns very closely to demands for respect of human rights and democratic institutions.

In relatively liberal states abuses of human rights or civil liberties are most likely to occur in times of war or emergency. Obvious examples are the role of French forces in Algeria resorting to torture and the policy of internment tried by the British in Northern Ireland. Governments are under more pressure to contravene peace-time standards when engaged in conventional or guerrilla war. When the state is threatened, temporary suspension of civil liberties has, indeed, often been seen as justifiable, though particular measures – such as internment of foreign nationals – have been criticized. When, for example, the British Government interned and deported a number of Iraqis and other Arabs during the Gulf War, although some were prominent opponents of Saddam Hussein or faced severe danger if deported, liberal circles queried the procedures and intervened on behalf of some individuals. Peace activists have tended to publicize abuses of power as an element in their case against a particular war.

Peace groups have, however, been very aware of more subtle and continuous threats to liberal and democratic principles posed by military practices and by the security services. A central issue is whether parliamentary democracies fully recognize the right of citizens to express dissent on defence policy. While peace groups have, in general, been allowed to organize and to demonstrate, security services have often made peace campaigns a target for surveillance. When a former M15 officer revealed in 1985 that M15 had used informers within CND, and tapped CND members' phones, CND took up the civil liberties implications by bringing a court case against a former Home Secretary for unlawfully agreeing to a warrant to tap the phone of a CND officer. The High Court rejected CND's case, but did confirm the existence of the warrant and the right of the courts to adjudicate.[9] In the USA, too, it emerged in the early 1980s that the FBI was investigating six peace organizations – ranging from the professional body Physicians for Social Responsibility to the pacifist War Resisters' League – when the FBI refused a request under the Freedom of Information Act to supply files on the peace groups, but confirmed that 'damaging' information existed.[10] Surveillance of peace campaigns not only raises questions of individual privacy and the right to dissent, but of possible penalties for peace action such as blacklisting for certain jobs.

The availability of military information bears both on the rights of free speech and publication and on the possibility of democratic scrutiny. Peace activists have claimed that the need for 'military security' has often been invoked not to keep information from the other side (whose intelligence services are almost certainly well-

informed), but from the press and general public. The charges
brought against the editors of the Norwegian pacifist paper which
revealed US involvement in a Norwegian base (see Chapter 8) seemed
to reflect these motives. Government attitudes vary markedly over
the issue of release of military information – the USA has been
notably more open than Britain. During the Vietnam War, however,
radical journalists and the peace movement unearthed a good deal of
hidden material about the realities of the war and US policy. Peace
researchers and peace papers have generally worked in all Western
countries to bring more knowledge about defence into the public
domain.

In challenging military policies peace campaigns have raised key
questions about the accountability of governments to Parliament and
public in this sphere, and about the right of the public to influence
defence decisions directly. There is a tradition of thought and
diplomacy which has regarded foreign policy and defence as the
prerogative of qualified élites; a realm for statesmanship and for
taking hard, but necessary, decisions. This conservative, *realpolitik*
approach has been repudiated since the nineteenth century by liberal
peace campaigns and by the early socialist movement. After 1945,
however, as social democratic parties entered government, they also
tended to move towards a consensus with more right-wing parties on
defence and on the US Alliance. Establishment critiques of peace
campaigns in the late 1950s and to a lesser extent in the 1980s, were
directed not only against their policies, but against the dangers of
submitting defence to the influence of public opinion. Critics implicitly embraced an 'élitist' theory of democracy to argue that the public,
and in particular peace activists, were ill-informed and swayed by
emotion.[11]

Peace campaigners have retorted that decision-making on defence
has frequently been exceptionally secretive and undemocratic – for
example the British Labour Government's decision to make the A
bomb was never debated in Parliament or even the full Cabinet.[12]
They have also argued that Western defence policy was based on
strategic arguments which operated at an abstract level, excluding
genuine human and moral considerations, and rested on political
assumptions which needed to be re-examined. In practical terms peace
movements have had to appeal to the public when trying to widen
the agenda of defence debate and to mobilize pressure for change. So
peace groups have advocated the right of the public to have a say in
defence decisions which affect their own lives.

In addition peace campaigners could justify their democratic role by pointing out that they have directly disseminated a good deal of information about weapons and strategic issues, and indirectly prompted a flood of documentaries, books and debates on defence. They have provided channels for expressing dissent through petitions and demonstrations, and have also used existing forms of participatory democracy – referenda in Switzerland, town meetings and resolutions on the ballot in the USA, city and town councils in Western Europe and Canada – to raise defence issues. So, given increasing acceptance of the importance of opinion polls and elections in influencing national policies on defence and war, peace groups have tended to provide alternative views and encourage more informed popular judgements.

Not all peace campaigns – or all actions by peace campaigners – can be justified in terms of liberal democratic theory. There has indeed been a lively debate about the justification of civil disobedience in a democracy, and the limits of valid resistance.[13] A moral right to conscientious objection, for instance, does not automatically extend to draft evasion. Marxists and anarchists within peace movements have sometimes explicitly rejected liberal principles and constraints and endorsed more militant forms of resistance, such as desertion. Whatever the motives of individuals, desertion fits better into a socialist call for war resistance than a liberal peace tradition. As we noted in Chapter 1, peace protests have often reflected the conflicts between opposed political traditions. In addition judgements of methods used in particular campaigns vary with the precise political context.

CONCLUSION

The role of peace activity in a liberal democracy raises many important questions, but peace campaigns have to be judged primarily in terms of their own goals of preventing war or violent conflict, and promoting effective disarmament. Since war, and preparations for it, have so far seemed to be inevitable in human affairs, it would be wholly unreasonable to dismiss peace movements because they have not promoted a more peaceful world. Peace campaigns might, however, be expected to prevent or curtail some wars, or stop particular weapons being produced and deployed. Previous chapters have examined the difficulties faced by individual campaigns and their degrees of success or failure. Given the variety of campaigns, and their very different circumstances, no simple generalizations are possible; but the bigger and better publicized movements have not necessarily had the best results.

Political success is not the only criterion for judging the value of dissenting groups. Individuals have often believed that it was essential to uphold certain principles even if their cause seemed hopeless. Pacifists have quite often seen their own role in this light, particularly in time of war. COs and pacifist organizations have reminded others that even just wars are inhumane and corrupting, and have dangerous and unpredictable long-term consequences. They have maintained the importance of a common humanity transcending national frontiers or sectarian divides, and have promoted tolerance and reconciliation where hatred seemed inevitable. They have also experimented with and advocated non-violent alternatives to violent forms of struggle where conflict has been necessary.

Pacifists have, nevertheless, been very aware that maintaining this kind of 'peace witness' has been a limited and limiting role. Indeed, their critics have often felt able to commend the purity of their motives while dismissing them as politically irrelevant. So, established peace bodies have usually been willing to join wider campaigns to pursue immediate goals, even though attitudes, styles of argument and forms of protest in these movements sometimes contravene strict tenets of tolerance and non-violence. Political action for peace, like other forms of politics, requires compromises.

Peace groups have not only upheld principles of non-violence and humanitarianism, but have called for the achievement of what are usually seen as utopian goals: an end to the arms trade, general disarmament and abolition of war. Utopianism can be seen as an indulgence, and an abdication from taking part in more realistic forms of politics. But it can also be welcomed for providing a vision and inspiration necessary to those taking on what appear to be over-whelming political odds, and challenging a narrowly defined 'reality'. Whether peace campaigners' goals are well conceived is an issue which, as we have seen, has been debated ever since peace organizations arose.

Although long-term peace movement goals appear utopian, world trends are making their achievement seem more urgent. Modern methods of warfare pose an increasing threat to world society and the world environment, and states are becoming more interdependent. The widespread nuclear disarmament movements have been a response to the threat of nuclear war. The Gulf War in 1991 has brought the danger of chemical warfare, and environmental pollution as a weapon of war, to the forefront of popular consciousness. The fact that peace activity has spread to so many parts of the world suggests a growing awareness of the need to organize across national frontiers to prevent major wars and promote measures of disarmament. It also reflects a new ease of communication and a new sense of belonging to a world society, which may possibly assist peace campaigns in the future to achieve greater political effectiveness.

NOTES AND REFERENCES

1. Anthony J.N. Judge and Kjell Skjelsbaek, 'Transnational Associations and their Functions' in A.J.R. Groom and P. Taylor (eds), *Functionalism: Theory and Practice in International Relations* (London, University of London Press, 1975). The authors note the rapid growth of international non-governmental organizations since 1945.
2. N. Bamba, 'Peace Movement at a Standstill: Roots of the Crisis', *Bulletin of Peace Proposals*, **13**, 1, 1982, p. 41 suggests post-war Japanese 'pacifism' included a disguised nationalism of the weak'.
3. See for example Ian Davison, 'Scotland Goes it Alone', *Sanity*, May 1988, pp. 15–16.
4. For example, the war tax resistance campaign began in Andalucia, see Chapter 8.
5. By January 1991 there were an estimated 8,000 to 10,000 draft-resisters in Estonia (*Guardian*, 26 January 1991, p. 9).
6. *Strategic Survey, 1983–1984* (London, IISS., 1984), p. 56.
7. R.J. Bresler, 'The Tangled Politics of SALT', *Arms Control*, 3, 1, May 1982. p. 7 on popular resistance to ABMs.
8. *Sanity*, September 1989 had a section discussing the Greens, and in its campaigning notes for CND Groups included details on how to campaign against low-flying military aircraft.
9. *Sanity*, April 1985, p. 3; October 1986, p. 4.
10. *New Statesman*, 5 August 1983, pp. 17–18.
11. J.A. Schumpeter, *Capitalism, Socialism and Democracy* (London, Allen and Unwin, 1965), Chapters 22 and 23 provide a classic argument for 'élitist democracy'.
12. John P. Mackintosh, *The British Cabinet* (London, Stevens, 1977), pp. 501–2.
13. See, for example, Michael Walzer, *Obligations: Essays on Disobedience, War and Citizenship* (Cambridge, Mass., Harvard University Press, 1970); and Ronald Dworkin, *Taking Rights Seriously* (London, Duckworth, 1977), Chapter 8.

Bibliographical Essay

The primary sources for studies of peace organizations and campaigns are the materials produced by the campaigners themselves: leaflets, pamphlets, and peace periodicals. Archives are available for some peace organizations, though not all have been preserved. Other internal sources are memoirs of individual activists and leaders of peace campaigns, and histories of particular peace organizations written by members or sympathizers. Liberal or left-wing newspapers and periodicals in some countries have provided sympathetic coverage of the major campaigns.

The response of governments and political parties to peace movements in parliamentary democracies can be found in the memoirs of leading political figures, in legislative records, party conference reports, party defence programmes and election manifestoes. Some information about governmental efforts to combat the public impact of peace campaigns or to maintain surveillance on peace activists can be unearthed by research in government records, though the sensitivities of police and security services tend to result in censorship of information available to the public, even where a Freedom of Information Act exists.

Institutions and organizations opposed to peace campaigns have also produced materials on peace movements and their impact. These sources range from serious scholarly studies by the London-based International Institute for Strategic Studies (which publishes *Survival*, the annual *Strategic Survey* and the Adelphi Papers), to polemical pamphlets by organizations set up to campaign against peace movements.

Analysis of the political context in which peace campaigns operate, and some assessment of their success or failure, can be derived from the serious press and current affairs journals. Political scientists and sociologists provide surveys of campaigns and of public opinion in the academic journals. Studies of the politics of individual countries and biographies of political leaders are also an important source for understanding many campaigns.

There is in addition a growing academic literature by political scientists, sociologists and historians focusing on peace movements, in particular the nuclear disarmament movements, which have been a source of PhD theses and academic specialization. Some authors are clearly sympathetic to the movements; others write from a more orthodox *realpolitik* stance.

The growth of small independent peace groups in Eastern Europe and the USSR in the 1980s, and their relationship with opposition ('dissident') circles, can be traced in part through some peace movements' journals (in particular the *END Journal*) and pamphlets. But much of the relevant material appears in journals directly related to Eastern Europe and the USSR, and the wider Western literature on Soviet and Eastern European politics is often necessary for Western readers seeking to understand the political context.

It is outside the scope of this essay to attempt an exhaustive survey of all possible sources, even those in the English language, but specific peace movement sources are discussed in more detail below.

PEACE PERIODICALS

Peace periodicals are, as the references in this book indicate, a valuable source for anyone seeking more information about peace organizations and peace protests. The newsletters, papers and journals produced by various peace organizations vary considerably in the amount of detailed information they convey, whether they attempt in-depth analysis of issues and their degree of objectivity, but all are interesting in the sense that they convey the tone, attitudes and assumptions associated with particular organizations and campaigns.

The international peace organizations produce their own newsletters or journals, which over time are liable to change their name and format. The War Resisters' International (WRI) for example has published the *War Resister*, *War Resistance* and the *WRI Newsletter*, and is now associated with *Peace News*. The European Nuclear Disarmament campaign in the 1980s initially promoted itself through the *END Bulletin* (published by the Bertrand Russell Peace Foundation) and then founded the *END Journal* (one of the best sources for the 1980s nuclear disarmament movement). *Disarmament Campaigns*, launched as a newsletter early in the 1980s to serve the growing transnational movement, and published in English and French from the Netherlands and Belgium, was later incorporated into the *END Journal*. *Peace News* has passed through varying phases in its editorial policy, but has generally been a source of news about the transnational peace movement. It began as a weekly organ of the pacifist Peace Pledge Union (PPU) in 1936, broke away to become independent in the early 1960s, and ran into difficulties in the late 1980s, to re-emerge in 1990 as a monthly linked to the WRI. The CND monthly, *Sanity*, concentrated on British issues in the early 1980s but acquired a more transnational perspective in its coverage in the later 1980s. PPU's *The Pacifist* includes articles and some news on international issues and campaigns.[1]

There are several informative American peace journals carrying articles and commentary on peace campaigns in various parts of the world as well as in the United States. Long-running journals include: *Fellowship* (linked to the Fellowship of Reconciliation), *Liberation* and *WIN* (the Committee for Non-violent Action magazine). *The Bulletin of the Atomic Scientists*, though primarily addressing itself to scientific and strategic issues, has carried assessments of various national and transnational peace initiatives. An academic peace research journal covering the history and analysis of peace movements is *Peace and Change* (edited in Boulder, Colorado), published by Sage and sponsored by the Council on Peace Research in History and the Consortium on Peace Research, Education and Development.

GUIDES TO PEACE ORGANIZATIONS AND PERIODICALS

There are a number of guides to the great number and variety of peace groups and peace research institutes in different countries. Susan Forrester (ed.), *Peace and Security: a Guide to Independent Groups and Grant Sources* (The Directory of Social Change, 1988), covers the UK (and includes a range of organizations concerned with security issues, not all of them part of the 'peace movement' as it is usually understood). A comprehensive and informative guide to peace organizations round the world, including historical background on each, was provided by Alan J. Day (ed.), *Peace Movements of the World: an*

International Directory (Longman, 1987). Although some peace groups have been long-lasting, others spring up to campaign on immediate issues and then disband. So *Housmans Peace Diary* (Housmans, London) which is published every year and carries a comprehensive and updated directory of peace organizations round the world, is indispensable for keeping abreast of a changing movement.

BOOKS AND PAMPHLETS ON PEACE ORGANIZATIONS AND CAMPAIGNS

There are histories of quite a number of national and international peace organizations, produced under their own auspices or written by sympathetic authors. These include: Jill Wallis, *Valiant for Peace: a History of the Fellowship of Reconciliation 1914–1989* (London, FOR, 1991); Bill Hetherington, *Resisting War* (pamphlet on fifty years of the PPU), (PPU, 1986); Gail Chester and Andrew Rigby (eds), *Articles of Peace: Celebrating Fifty Years of Peace News* (Prism Press, 1986); and Albert Beale, *Against All War: Fifty Years of Peace News 1936–1986* (Peace News, 1986). Histories of international peace bodies include: The International Peace Bureau, *100 Years of Peacemaking* (IPB, 1991); Professor J. Rotblat, *History of the Pugwash Conferences* (Taylor and Francis, 1962); and Vera Brittain, *The Rebel Passion* (Allen and Unwin, 1964), on the International Fellowship of Reconciliation. There are two books covering the Women's International League: Gertrude Bussey and Margaret Tims, *Women's International League for Peace and Freedom: a Record of Fifty Years* (Allen and Unwin, 1965); and Catherine Foster, *Women for All Seasons* (The University of Georgia Press, 1989).

The upsurge of peace activity in the 1980s stimulated a number of studies of that period and also encouraged the growth of scholarship on peace movements in the nineteenth and twentieth centuries. In the former category are Thomas R. Rochon, *Mobilizing for Peace: the Antinuclear Movements in Western Europe* (Princeton University Press, 1988); and F. E. McCrea and G. E. Markle, *Minutes to Midnight: Nuclear Weapons Protest in America 1950s–80s* (Sage, 1989). The latter category includes the first comprehensive history of the movement against the Vietnam War: Charles de Benedetti and Charles Chatfield, *An American Ordeal: the Antiwar Movement of the Vietnam Era* (Syracuse University Press, 1990); and a detailed history of the Australian peace movement: Ralph Summy and Malcolm Saunders, *Australian Peace*

Traditions: Two Centuries of Opposition to War (Cambridge University Press, 1992). Charles F. Howlett and Glen Zeitman, *The American Peace Movement: History and Historiography* (American Historical Association, 1985), is a guide to literature on the American movement. Harold S. Josephson (ed.), *The Biographical Dictionary of Modern Peace Leaders* (Greenwood Press, 1985), covers 750 individuals who lived between 1800 and 1980. Linus Pauling, Ervin Laszlo and Jong Youl Yoo (eds), *World Encyclopaedia of Peace* (Pergamon Press, 1986), provides an initial guide not only to peace organizations but to the much wider field of peace movement policies and theoretical approaches to war and peace.

ARCHIVES AND LIBRARY RESOURCES

There are two major archival sources for peace movement materials in the United States: the Swarthmore College Peace Collection (Swarthmore, Pennsylvania) holds the archives of many American peace organizations; and the Hoover Institution of War, Revolution and Peace (Stanford, California), which *inter alia* has materials on the 1980s European campaigns. The Garland publishers (New York) have provided an important source for student and researchers by republishing in the 1970s 360 titles of American and European books and pamphlets, including histories, biographies and memoirs and theoretical writings, under the heading of the *Garland Library of War and Peace*. The reprints include introductory essays setting them in context.

In the UK the London School of Economics holds some peace movement archives. Friends House and the PPU in London have selective archives and peace libraries, and the Imperial War Museum is collecting materials on conscientious objection and peace campaigns. The Commonweal Collection, the J.B. Priestley Library (University of Bradford), has a good selection of books (including the *Garland Library of War and Peace*) and an even more valuable collection of peace periodicals, plus some archives.

NOTES

1. Both the *END Journal* and *Sanity* closed down before publication of this book.

Index